TAKING THE

BIBLE

AT ITS

WORD

There is no issue more important to the church than the authority of Scripture. Now more than ever Christians need clarity and reassurance about this critical doctrine. For this reason, I am grateful for Paul Wells' new book which provides such a well-written, accessible, and faithful introduction to the doctrine of the Word of God. Deep enough for the scholar and clear enough for the layman, it is a book that deserves to be widely read.

Michael J. Kruger,
President, Reformed Theological Seminary,
Charlotte, North Carolina

TAKING THE

BIBLE

AT ITS

WORD

PAUL WELLS

CHRISTIAN FOCUS

Paul Wells is adjunct dean of the Faculte Jean Calvin in Aix-en-Provence, France and editor of La Revue reformee. After working in France as a theological educator for many years, he now lives in Sussex. He is also a director of the Greenwich school of theology.

All Scripture quotations are taken from *The Holy Bible, English Standard Version*, copyright © 2001 by Crossway Bibles, a division of Good News Publishers. Used by permission. All rights reserved. ESV Text Edition: 2007.

Copyright © Paul Wells 2013

paperback ISBN 978-1-84550-969-9
epub ISBN 978-1-78191-166-2
mobi ISBN 978-1-78191-171-6

Published in 2013
by
Christian Focus Publications
Geanies House, Fearn, Ross-shire,
IV20 1TW, Scotland

www.christianfocus.com

Cover design by Daniel van Straaten

Printed by Bell and Bain, Glasgow

All rights reserved. No part of this publication may be reproduced, stored in a retrieval system, or transmitted, in any form, by any means, electronic, mechanical, photocopying, recording or otherwise without the prior permission of the publisher or a license permitting restricted copying. In the U.K. such licenses are issued by the Copyright Licensing Agency, Saffron House, 6-10 Kirby Street, London, EC1 8TS www.cla.co.uk.

Contents

    Introduction—Is Anyone Listening? 7
1. Only a Book 11
2. The Person in the Book 27
3. A Book with a Story 41
4. Divine Revelation 55
5. God's Special Revelation 71
6. Word Revelation 85
7. Revelation and Inspiration 101
8. Inspiration: What it Isn't, What it Is 119
9. The Word of God 135
10. The Human Word 153
11. Authority and Clarity 171
12. Truth and Unity 191
13. The Canon of Holy Scripture 209
14. Reading the Bible 227
15. Sola Scriptura, the Bible Alone 245
16. Conclusion 265
    Appendix—Historical Criticism and After 269

For Alison,

Aix-en-Provence, 1972–2012,

with more adventures to follow.

Introduction

Is Anyone Listening?

Shortly after dawn on a glorious June morning I found myself toiling up the wooded slopes of the Achasaseung hill fortress overlooking the river Han in Seoul, South Korea. I had time to kill as Starbucks didn't open till seven.

Suddenly, a monotonous wail broke the silence. It lasted about ten seconds before trailing away like a siren. Two minutes later up the steep slope, I heard it again, and then a third time.

I was intrigued. Was someone in danger?

Finally I reached a glade, where a wizened old man, surprised by my unexpected appearance, swung sharply to face me.

He greeted me cordially, bowing slightly as Koreans do:

'Morning' he said in English, observing that I was not from that neck of the woods.

'May I ask what you were doing?'

'Speaking to spirits', he replied, rotating an index finger upward.

The aspens trembled in the breeze but the ancestral spirits were mute. His searching cry reached for something in the silent void, something inscrutable and mysterious.

I went on my way, feeling tinged with sadness by the plight of this old man who had trudged up there on a fine morning to be alone with the spirits.

Reality is so constituted that human beings only hear the echo of their own voices when they reach out. The infinite silence of the void is unnerving, as French philosopher Blaise Pascal once remarked. But we keep on trying to make contact, hoping desperately that someone out there wants to hear us.

Atheism tells us that nothing is there to answer. The void is a void. Agnosticism says that if anything is there, it is always out of reach.

Our desire for God is all too often a tragic dead-end. Our cries for help go no higher than the ceiling. We are frustrated at not finding God, even when it is our heart's greatest desire, and we give up on believing.

There seems to be no way up; man can climb every mountain or launch telescopes toward the black holes, but there the road ends.

Our only hope must lie in movement from the other direction, in a God who comes down to us.

The Christian faith proposes just this. God revealed himself on two mountains: on Sinai, to give his words to Moses, and on Calvary to reveal his ultimate purpose through Jesus-Christ. To these two central events can be added the many other times when God was present in a special way. The Bible tells the story of God coming to us for our salvation and restoration.

Christianity is often called a 'religion of the book'. However that is not its main feature. It is not primarily a set of rules or a collection of meditations, but a book that tells the story about the living relationship between God and men. For this reason the Bible speaks personally about the God who makes himself known to his people in the Old Testament and by the coming of Jesus Christ in the New.

Bible history unfolds through a covenant between God and man. The goal of the covenant is to demonstrate God's saving love for his people. The doctrines or teachings of the Bible are all rooted in the events of history by which God is known.

This story covers a span of more than two thousand years. During that lengthy period divinely chosen witnesses penned inspired writings. Most of the Old Testament was in existence before the major texts of the Eastern religions, which originated after 600 BC (the Gautama Buddah died around 480) and the writings of the great Greek philosophers. Aristotle, the teacher of Alexander the Great who died around 320, probably had no knowledge of the writings of Moses. The Old Testament was only translated into Greek during the second century before Christ and probably reached completion around 130 BC.

The New Testament collection was completed within 35 or so years after the crucifixion and resurrection of Jesus, written by his apostles or their associates. The Islamic Scriptures, the Qur'an, came several centuries later. Muhammad died around 630 AD, a good while after the major Councils of the Christian church had made their declarations about the Trinity and the divinity of Christ.

None of the original manuscripts of the Bible (called autographs) have survived, which is not surprising. After all, nor have the manuscripts of plays by William Shakespeare or most other great books, even quite recent ones. Thanks to many surviving manuscript copies, it is possible to reconstruct a trustworthy biblical text that reproduces what the originals must have been like. For Christians, the transmission and the preservation of the Bible has been the object of particular divine care, without which the Bible would not have come to us over the centuries.

The Bible gives us the chance to know God and what he did for us. *Taking the Bible at its Word* plans to take you through how the Bible is the place where God speaks, and what that means.

Beginning with the way the Bible functions as a book, we will look at how God speaks to us personally in it through Jesus Christ. We will describe how God manifests himself in acts and words in the ongoing story of salvation. In order to give us a true witness to what he has done, God completes his revelation in acts with the inspired words of Scripture. Holy Scripture is therefore called God's word and has an authority and a truthfulness all of its own.

However, if Scripture is inspired, it is also undeniably human. God speaks to us in our own language. God's revelation is finished, as is his salvation, and therefore the canon of Scripture is closed.

The Bible is a book that speaks for itself and we are called to listen to it and learn from it on its own terms, not ours.

Now you have read this brief introduction, I suggest you do two things before starting on the first chapter. Read the table of contents to get an overview of where the book is going (if you have not already done so) and then read the conclusion that provides an overview of the outcome, to see where you will end up.

I

Only a Book

The Bible is a *book* and only a book.

A world of misunderstanding lies behind this idea. People want books for what they can get out of them, be it information, relaxation or passing the time in the departure lounge. A 500-page manual about exploring iPhone might well convince you that neither the phone nor the book is for you, quite apart from the cost!

About a Book

Any book you pick up has two sides, one you see and one you don't. That's what's fascinating about them. You now have this book open at this page but you can't see me writing it with the southern French sun streaming in my window.

There's a hidden world behind books made up of the thoughts, experiences, observations, and the life of the authors. A book says a lot about an author you will never meet, but you may well feel you know him or her already.

Many people have an 'inner book' in their mind. They never get round to writing it, like my father-in-law who wanted to write the story of his childhood in rural Cheshire.

Books, however, have no existence apart from their outer side, which can take many forms. Throughout history they have existed as clay tablets, papyrus scrolls or manuscripts written long hand, long before today's e-books. Someday maybe someone will even write a book that is an extended text message :-) —if it has not been done already.

Whatever the form, the words recorded always depend on what goes on behind the scenes.

Both sides of the Bible as a book are important. Outwardly, it seems much like any other book. No one imagines that the paper and ink are 'the Word of God'. The proof of the pudding is not in the eating in this case, but in the mixing. If we think the Bible is special it is because unseen factors have gone into its making—the stories of the authors and their claim that God was speaking through them.

Above all, the Bible is important because of its central figure— the person of Jesus Christ presented by eyewitnesses who wandered around the Holy Land with him for three years.

When we think about the Bible we have to consider not only its final form but also how it was made, what and who were 'behind' it.

From time immemorial people have recognised the usefulness of books. Some books are epoch-making. *The King James Bible* or Shakespeare's plays helped to make the English language what it is.

We also know their limitations as yellowing charity shop discards, to the chagrin of aspiring authors. When people finish with books, they junk them. Unfortunately many people have done that with the Bible because they think it's no longer related to modern life.

This book attempts to show why we should hold on to the Bible, because of the mixing and the pudding, its 'inner' and 'outer' sides.

The Bible as a Book

All this seems self-evident. We tend to forget that *written* words have had a wide variety of functions throughout history. Books aren't just for bookworms; they have many varied social functions.

The Bible too is made up of all sorts of documents, stories, history, genealogies, law codes, instruction, poetry, future predictions and proverbial wisdom.

The historical reality behind our word 'Bible' is ancient and complex. It is the equivalent of a Greek word *biblia* (from *biblos*, the inner bark of papyrus) and originally meant 'books'. It is found in the Greek translation of the Old Testament in Daniel 9:2: 'I Daniel perceived in the books the number of years that, according to the word of the Lord to Jeremiah the prophet, must pass before the end of the desolation of Jerusalem, namely, seventy years.' It refers here to prophetic writings or scrolls that had come down to Daniel from Jeremiah (25:11), who lived several centuries before.

The expression 'books' passed over from Judaism into Christian usage and came to refer to the Old Testament. Jerome, the translator of the Bible into its Latin version (called the Vulgate) in the fourth century, used the expression 'the divine library'. This lends some historical credence to the statement that the Bible is a library of sixty-six books and not just one book.

By and by, the 'books' came to refer to the whole of the Bible as an ensemble, 'the Book' in the singular. The earliest use of 'the Bible' in English seems to be toward the end of the fourteenth century in *Piers Ploughman*, Chaucer and Wycliffe.

Most Christians today own a Bible and read it regularly, apart from in places where poverty is rife and literacy low. But over the period when the Old Testament was written writing materials were expensive and the scrolls of Scripture were copied carefully and kept in safe deposit. In the apostle Paul's time, his epistle to the Romans was a good deal longer than many texts of the day. Christians in Rome would not have thought of having a pocket copy.

Between 200 BC and 300 AD the material on which the Romans wrote, papyrus, the dried leaves of a grass grown along the Nile, was replaced by vellum, calfskin soaked in lime, which was a durable luxury material. Some of the letters of the New Testament were thus written and bound in codices, forming small pamphlets.

It was not until much later that books became more available. Around 1450 Johann Gutenberg began work on a printed Bible using movable type for letterpress, known as the Forty-two line

Bible (from the number of lines on a page). It was finished five years later and was the first printed book. Before Gutenberg even the largest libraries in Europe contained less than a thousand hand-copied books, but things soon changed. William Caxton who had learned printing in Cologne published ninety new books in England after 1474. By 1500 nine million printed books were in circulation in Europe. The Bible became a best-seller. Thomas à Kempis' *Imitation of Christ* was in second place, with 99 editions in the last thirty years of the fifteenth century.

Around the time of the rise of the modern world, national languages were 'fixed' in religious and legal texts. Martin Luther did this with his German Bible and Calvin, with Rabelais, was one of the first to write a major book in French.

Personal agreements in the past were made on word of mouth by oaths and a shake of the hand. With the development of printing, written documents of all kinds became more widely available and as literacy spread, books gained social functions previously unknown.

In this context, and particularly with the advent of printing and translations, the Bible was distinguished from other writings as the Holy Bible or later, 'the Good Book'. One difference between Roman Catholic and Protestant cultures was that Protestants had and read their Bibles. The Bible was used in many ways apart from in church or in public preaching. It guaranteed evidence under oath in law courts, it was popularly used in soothsaying to make decisions and it comforted dying soldiers in craters at Ypres. One of its pages was even used to cast lots and mark the 'black spot' in R.L. Stevenson's *Treasure Island*. That must have been more shocking for readers at the time than it is today when blasphemy laws are off the statute book.

In other words, the Bible has had an important place in public life and in personal spirituality. Some of the uses it was put to were even superstitious. The Bible came to be used or abused in many circumstances and often in ways for which it was not intended. People knew snippets of it and used it proverbially in expressions like 'an eye for an eye', 'all things work for the good' or 'love your neighbour'.

A Closed Book

The technological revolution of the last half-century has changed the way we look at books.

Not only does the written word not hold the sway it once did in communication but books in general have lost their aura. A French sociologist, Jacques Ellul even published a book in the 1980's entitled *The Humiliation of the Word*, warning against the domination of non-verbal communication.

Written texts have been relegated to a secondary role, above all in leisure and cultural activities. Pictorial communication rules supreme in film, comic strips and advertising. Graphics have a central place in communication. Even when words are important, visual images are vital. François Mittérand was elected President of France in 1982 not so much because of his slogan 'Quiet strength' but because posters showed his Gallic features against the backdrop of archetypal France, an old village coiffed by a church. My children who were young at the time got the message and called him 'the man with the golden eyes'.

It is said that in the USA around ten million people suffer from illiteracy with a larger number having reading disabilities. In the UK in 2009 members of Parliament warned about an unacceptably high level of adult illiteracy. You don't have to look up the statistics to know we are no longer in the Gutenberg galaxy but in cyberspace.

Many people today never open a book, some do so only to consult a manufacturer's instructions, and some do not even own a single one. This is not just the case in certain sections of society, it also applies to leading people in their profession, who rarely read anything outside their field other than a biography of Eric Clapton or David Beckham. Young people are more likely to spend their free time on Facebook rather than opening a book or even switching on the TV. Adults, on the other hand, read children's books, as the success of Harry Potter shows.

Some Christians may view these developments with a sense of foreboding. If books remain closed, what will become of the Bible, an old book very much distant from modern people's concerns?

One reaction is to hang on to King James' *Authorised Version*, 'thous' and 'thees' included.

Efforts have also been made to ride the wave: picture Bibles come in comic strip format or manga versions. Bibles appear in basic English and are edited with presentations adapted to specific reader groups. Films are used to make the Bible story or the life of Jesus accessible. Sunday school is more likely to be a DVD rather than a good old Bible story. If you are an aficionado of *The New Geneva Study Bible* it certainly says a lot about who you are!

The 'Good Book' has become a closed book for many of our contemporaries. This raises important questions about the status of the Bible beyond present cultural trends and concerns. Such an elevated status has been bestowed on this book in the past—the Holy Bible, Sacred Scripture, the Word of God—that the present predicament seems to belie the claims that have been made for it. TV quiz shows reveal profound ignorance even of the basic facts of Scripture. It may be sold in supermarkets and presented at weddings but why on earth would anyone apart from some otherworldly fuddy-duddies want to read it?

New Challenges

In addition, the Bible has recently acquired some powerful competitors, known only to specialists in the past. The Buddhist Scriptures, the Qur'an, the I Ching and the folklore of animism or witchcraft offer new and exciting spiritual alternatives. In any case, at Christmas and Easter the media are apt to roundly dismiss claims about the star of Bethlehem or the empty tomb, and children are brought up to feel that Noah's ark is about as real as the babes in the wood.

How can a rather worn Bible maintain its 'street cred' faced by such an exotic market choice? The present climate seems to indicate that the future shelf-life of the once best-seller is in danger.

So why did God bother giving a book in the first place if books themselves have such limited value? Doesn't the thought that God chose a form of communication vulnerable to the vicissitudes of changing situations raise doubts about divine wisdom?

Reputable theologians have been known to say things such as 'If God had wished he could have made himself known to humanity in ways other than through written words. For instance he could have revealed his truth directly to the human conscience.' True, nothing could have prevented this, even man's innate unbelief.

The fact is, however, that God *did* choose the process of writing, the accumulation of sacred texts and finally an entity known as the Bible to make his ways known to humanity. So even though the Bible itself does not tell us why God saw fit to give us a book, there must be some reasons why, in his wisdom, he did it his way.

The three following ideas can help us to understand why the forming of a book of sacred oracles was no coincidence but the outcome of a divine plan. Something is present that is more than the conventions of a time.

How Sacred Texts Work

Firstly, we might think that the social usefulness of a book implies wide popularity and personal use. Evidently, this has not always been the case. Our ideas about how the Bible should function as a sacred text might well be conditioned by modern individualism and Victorian views of education more than by the Bible itself. We may too often take it for granted that the Bible must work best by being a pocket textbook for those who like its teachings or a spiritual booster for those who need a quick prayer.

It is obvious, however, that the *Qur'an* holds sway over many lives, even where few read Arabic. Likewise, Jesus and Paul knew and quoted from the Old Testament Scriptures without transporting the Torah with them on their journeys. Even if the Ethiopian eunuch had a copy of the scroll of Isaiah in his chariot (Acts 8:28), he must have bought this at a cost prohibitive to common people.

Books have a wide variety of social uses and can be influential in non-literate societies. That a sacred text is unavailable to many does not mean that it is a closed book to the public. Reading and listening, repetition and memorisation, texts used in public and private prayer and song made an impression on the daily lives of believers throughout the ages. One only has to think of the lining-out in the singing of Psalms and how it influenced Afro-American musical tradition. In a day when reading books holds limited appeal, some of these practises could be useful for church services and instruction. They could renew the quality of reading and change the liturgical monotony in our churches. Why should we not hear all of Ephesians read well and not just some verses from chapter one? Why not sing more Psalms or New Testament passages instead of some dumbed-down feel-good mantras? Such listening practice seems to have been current in the early churches and in the Old Testament the people of God assembled to hear the Law read, not just a few verses.

Word and Spirit

Secondly, we often think of the Bible in terms of 'quiet times' and personal Bible reading. No one is against that, but should it be the primary function of the Bible? The reason the Bible is 'open' is not because we chose to open it, but because the Holy Spirit does. More of this later, but the Word God gave was never meant to exist apart from the work of the Holy Spirit. In fact the written text had its origin in acts of God, accompanied by spoken words, and was subsequently written down and then used in witnessing.

This was so even when the texts had a legal nature. For instance, when Moses was with God on Mount Sinai, he had heard the words of the Lord. After coming down from the mountain 'he told the people all the words of the Lord and all the rules. And the people answered in one voice and said, "All the words the Lord has spoken we shall do."' Moses must have had a good memory, as it was only after this that he 'wrote down all the words of the Lord' and went back up the mountain to receive the two tables of the law that the Lord had 'written for their instruction' (Exod. 24:4, 12).

The 'great commission' of Matthew 28:20 to 'go into all the world and preach the gospel' made the apostles understand the importance of preaching. The word is the prime agency under the Spirit of God for the mission of the Church in evangelism. The apostles preached a person, they proclaimed the gift of salvation through faith and they looked for a response. Whether it be in the Old or in the New Testament, we are reminded that word and Spirit go together. The inspired record of foundational events calls for exposition in preaching or witnessing plus the work of the Holy Spirit.

A friend of mine was mind gone when an Indian Christian gave him a gospel on the banks of the Ganges. He read it and found the truth. For most of us it happens the other way round. We hear the gospel as adults or receive Christian teaching from a young age before we open the Bible and dig in ourselves. This reminds us that the Word is never given without witnesses and that preaching is the natural extension of the Word.

Contemporary Christianity has often been too coy about this. In a day when books are marginal, the importance of proclamation and witness as the place where the Spirit acts becomes evident with renewed urgency. Dr Martyn Lloyd-Jones brought it down to grass roots level when he encouraged Christians to 'gossip the gospel'. It's tragic that in many churches the preachers bore the pants off people. Why? Because absence of conviction and passion for the truth give the impression it doesn't matter.

Sola Scriptura, When Closed Is Open

Finally, we should not forget that a book is a completed whole, a unit, and therefore has a particular status. The fact that it is 'closed' gives it finality. This tallies with the New Testament message that the work of salvation is wrapped up by Jesus Christ. The once-for-all completed work of Christ is mirrored in the final witness to Christ we have in the Bible. The New Testament seals and closes the witness. This is one of the meanings of the expression *sola Scriptura,* Scripture alone. It indicates the sufficiency of the Bible to tell us all we need to know for life and hope.

The fact that nothing more is to be added means that nothing is expected from the outside to round it off. This was the point at issue when the Reformers insisted on Scripture over against non-biblical traditions being added to its message.

When a book is incomplete, whether it be a scientific textbook, a novel or a telephone directory, its use is rather limited. The awaited next instalment will sort out the problem, a factor that makes television soaps a great talking point. An incomplete text lacks in authority and leaves loose ends. That might be attractive in a novel like *The French Lieutenant's Woman*, where the author presents different possible endings to intrigue his readers and get their imagination going.

Luke, a consummate storyteller, also used a similar technique. At the end of the story of Martha and Mary (Luke 10:38–42) after Jesus' words—'Mary has chosen the good portion, which will not be taken away from her'—Luke does not tell us what the two sisters did after that. Did Martha leave off the chores to listen to the Master, or did Mary go and give her a hand in the kitchen? Or did they both do one and then the other? That's what I imagine, but perhaps you have a different idea!

Obviously inconclusive endings are not a problem when they are intentional. In other cases, they would be seriously inadequate, for instance in any text that claims to authority, whether it be of a legal, a factual or a religious nature. The lack of an ending would amount to a deficit in meaning.

Furthermore, when a text is thought to be complete, like the painting of a great artist, it contains its own internal message. 'The meaning is in the text', which is self-interpreting. One part of a book or painting is the key to the meaning of another part, and because it is a whole no *additional* information is necessary for understanding the meaning. Recently on *You Tube* I saw Van Gogh's self-portraits projected in sequence one after the other. It was most interesting, as you could see clearly the development of the painter's decline right to his sad end. It's rather like that with the Bible too, but in a positive sense. Through the books you can see the development to the conclusion.

This is what the Protestant Reformers meant when they mooted the principle 'the Scriptures interpret the Scriptures' or 'the Scriptures are self-interpreting'. Because divine revelation is complete, one need not go outside to the canons of church tradition or to the arguments of human reason to know what the message of Scripture means. The authority of the text lies in its unity as a whole.

Interpretation is turned back on the text itself. This is fundamental to the idea that one needs the New Testament to understand the Old, a principle stated by Augustine: the truth of the gospel that is latent in the Old Testament is made clear in the New.

Opening Understanding

With the Bible, the closing of the witness makes the opening of our understanding possible.

We can ask, where are the beginning and the end of the Bible to be found? The answer will be very different according to whether one approaches the text of Scripture from a critical 'modernistic' perspective or from an evangelical one. From the evangelical point of view, the beginning and end of the Bible that make it a unit can only be found in the first and the last verses of the Bible, the text as it stands. This is not a form of fundamentalist literalism, because it is simply what we expect of any text we find between two covers.

The beginning is unproblematic because it is an absolute beginning. The Bible starts with the creation story and its history develops from there, not from the call of Abraham or the Exodus of Israel from Egypt. The natural and the textual beginning coincide in the words 'In the beginning God created the heavens and the earth...God created man in his own image...male and female he created them.' Genesis 1 uses *bara*, the Hebrew word meaning to create, five times to mark the beginning as an act of God. This means that before anything else was, God was. There is no better way to say that the story of the Bible is God's story and begins and ends with Him.

But what about the end? If we look at the end of the Old Testament it is inconclusive: 'I will send you Elijah the prophet before the great and awesome day of the Lord comes' (Mal. 4:5). Mark's Gospel picks it up in a new beginning: 'The beginning of the gospel of Jesus Christ, the Son of God', with a reference to the appearance of John the Baptist (Mark 1:1–3 quoting Isaiah 40:3).

The end of the apostle John's Revelation, the last book in our Bibles, is interesting:

> I warn everyone who hears the words of the prophecy of this book: if anyone adds to them, God will add the plagues described in this book, and if anyone takes away from the words of the book of this prophecy, God will take away his share in the tree of life and in the holy city which are described in this book. He who testifies to these things says, 'Surely I am coming soon.' Amen. Come Lord Jesus!
>
> Rev. 22:18–20

The word 'book' (*biblion*), used four times here, refers undoubtedly to the scroll of John's Revelation. The adding and subtraction referred to indicate the finality of what is written, its divine character, and is underlined by a threat of judgment. Yet at the same time because the book is closed, it also opens up a final prophetic event. The 'I am coming soon' echoes the words of Jesus himself (Rev. 1:3, 7). The future coming of the Lord Jesus will be marked by a final Amen. The book is closed precisely to prevent any tampering with this promise.

It would be impossible to demonstrate that John had in mind anything other than this specific text when he wrote these concluding words. Maybe at this time, no doubt before the year AD 70 and the destruction of the Jerusalem temple, he had no clear view of what made up the whole of the prophetic writings we now call the New Testament. However, for anyone who believes that 'God does not play dice', the placing of this text at the conclusion of our Bible does not seem to be a hit-or-miss affair. The church understood that the books were closed until opened again by the final event of revelation, the appearing of Jesus a second time.

In this case as well, closing leads to opening in an unexpected way. When the new earth appears resplendent under the new heaven the final goal of God's original creation and of His saving grace will become evident to all. The beginning, the end and the middle are tied together in God's story.

These thoughts lead us to a final question in this chapter and one that is often raised in our multicultural societies. What is the relation between the Christian Bible and the texts of the two other recognised 'religions of the book', Judaism and Islam?

Three Religions of the Book

In the past the Christian Bible was a recognised authority. Today, however, people are likely to ask: 'Why the Bible, aren't there a lot of religious books?'

In particular, three types of monotheism, religions that confess there is only one God, are recognised among world religions. They all stem from the patriarch Abraham and are crystallised in canonical books. It is widely thought that they are essentially similar, like three branches of one tree. People get the idea that underneath the external differences it's fundamentally the same religion and the same God, so there is nothing to stop Jews, Christians and Muslims from praying together.

Appearances deceive. The differences are deep and across the board. A French philosopher once said, tongue in cheek, that the religions of the book don't owe so much to Abraham as to three women—Sarah, Hagar and Mary! There are also three distinct concepts of sin, grace and salvation in Judaism (as distinguished from the teaching of the Old Testament), Christianity and Islam, to say nothing of how God is known and approached. The worldviews of Christianity and Islam are dissimilar in crucial ways. For this reason, their sacred texts work differently. The same is true of Christianity and Judaism, although to a lesser extent. How can this be understood?

The Old Testament revelation is like a flower still in bud, waiting to burst open. Its prophecies call for accomplishment, for the appearing of the promised saviour, the long awaited Messiah. It is an incomplete religion and an unfulfilled faith. Whether the Messiah be understood as a collective body, the people of Israel, or as a person, fulfilment can only come from outside the book through a new unveiling of God's redemptive purpose in fulfilling his promise. Believing Jews are still waiting for something outside the Torah, the writings and the prophecies of their Bible, which make up our Old Testament. They wonder whether the Lord would intervene and save if Jews obeyed the Torah perfectly. The silence of God is a terrible burden. Is the Master of the Universe indifferent to the suffering of his people?

Christianity claims that God accomplished what he promised. The Messiah has appeared in the person of Christ. Sin has been paid for, salvation has been accomplished and a new creation has appeared in the resurrection of Jesus. If the kingdom of God is spiritual and is still to be unveiled in the future, by faith the believer lays hold on a free and perfect salvation. There is nothing to add. The Spirit of the living Christ bears witness to the facts. Salvation is done and Scripture is closed as God has spoken finally in the Son (Heb. 1:1).

Christianity from the start has claimed that what the Jews were waiting for is Christ, who is the true Israel. The New Testament completes and rounds off the Old because the terminus has been reached.

Islam claims that it is the awaited conclusion not only of Judaism but also of Christianity. The *Qur'an* was revealed to Muhammad, the final prophet, by the angel Gabriel from 610 AD until his death in 632. Some of the *Qur'an* was written down by Muhammad's companions while he was still alive, but the main method of transmission was oral. After his death the written text was compiled, and over the next decades it was standardized and distributed in what became the Islamic empire.

The *Qur'an* appeared around six centuries after the texts of the New Testament were penned, although a good many people, including Muslims, are ignorant of this fact. Islam claims that Muhammad was the last prophet and that the *Qur'an* completes the Judeo-Christian revelation. However, many historical facts and teachings of the *Qur'an* contradict the Bible.

Only two explanations are possible:

1. Muhammad did, in fact, record the correct version of divine truth and biblical history in the *Qur'an*. The authentic revelation that had been given was changed in the course of time in the Christian Bible. The Bible contains false information and the *Qur'an* restored the truth that had been lost. This is unlikely because historical evidences for what is found in the Bible exist in a wide variety of sources, from the

earliest times, and in different geographical locations. None of these sources say, for instance, that Simon of Cyrene took Jesus' place and died on the cross as Islam claims.
2. The other possibility is that Muhammad's information in the *Qur'an* is incorrect and the Bible record is true, which is historically more likely.

For Muslims the first position is the only feasible one, as Muhammad received the *Qur'an* by direct revelation. The Bible texts must have been tampered with and become incorrect by teaching things like the divinity of Jesus Christ. However, the historical problem remains. The fact must be faced that information, confirmed in a wide range of sources from the first century close to the events of the life of Jesus, is far more likely to be correct than ideas that appeared several centuries later.

The historical question is not the main difference between the Bible and the *Qur'an*. The Bible zeroes in on a person in whom salvation is fulfilled. Christianity may be a religion of the book, but it is more than that. It is faith in a mediator who bridges the gap between an unapproachable God and man's need of salvation. It is the religion of a person and what he claims to be as Son of God and Son of Man. The essence of Christianity is not a series of rules but a person and a new relationship of reconciliation and forgiveness in which the eternal God is also a personal God.

Conclusion

So the Bible is not simply a book. It is unique, being a book about a personal God who reveals himself in Jesus the Messiah.

In the history of Christian thought this emphasis reached its pinnacle at the time of the Reformation in Martin Luther's theology of the cross and John Calvin's presentation of Christ as the mediator.

However, Christ and the Bible are inseparable. The Christ of faith is the person disclosed in the text of Scripture and the texts of the two testaments have Christ at their centre. If we had no Bible we would not know Christ and if there were no incarnate Christ there would have been no textual revelation. This is why the status of Scripture expressed by the Reformers' *sola Scriptura* is vital.

Having said that, there is an order of priorities to respect: first the incarnate personal Word and then the in-Scripture textual Word. Person and text go together. In the next chapter we will look at what Christ himself said about the texts.

2

The Person in the Book

The Bible is a book in which a *person*, Jesus, is central. This statement will seem surprising to anyone who flicks through the content of the book. After all, the main actor in a book would be expected to be present on almost every page, but Jesus' on-stage appearance seems limited to the four Gospels. How then can he be the central figure of the book?

The answer to this question lies in how Jesus himself viewed the Scriptures, how he interpreted them and modelled himself on them. What role did they play in his life? As with the master, so must it be with the disciple. If we are Christians we cannot consistently adopt a policy other than the one that motivated Jesus.

Many Christians, to say nothing of the uninitiated, may never have thought about the Bible in this light. Others who have done so sometimes reject it outright. They think that we cannot ultimately know what Jesus' attitude to the Bible was, as it's the Bible itself that tells us. So we're trapped in a circular argument. Or others ask, what does it matter anyway because that was so long ago?

A more serious objection puts forward the idea that attitudes are always conditioned by their situation. The argument develops like this:

> Jesus was a person of his time;
> like everyone he was affected by contemporary attitudes;
> therefore what Jesus thought is simply the accepted wisdom of his day.

A further step is taken:

> we live in a totally different world with other values;
> there is no reason to perpetuate outmoded ways of thinking;
> what was acceptable for Jesus need not be for us.

The conclusion drawn is that just like Jesus was a person of his time and culture, so we must be of ours.

The problem with this approach is that it takes for granted the relativism that characterises modern Western thought. It's not only patronising but also it fails to face an important fact. If the opinion of Jesus' contemporaries regarding the status of the Scriptures was faithful to God's revelation it will for this reason be the true view on the subject. In other words the problem of relativism is an implicit refusal to accept the notion of revelation. It's a denial of the biblical worldview in which a personal God who speaks is central.

From an evangelical perspective there is a more important consideration. It concerns Jesus himself. For Christians, the person, words and acts of Jesus must be the standard of true humanity. When Jesus made known his attitude on Scripture he didn't do so like any random punter who might say, 'Here is my take on this question…' He was expressing himself as a divine-human person.

What Jesus knew and did in his human nature could not be inconsistent with his divine nature; if it were the case, the unity of his unique person would be broken. During his time on earth Jesus was willingly subject to limitations in knowledge, but the idea that he could have been in error is no more feasible than the thought that he could have been sinful. On a vital question like the nature of God's revelation it seems only fair to expect Jesus to be a source of reliable information. Much more so than some hardened modern rationalist.

To sum up: for followers of Jesus, his attitude to the holy Scriptures is not optional for their faith, but ought to be normative. This is fundamental because of the consequences of adopting a view of Scripture deviant from the one proposed by Jesus himself. If we do not tread Jesus' way, we will not tune into Scripture in the same way as the master and will run the risk of misinterpretation and error at every point. The outcome will inevitably be that what is thought to be the message of the Bible will not come within hailing distance of what the Bible actually says. What Christians say about Christianity will not tally with the Bible.

No illustrations need be given of this problem—just look at the reactions of many outsiders when 'experts' or establishment clerics pontificate in the name of 'Christianity' in the media. Their ability to deconstruct the Bible and reconstruct a bible mark II is an awesome feat of intellectual juggling, but people are not fooled.

It might seem extreme to put it this way, but these conclusions are simply the logical consequence of working with an approach to Scripture not authorised by Jesus himself and which does not tally with what Scripture itself clearly demands. Of course, critical modernism will always deny that there is an approach to Scripture authorised by Jesus or that there are beliefs, 'Bible doctrine', proposed by Scripture itself. But they can never catch the truths of the Bible on any subject in their net.

Jesus' point of view is fundamental to determine the nature of the authority of the Bible. It does so in two ways, firstly concerning his stance to the Old Testament and secondly concerning the New Testament. Since the incarnation, when Jesus came among humans in our humanity, lies between the two testaments, and Jesus stands at a middle point in the history of God's revelation, his attitude to the first will be a flash-back and to the second a fast-forward.

Sometimes it is asked why Jesus himself penned nothing if the written word is so important? The answer is that he *did* write something, but he did it through those he had prepared for the task and by giving them his Holy Spirit as witness. Just as the Acts of the Apostles are acts empowered by the risen Lord, so the words of the apostles in their letters which became our New Testament, are the speech of the communicating Lord.

In the rest of this chapter we will look at what lines can be drawn from the person of Jesus to the two Testaments of the Bible.

Historical Persons, Real Events

When Jesus refers to the Old Testament there can be little doubt that he considers the events it relates to have happened in the real world They are authentic and historic. The saints of biblical history are not parabolic cameos or mythical figurines. We can talk about the first couple in creation, Noah, Abraham, Moses, David, Elijah and the prophets as a whole. Jesus refers to the visit of the queen of Sheba to Solomon and the maritime experiences of Jonah as clinchers in debate with his critics. In Matthew 12:41 Jesus takes Jonah as a reference in his argument for the reality of future judgment. 'The men of Nineveh will rise up at the judgement with this generation and condemn it, for they repented at the preaching of Jonah, and behold, a greater than Jonah is here.' If Jonah is a mythical figure then Jesus' whole line of argument becomes nonsense. To say that he thought Jonah was historical, but really he wasn't, begs the question by inventing something that can't be shown from the text itself.

In his teaching, Jesus bore witness to many Old Testament events: the creation, the exodus, the giving of the law on Sinai and the forty years in the desert, the time of David, the exile and the repeated prophecies given at various times regarding God's judgement of an unfaithful people. In fact Jesus goes further than a simple historical reference. He sees the whole of this history as predictive. It ends up in his life, death, resurrection and glorification. As the serpent was lifted up in the desert so will it be for the Son of Man. His Sermon on the Mount picks up and completes the laws of Moses. All that is written in the law of Moses, the prophets and the psalms is accomplished in him. All his teaching about this is with 'authority and not as the scribes' (John 3:1–14, Matt. 5–7, 7:29, Luke 24:44f).

Jesus includes his person and work in the historical continuum set in motion in the Old Testament. In the parable of the vineyard planted by the master the tenants repeatedly beat up his messengers before deciding to kill the son. (Matt. 20:1–9) Jesus resumes the whole of this history in one sweep when he challenges the leaders of Israel of his day: 'You build the tombs of the prophets whom your fathers killed...the blood of the prophets shed from the foundation of the world will be charged against this generation, from the blood of Abel to the blood of Zechariah... it will be required of this generation' (Luke 11:46-51, Matt. 23:34-6).

Jesus accepts the authority of the Old Testament in such a way that it is the template that provides the structure and the substance of his own ministry. In his person and work, the age-old story of ingratitude, rebellion and hardness of heart is played out one final time. Because Jesus completes the Old Testament pattern, salvation also emerges from judgment.

Why is the historical nature of events from the distant past of such vital importance, one might ask? Wouldn't a meaningful story produce the same effects and suggest the same themes of suffering and salvation? No doubt it could be the case if the subjective reaction was all that mattered. However, if nothing happened other than what happens when a fairy tale or a redemption myth is read, nothing has *really* happened in reality. There is no real change from sin to grace in history and there is no future hope either. There is no real demonstration beyond the level of feeling that God is a pardoning and saving God. We are adrift in a sea of imagination with no moorings to reality. It might be a nice feeling in passing, but in the end it's all an illusion. The Bible story depends on there being a living and acting God who is behind all that goes on.

Fulfilled Expectations

Not only did Jesus make claims about the historical character of the Old Testament writings and shape his own life goals according to their pattern, he also confirmed their authority by placing himself under their umbrella.

When Jesus dialogues with his contemporaries and particularly with the Jewish authorities, final arbitration belongs to the texts of the Old Testament that put an end to discussion. Jesus questions the Jewish authorities about how they understand the law. He does not criticise their attachment to it but their false understanding and the rigidity of their trumped-up interpretations. Jesus never undermines the authority of the Old Testament. When he elaborates it, as he does on several occasions in the Sermon on the Mount and elsewhere, it is not to amend it but to ratchet it up a notch. He applies its requirements to the inner motivations of his hearers with a pointed 'but I say unto you'. The tactic is not to abolish but to fulfil the law. (Matt. 5:17, 22, 28, 32, 34, 39, 44)

However not only does Jesus recognise the sacred word as a general principle, he also applies it to his own case and needs. The word is 'a guide to the feet and a lamp to the path' of the anointed Son as well as to the children of Israel. (Ps. 119:105, 132:17)

Illustrations are always instructive. We have chosen two from Jesus' life experiences.

In the first act of Jesus' ministry, after his baptism, he finds himself not face to face with God, as Moses did during forty days on Sinai (Exod. 24:18), but locked in combat with Satan for forty days in the desert. How does Jesus emerge victorious from this struggle? By appealing to his own power and authority? No, but by turning to Scripture. Satan's fraudulent distortions of the word are exposed in each case by a counter thrust. Jesus defends himself by giving the true meaning of Scripture.

This is no mental joust of masterminds. Its significance lies in the fact that Jesus' success hangs in the balance in his replies. His life's work will be to live by 'every word that comes from the mouth of God'. Worshipping and serving God are demonstrated by submission rather than by 'putting God to the test'. (Matt. 4:4, 8, 10)

Notice also that Jesus is alone in this confrontation. The Word of God is all he has to defend himself. It is only subsequently that the angels come and minister to him. When the tempter appears he always uses the words of God perversely. As the liar 'from the beginning' (John 8:44) he is incapable of saying 'It is written', because he has no trust in or respect for the Word of God. Jesus, on the other hand, in his inspired answers says 'It is written' three times. This shows he commits his fate to the power and truth of God's Word.

Many lessons could be learned from this apocalyptic encounter. One could be that in a strange way God's words can become the devil's when they are not used to the end for which they were given. Another might be that deviance from the Word of truth is invariably the work of the great liar and murderer. When men twist God's Word it reveals a profound hatred for the divine Lord and his authority. This is surely enough to make any of us think twice about some of the glib things said and done in the name of Christianity. A further thought is that Jesus shows us what true obedience to God is: it lies in serving and worshipping God and by following the divine guidelines of his Word.

For a second example let's switch to a further dramatic moment at the end of Jesus' earthly ministry. Satan again appears using the same ploys as those he used in the temptation in the desert: 'If you are the Son of God, come down from the cross' (Matt. 27:40). What a mind-jogging flashback this must have been for Jesus, laying his whole ministry out before him. Yet by a strange providence the very temptation that was meant to trip him up kept him on track in following his calling.

The importance of Scripture in Jesus' life is nowhere more striking than in his central fourth word from the cross, called the word of dereliction. Jesus refers to Psalm 22:1, 'My God, my God why have you forsaken me' to express abandonment in judgment. It seems that in the context of the events described in Mark 15:24–34 the Father has mentally led his Son back from the end of the Psalm to its beginning. Jesus lives through the experience of Psalm 22 on the cross in reverse order from the sequence in the psalm.

The reverse order of events in the psalm and in Mark's gospel is shown by the verse numbers going up in the left column and down on the right:

Mark 15	Topic	Psalm 22
24	division of garments	18
29	mockery/head wagging	7
30–31	save yourself!	8
32	reviling	6
34	cry of dereliction	1

Jesus had probably sung this psalm the previous evening with his disciples at the Passover meal. Could he have failed to heed the warning lights as the scene unfolded the following day? If he knew his psalms, and he must have done, if he was alert to each new incident, as he must have been, if Mark gives a faithful historical narrative, and we believe he does, then it is difficult not to conclude that when Jesus uttered the first verse of the psalm in the fourth word on the cross, he knew he had reached the *very end* of what he had to live through. From this point there was no going back, no going forward, only going *out*, to the judgment of death.

Jesus knew that the whole experience described in the psalm was about him. It is his own psalm, the one he inspired for himself to pray, but more than that, Jesus the Word incarnate, in his experience *was* the psalm made flesh in his suffering.

So we see the extent of Jesus' commitment to Scripture as God's Word at the start and end of his earthly ministry. This was a full embrace of the sacred text as the expression of ultimate good. No formal or servile submission was this, but complete engagement of body, mind and strength in the service of the Lord, and it was perfect obedience to the great commandment. (Matt. 22:37)

Why was such involvement necessary on the part of the Son of God? The reason lies in the divine covenant. If humanity can only be saved by humanity, it can only be saved by God himself becoming man. Man since Adam can never be his own mediator. In order to reach fulfilment, the conditions of God's covenant with man had to be fully internalised and brought to fruition. In this Adam had failed, but the second Adam prevailed in active obedience to God and brought into being the new humanity by his obedience to the Word.

This is why the authority of the Word is essential to shaping what Christ should be personally as mediator between God and man and why Christ himself validated its authority.

Inspired Words

Not only does Jesus attest to the historical nature of the Scriptures and consider it his calling to bring them to fulfilment, he also refers to them as the ultimate authority. This applies to their content and to the formulation, the words themselves.

A century ago B.B. Warfield wrote extensively to demonstrate that the expressions 'it is written', 'it says' and 'Scripture says' are the New Testament writers' equivalent of 'God says'. They are used unsparingly in the Gospels, perhaps with most frequency in Luke. In the same class are expressions such as 'Moses said', 'Isaiah prophesied aright' and 'David said by the Holy Spirit' (Mark 12:36, Acts 1:16). Such is also the practise of Jesus, as we have seen in connection with his temptation. This form of use is so constant that it is difficult to avoid what underlies it: that God himself speaks through his servants and their writings.

Let's take some illustrations. An interesting case in point that underlines this principle is found in Matthew 19:4–5, when Jesus discusses divorce law with the Pharisees. His answer to their question is: 'Have you not read that he who created them from the beginning made them male and female and said, "Therefore a man shall leave his father and his mother and hold fast to his wife and they shall become one flesh?".' Jesus argues that the act of creation and the word of interpretation go together and that both are divine actions. When we turn to the quotation in Genesis 2:24, however, it is evident that it is not a direct word spoken by God as Jesus affirmed, but an inspired comment by the author of the text. Either Jesus got his facts wrong, or he considered that the human written word was God's own word. The second possibility is preferable.

In John 5:30–47 Jesus chides the Pharisees because of their unbelief. If they believed Moses, they would believe in him, 'because he wrote of me' (47). Not that Jesus himself need rely on Moses or John the Baptist as witnesses (32–6), because he has a greater witness, the Father himself. The Father has sent him. (36–7) However, if his opponents cannot see this in his works, all their searching of the Scripture will be in vain. 'You search the Scriptures because you think that in them you have eternal life; and it is they that bear witness about me, yet you refuse to come to me that you may have life' (39–40). Jesus' opponents are not wrong in thinking they can find eternal life in the Scriptures, but they are mistaken in not seeing that the person of Christ and the words of Scripture are of the same ilk because of divine authorisation. The authority of God the Father guarantees both.

Finally, there is a complex argument in John 10:33–6. It may be difficult for us to follow, but there can be little doubt that Jesus' enemies got the point because immediately after they wanted to arrest him.(39). Horrors, he claims he is the Son of God, a shocking blasphemy. Jesus replies in substance, quoting Psalm 82:6 'you are gods'. The 'gods' refers to the forerunners of the Pharisees, the judges of Israel, who are sons of the Most High, who were also to die. We can paraphrase: 'If in any sense the psalm can apply the term 'gods' to mere men, then much more may it be applied to One who is sanctified and sent into the world by God.' Verse 35 backs this up: 'the Scripture cannot be broken'.

Several comments can be made about this in the context. Firstly, Jesus refers to the statement 'you are gods' as Scripture. He is not talking about the whole of the Old Testament, but just about this one sentence. Secondly, this small unit is considered as sacred text and something that 'cannot be broken'. Thirdly, if it cannot be broken, it is because of its divine authority as Word of God. Finally, if this is true of a small and relatively obscure text, what is true in this case must also be the case for all of God's utterances in sacred Scripture. Such was Jesus' view of the divine Word.

Why should we accept Jesus' teaching on this subject? There is only one valid reason—because of the personal authority he wields as Lord and Saviour. We accept his witness about Scripture and believe it to be of divine origin. If it is exhaustive rational demonstration that we want, we will never be satisfied, which is not to say that evidence is lacking.

For the believer, the Master's approach is canonical. It constitutes an objective witness superior to that of all other authorities, including ecclesiastical and scientific ones. Most striking is the fact that it is not the testimony of the intelligencia but of someone they excommunicated. Jesus argues in favour of the Jewish Old Testament, of the historicity and authenticity of innumerable facts and the Holy Spirit bears witness in our hearts to confirm what Jesus said.

Chosen Witnesses

What Jesus thought about the Old Testament Scriptures cannot be gainsaid. He put the weight of his authority behind the New Testament too, but in a very different way.

It is evident from his words and deeds that Jesus anticipated the formation of a new body of sacred Scripture. Just as he predicted other events that would follow his resurrection, such as the destruction of the Jerusalem temple, the persecution of his disciples, the world mission and Peter's long life and martyr's death, so also Jesus took positive steps to assure the existence of an authorised witness to what he had done.

How could the knowledge of what he did, his message and its meaning be passed on and guaranteed? Should it be left to his hearers' discretion, whether disciples, sceptics or enemies, to their power of recall and their integrity? Jesus never entertained such a thought. From the start of his ministry, right down to his final farewell, Jesus paid attention to this matter. This point of view has little difficulty finding support in the New Testament. For instance, 2 Peter 3:2: 'remember the predictions of the holy prophets and the commandment of the Lord and Saviour through your apostles...' weaves together references to the message of the Old Testament prophets, the commandment of Jesus and the apostolic witness.

What about the witness of Jesus himself to future revelation? The principal texts on the subject are found in the Gospel of John and exist in three layers. First of all, John 14:26:

> These things I have spoken to you while I am still with you. But the Helper, the Holy Spirit, whom the Father will send in my name, he will teach you all things and bring to your remembrance all that I have said to you.

Jesus is 'going away' to the Father but he will come again in the person of the Holy Spirit. The Spirit will come in Christ's name as his witness. His function will be twofold, both teaching all things and recalling Christ's words. The word 'helper' (*paracletos* in Greek, meaning intercessor or advocate) has the sense of a counsellor in justice. It is also used of Jesus himself in 1 John 2:1 where 'Jesus Christ the righteous' is presented as an advocate with the Father. In John 14 it means that the Spirit will be the counsellor who directs the witness of the apostles so it will be truthful not only with relation to men but in faithfulness to God. Secondly, John 16:12–14:

> I have still many things to say to you but you cannot hear them now. When the Spirit of truth comes, he will guide you into all truth, for he will not speak on his own authority, but whatever he hears he will speak, and he will declare to you the things that are to come. He will glorify me, for he will take what is mine and declare it to you. All that the Father has is mine, therefore I said that he will take what is mine and declare it to you.

The accent in this passage is slightly different from the previous case, even though once again the Spirit is seen as working in harmony with the Father and the Son, speaking on their authority. More specifically, the Holy Spirit expresses the truth of God as the one who will show the apostles the way into all truth. His function is to announce truth in such a way that Christ will be glorified. It also concerns 'the things to come'. This expression presents Christ as the 'coming one' (see Rev. 1:7), his future glory, reign and return. It is more than a simple recall of the past; it entails a vision of the future glory of the Risen Christ and is a prophecy of his return. Finally, John 17:14–19:

> I have given them your word, and the world has hated them because they are not of the world, just as I am not of the world… Sanctify them in the truth; your word is truth. As you sent me into the world, so I sent them into the world. And for their sake I consecrate myself, that they may also be sanctified in the truth.

Here, in Jesus' high-priestly prayer, his apostles are singled out for special intercession because of the task that lies before them. What is the difference between Jesus, his apostles and the world? They are separated from the world because knowing the truth makes for a situation of hostility. Divine truth and worldly truths never make good bedfellows. When this is not recognised, unsatisfactory compromises are invariably brokered. The word that sanctifies or sets apart from the world is the word that is true. Just as Jesus was sent into a hostile environment, so will it be for his apostles. The same verb used in the past tense in both cases is *apostello* in Greek, to send out, meaning that Jesus is the first 'apostle'. Of course the sending of the apostles is still future, but Jesus is praying about it in a prophetic way, speaking of it as though it were something that had already happened. In a sense it has, because both the sending of Jesus and that of his apostles are according to the prior divine plan for making salvation known.

In a mysterious way, the apostles share in the unique consecration and sanctification of Jesus who was sent into the world. Jesus' action and their action are bound together as two aspects of the one plan of God in the revelation of truth through the Word. Nothing could illustrate more clearly how the presence of the divine Son is of a piece with the presence of the divine Word. This is, of course, why witness, proclamation and preaching are the prime tasks of the apostolic ministry.

It would be exaggerated to pretend that we have an explicit promise of the New Testament Scriptures and canon in these words. However the fundamental principle for the formation of new Scriptures is laid down. This principle will be confirmed later by the self-understanding of the apostles. It will allow Paul to say that Christians are 'members of the household of God built on the foundation of the apostles and the prophets, Christ Jesus himself being the cornerstone' (Eph. 2:20).

The new people of God will find their unity and truth in terms of the apostolic gospel. The disciples who have been with Christ from the beginning and are eyewitnesses will becomes apostles, sent by Christ and empowered with his Spirit (John 15:26–7).

Conclusion

In his preface to the 1541 translation of the psalms in French, commissioned by John Calvin, the poet Clément Marot used a word-picture from the Church Fathers to portray the fact that when we hear the words of the psalms we hear the music of the Spirit: 'Here, wrote Marot, we hear the Spirit of God who speaks through David when David prays, making him like a flute played with all the skill of a perfect musician.'

How difficult it is not to let the Spirit's tune be drowned out by the din of the madding crowd! When and if Scripture feels distant and cold to us, it is more often than not we who have become distant from its Lord and cold to its message.

God spoke by his prophets: Moses, David, Isaiah, Jeremiah and the rest. He will speak by his apostles, Peter, Paul, John and the rest. That is the clear message of Jesus, a truth that he was prepared to give his own life for. By doing that, he made all the promises of the Old and New Testaments come true in reality.

3

A Book with a Story

The Bible is a book with *a story*, which is quite different from saying that it is a story book.

Many people think the Bible is chock-a-block with good, bad or indifferent stories. Some are like fairy tales, others are so offensive that they can't be told to children, but whether true or false most are thought to be irrelevant because they are so far in the past. Best-selling atheist or agnostic pundits like Richard Dawkins, Robin Lane Fox or Christopher Hitchens take it for granted that the Bible is fictional and full of errors. The latter stated that the Old Testament is a 'nightmare' and the New is 'evil'. The miracles of the Bible are ridiculous and tawdry.

Why do highly intelligent people say things like this? They are devoid of spiritual sensitivity and have little sense of the greatness of God or the baseness of man. Lacking those two vital faculties they can only have foggy ideas about ultimate reality.

It is often forgotten that such judgments don't rest directly on facts, but on preconceived ideas that determine the interpretation of the facts in question. It makes a whole world of difference if you think there is a living God who speaks or not. These opinions are popular currency and give the impression that the inadequacy of the Bible is an open-and-shut case. If it has any value it can only be to foster a sort of religious piety, and that itself is of doubtful value.

For Christians, the stories of the Bible can only be understood in the light of the story of the whole Bible. It is often said that the Bible has a 'story-line' that runs through it and that it is essential to grasp the big picture to understand the details.

For many readers the question is: how do we get at the Bible's story line, so we can fit the pieces together and make something of the whole? Where does one start?

Story Set-Up

The vital thing about a good story is the contrast between the start and the end and what happens to make things zip along between the two. These ingredients go into making a good thriller.

The Bible obviously moves along very differently from a John Grisham novel but what's important in both is the start, the end and the plot between. It's often pointed out that the Bible begins in a garden and ends in a glorious city, which itself implies construction and progression. One of the best ways for accessing the Bible for an uninformed reader would be to read Genesis chapters 1–3, then Revelation 21–2 and finally John 1. Then the beginning, the end and the middle are well in focus and everything else fits somewhere into this basic pattern.

The real difficulty for agnostics or atheists, like the authors referred to above, is that there *is* something and not nothing. In a way they need a concept of 'nothing' to prove there is no God. If there were nothing, there would be no God either. But the fact that something is there leads to the idea that there is a cause behind the something we can see before our eyes. Similar reasons led a sceptic like Anthony Flew to have second thoughts on 'no-God-ism'.

Psalm 14 states it is silly to toy with the idea that 'there is no God'. Atheists are self-deluding fools not to get it. From a Christian perspective, there is someone behind the *everything* going on in the cosmos. Between the 'there *is not* nothing' at the start and 'there *will not* be nothing' at the end, something happens, a story in which

God speaks and interacts with human beings. The Bible is made up of the story that moves between the start and the end. Someone is there to give life its ultimate meaning.

But concretely, how do we unpack the story? The classic way is to begin at the start and work forward. Biblical theologies that describe the 'history of salvation' generally work with this model. They begin with the account of creation and end with heaven, the paradise of the new creation. This approach is useful and understandable. On the one hand, the Bible is a narrative with movement from one beginning to a new beginning; on the other hand, the biblical story shows that God does not abandon his creation, but instigates a process of restoration. Biblical history develops like a story with a plot.

There is, however, another equally valid way of considering it, and one that makes the vitality of the story starkly evident. Take the idea of a growing organism. It's the oak tree the king hid in that interests us more than the acorn, the beauty of the tulip rather than the bulb in the ground. The end product gives meaning to the whole process and its wonder—how ever did such beauty come from that?

This is also true with stories. We often classify them into those that have satisfying endings and those that don't. 'I felt let down by the ending' is a common lament. The art of the story-teller is the ability to lead up to the final unexpected twist. How frustrating it is to have someone spill the beans by telling you the end when you're only half way through!

For this reason, I think the important thing for understanding the Bible is its *end*. We already know many things about the future from what the Bible tells us, even if many more remain mysterious. When you look at the future in the Bible it gives a meaning to time from the perspective of eternity.

In this respect, the Bible is different from other books. You read a story or see a film once, twice perhaps if you really enjoy it. You read the Bible all your life, however, and every time you already know what the end is and understand it in that perspective. What could be more engaging? This is *your* life in the perspective of eternity and *your* future too. It's also scary as the Bible speaks about the ultimate tragedy that is not death but worse—existence in hell. The awful fact is that we can lose our lives as well as save them. Many of Jesus' parables carried this warning.

To trace the story line of the Bible we will start at the end and with what we know about the future. Then we will see the vital place of Jesus in the middle, as the one who prepares this special future. There is an 'after Jesus' before the end comes, the AD intermezzo we live in at present. Before Jesus, in the BC period of history, enveloped in the mists of the past there is the creation and a long time of unfulfilled hope. Jesus himself is the fulcrum of the whole story. The hour may be late but the clock is still ticking.

Unpacking the Story from the End

The kingdom of God has three aspects: it is the realm of God's perfect rule, it is a future expectation and it will be a spiritual kingdom unlike anything on earth. The Reformer John Calvin said that 'it would be pointless to speak about the kingdom without first warning readers that it is spiritual in nature. From this we infer its benefit for us as well as its power and eternity.'

However, God also shows his future reign in the world by his *presence* throughout the whole history of salvation. Heaven is not a place distant from the present world, but an aspect, normally kept secret, of present reality. When you are facing the sun your shadow is always behind you. The future of God's kingdom casts its shadow back through all of history.

What do we know about the future? Here are a few things from Revelation 21, the penultimate chapter of the book we are considering.

The Bible ends with happiness and joy. The conclusion of human existence is glory after constant suffering, being with God in a new and united humanity. Fellowship with God in our world, even under the new covenant with the coming of the Holy Spirit, is always only a forerunner of eternal glory. The promise 'I will be their God, they will be my people', repeated all through the Bible, reaches its conclusion (Rev. 21:3).

When God 'makes all things new' (Rev. 21:5) he becomes the 'all in all' of the new creation (Rev. 21:6, Rom. 11:38, 1 Cor. 8:6, 15:28). If our experience in this old world sometimes hints at this perfection, the new world reaches a fullness of joy, of life, of knowledge, of holiness and of justice in the new Jerusalem. God dwells in Sion; all that falls short of its perfection, 'all that is unclean', is excluded from the city (Rev. 21:27, Ps. 24) God will 'wipe away every tear from their eyes, and death shall be no more, neither shall there be mourning nor crying, nor pain any more, for the former things have passed away' (Rev. 21:4). The sea, a symbol of the turmoil and toil that toss us about in this life, will be no more (Rev. 21:1) Beyond the murky horizon of earthly vision the sky is royal blue.

Jesus Christ, 'the author and finisher of faith' (Heb. 12:2) is the centre, the craftsman and substance of this new world. His visiting card, presented in the first person singular, is I am *alpha and omega*. The first and last letters of the Greek alphabet indicate his rule over all history (Rev. 1:8, 11, 21:6, 22:13). He was there at the start and he will be there at the end. He is the summit and the beginning of a new order of created things. Jesus fulfils the Old Testament promise; but what he will do in the future sends us right back to the beginning:

> I am he; I am the first,
> and I am the last...
> from the beginning I have not spoken in secret,
> from the time it came to be I have been there.
> And now the Lord God has sent me,
> And his Spirit. (Isa. 48:12, 16, *cf.* 3, 7)

God declares 'the end from the beginning and from ancient times things not yet done' (Isa. 46:10 *cf.* Prov. 8:22). As author of the creation of God, Christ who is 'pre-eminent' (Col. 1:18) reigns over the universe, over everything.

A Story of Life, Knowledge and Justice

Human beings have always been fascinated and terrified by eternity. Variety is the spice of life; change, movement, progress and freedom are of the essence. Being tied down in a state of permanence seems like a living death. In his song, *Visions of Johanna,* Bob Dylan wrote 'Inside of the museums infinity goes up on trial/ Voices say this is what salvation must be like after a while'. There's the fear that living in eternity is being hung in a museum forever like a painting. Whatever could we do for all eternity?

The Bible mostly uses negative expressions to describe a dynamic new creation because the future world is not like the present. What we have to lose is darkness. It is a story of new life and light, new knowledge and final justice.

LIFE. Jesus is not only the first, the *alpha,* in creation but he also 'grants to eat of the tree of life which is in the paradise of God' (Rev. 2:7). What is this mysterious tree of life? The book of Proverbs tells us that 'wisdom is a tree of life to those who lay hold of her' (Prov. 3:18). The tree symbolises nothing less than the fullness of living with the boundless energy that comes from God who is life. Who is this wisdom if it is not Jesus Christ himself? He was the tree of life in the primeval garden of Eden (Gen. 2:9) to which man has no longer access. Human life ends in death. But in heaven the river of the water of life flows, watering the tree of life, the leaves of which are 'for the healing of the nations' (Rev. 22:1–5 *cf.* Ezek. 47:12). Eternity is the place where we will receive wisdom and life from Christ himself and live with him for ever.

Heaven is never presented in the Scriptures as being other than a place. Biblical symbols often show that heaven is not an ethereal state. For example, the Biblical images of the city, the promise of Jesus in John 14 where he announces that he is preparing a 'dwelling', the ascension described in Ephesians 4 as the passage from one place to another, the welcome of the brigand on the cross to paradise… Paul, in 1 Corinthians 15 presents the resurrection of Jesus as being the reconstitution of a glorified body; it precedes the resurrection of everyone, it is the first fruits.

Heaven is therefore the final place where Jesus is now, the *omega* in person, and in bodily form.

KNOWLEDGE. The present state of the knowledge of God in our world is partial, like that of a child. The apostle Paul says that in the 'adult' stage to come, 'I shall know fully, even as I have been fully known.' At present, our knowledge of God is like seeing 'in a mirror dimly, but then face to face' (1 Cor. 13:11–12). Revelation states, in a symbolic way, that the earthly lights will no longer be needed 'for the glory of God gives it light, and its lamp is the Lamb' (21:23). The eternal city itself is as 'transparent as glass.'

The knowledge of God will be transformed as the Old Testament prophet anticipated: 'for the earth shall be full of the knowledge of the Lord as the waters cover the sea' (Isa. 11:9; Hab. 2:14). The prophecy of Jeremiah concerning the new covenant, 'they shall all know me, from the least of them to the greatest' (Jer. 31:31–4; Heb. 8:11) already anticipates this glorious future reality.

Renewed knowledge in heaven will be the power to do things in the light and to benefit from transparency in every activity.

JUSTICE. Heaven is a place of supreme good, love and justice, where the blessing of perfect ethical harmony joins with divine holiness. The infidel Babylon, the great prostitute, must be judged and annihilated (Rev. 18:21, 19:2). God shows that 'his judgments are true and just.' The devil, the antichrist and the false prophet are all condemned to be thrown into the lake of fire (20:10). Those whose names do not appear in the book of life, the 'dead', the 'idolaters', suffer 'the second death' (20:15, 21:7–8).

The purification of creation introduces divine justice. Like the first creation, everything there will be 'very good'. Without this good God's reign would not be achieved. The terrible reality of hell is the demonstration of the justice and the holiness of God.

Entering the new creation is like an invitation to a wedding. (Matt. 22:1–14) The wedding of the Lamb is consummated with a pure bride, the new Jerusalem which comes down from heaven. (Rev. 21:2, 10) The wedding guests, 'those who are written in the Lamb's book of life' (Rev. 21:27), will be clothed in fine linen, that is 'the righteous deeds of the saints' (Rev. 19:7–8). So begins the history of the new creation where 'his servants will worship him. They will see his face' (Rev. 22:3–4).

God's presence banishes all ignorance, injustice and evil, a thing we can only dream about in this unhappy world. The mission entrusted to Adam will be an eternal occupation for the people of the last Adam, Jesus-Christ. Their life will be in truth, justice and holiness. The satisfaction and joy they will know are unimaginable.

Real life, true knowledge and pure justice are the things to which human beings aspire most. The end of the Bible's story brings them to life in the fullest way possible, because they will be complete and eternal.

The View from the Middle

God has spoken 'in these last days' by his Son. Jesus 'appeared once for all at the end of the ages to put away sin' (Heb. 1:2, 9:26). His appearance, called the incarnation, means that God has finally come to set things right in a world gone wrong. A new and different time has begun. The apostle Peter says that Christ 'was foreknown before the foundation of the world but was made manifest in the last times for your sake' (1 Pet. 1:20). Here are two contrasted but similar events: the foundation of the world and the end of time. The link between the two is the coming of Christ, who is the key that opens the door of the Bible's story line and does so in three complementary ways.

JESUS IS THE BEGINNING OF THE END. God's 'year of grace' is announced and has begun with Jesus (Luke 4:18–21). Slaves are set free because Satan is bound and dethroned. Satan falls from heaven; he no longer has the same power on earth as before because the kingdom has come. (Matt. 12:28, Luke 11:20) Note the manner in which the demons react to Jesus in the Gospels: 'if by the Spirit of God I cast out demons, then the kingdom of God has come upon you.' Jesus conquers evil, delivers men from its power and gives them access to the blessings of God's reign.

THE CRUCIFIXION BEGINS SOMETHING NEW. On the cross Jesus announced in the sixth of the seven words he pronounced 'it is accomplished' (John 19:30, also translated 'it is finished', Greek, *tetelestai*). It means that Jesus had done everything that had been foretold in order to save humanity. It also indicates that the end of the story begins at Calvary. The crucifixion is the judgment of the world (John 12:31). It is a final event that begins something new. Salvation was complete and Jesus left this world to enter another, his real home. The resurrection and the ascension begin a new creation. This story holds the secret of the new world.

JESUS AND WHAT LIES AHEAD. Since Jesus' life and death make known the truth of God's salvation, the end of the story is present in the way people respond to him. In John's Gospel Jesus himself is said to condemn no one. But his message—of which salvation is the goal—is a witness against those who reject him; it is also their judge (John 3:17–21, 12:46–8). Between the incarnation and the return of Jesus in glory, God's policy does not change. The conditions of salvation and judgment, which will be evident on the last day, are already there now. In a certain respect the end has already come in Christ. The last judgment makes evident what has been decided once and for all at the cross and in sinners' response to the good news of salvation.

As the story moves on from the cross and the resurrection to the end, the train leaves the platform. We can get on board or stay on the platform and our decision will decide our destination.

Half Time: After the Middle, Before the End

New wine needs new wineskins. The appearance of Jesus marks a turn in the story. The fact we have an Old and New Testament in the Bible underlines that.

The *new element* in the New Testament is not that the end is in sight. That has been the case from the start of the story. It is the *tension* between the decisive 'already' and the 'not yet completed', between the present and the future. A well-worn comparison suggests that the cross and the resurrection of Jesus are like D-day anticipating the final victory of V-day. The landing of 1944 was not the end of the war but its outcome is already on the cards. The battle that sets the scene for the rest of history has been won by Jesus.

We are now in an interim period, a 'time between' the resurrection and the future coming of Jesus in glory. Four new twists to the story appear.

SALVATION IS NOW. The New Testament story weaves a complex relationship between the past, the present and the future. The author of the Epistle to the Hebrews uses the words 'once for all' (Greek, *hapax, ephapax*: Heb. 7:27, 9:11–12, 26–8, 10:10, 12:26–7 and Rom. 6:10) to show that Jesus has procured salvation for his people. Similarly, 1 Peter 3:18: 'For Christ also suffered once for sins, the righteous for the unrighteous, that he might bring us to God'. The past, present and future are conditioned by one another. The story supposes that the salvation already revealed in Christ will be finalised when he appears a second time for those who wait for him (Heb. 9:28).

RECONCILIATION. The 'Berlin wall' separating God and man and between men has come down because Jesus dismantled it (Col. 1:20, Eph. 2:15–16). It is not a question of two enemies who make peace, because God was never man's opponent. The message of the gospel takes away *our* hatred for God. God reconciles the world to himself in Christ (2 Cor. 5:19). Man's sin brought his own loss on him. This breach is abolished by the obedience of Christ who stands for us. Christ destroyed the enmity by his death on the cross, while men were still his enemies (Rom. 5:10). Reconciliation is not a change in God. Christ took away man's sin. The door for forgiveness and new life is opened for those who believe. This is the 'now' of salvation.

VICTORY OVER DEATH IS ALREADY PRESENT. Christ is the conqueror of death and delivers from its inevitability and from its power (Rom. 6:9–10). Christ has destroyed death and brought immortality to light (2 Tim. 1:10). Death is conjugated in the past tense: death died when Jesus died. That is how the believer now experiences the victory of the kingdom in this life. He knows, by faith, that nothing can separate him from the love of God in Christ (Rom. 8:39). Christ presents himself to suffering Christians in Revelation 1:18 with the title 'first and last' and 'the living one': 'I died, and behold I am alive for evermore, and I have the keys of death and hell.' He is their master because he is their conqueror.

THE AGE OF THE SPIRIT. The Holy Spirit, promised in the Old Testament to bless the work of the Saviour (Isa. 61:1–2, 42:1), was received by Jesus and given to his apostles on the day of Pentecost. The gift of the Spirit places Christ's people under his care (Acts 2:16–17, Matt. 28:16–20). The Spirit of promise is a guarantee (2 Cor. 1:22, 5:5, Eph. 1:14). They already have some of the future blessings in faith, hope and love, if not their fullness. The Spirit lives 'forever' (John 14:16) with the people of God and allows them to recognise the Father (Gal. 4:4–6; Rom. 8:14–16) and to be part of God's family. The Spirit is the ongoing Spirit of the new creation who transforms the children of God to the likeness of Jesus (2 Cor. 4:6, 5:17, Col. 3:10).

These four new elements in the story mean that the life of believers is new life and one that looks forward in hope to the inevitable last act of the story, when Jesus will confirm it all as true by appearing a second time. In this new perspective 'the last days' are already here.

Before Half Time

The first half of the Bible, the Old Testament, is the part that gives people the most problems. Look at any regularly read Bible (perhaps your own) and you will probably see the pages of the New show more use than those of the Old.

In spite of its historical and cultural diversity, the Old Testament has a unified story. Its expectation looks to the coming day of the Lord when God will come and save his people. The footprints of Jesus are everywhere even if you have to be a good tracker to follow them.

It is impossible to draw an identikit picture of the person of Christ from the Old Testament story. The coming of Christ—God in person—into history far exceeds what could be seen from its prophecies. However, three themes run through the story.

CREATION LOOKS FORWARD. At the start of the Bible story in Genesis 2 and 3, the expression 'Lord God' is used a remarkable 20 times (out of 36 in the entire Old Testament). It indicates that God the Creator is also the Lord of nature and history.

God proposed to man the *modus vivendi* found in Genesis 2:16–17: 'You may eat of every tree of the garden, but the tree of the knowledge of good and evil you shall not eat, for in the day that you eat of it you shall surely die'. If a threat of death hangs in the air, it is because everything was created 'very good' and placed under a sign of blessing (1:28–2:2). Man's goal is a fellowship of love with God and harmony in all created reality. Once man sinned, the story took a nosedive. The grace of God that had been general, for all creation, became a common catastrophe, with life ending in death.

After man fouled up, God in his grace proposed a new start. He would take things in hand to deliver man from death and from himself, but most of all from Satan and evil (Gen. 3:15). This redemption of creation is realised ultimately in Christ. Thus, the successive high points of the Old Testament all have their particular character but they are all part of one story ending up in salvation.

ADAM'S CALLING. If in 'Adam all died, so also in Christ shall all be made alive' (1 Cor. 15:22). Christ is 'the last Adam' (15:45). In the development of the story in the first half of the Bible, there have been many 'Adams'—Noah, Abraham, Moses, Saul, David or Elijah—who all failed in the mission to lead the people of God to new life. Jesus epitomizes all that had gone before and succeeds where others had been found wanting. That explains why the Old Testament is a sad and sorry story, full of blood, sweat and tears. No human being can supply what is required to make things good with God. The Bible never brushes under the carpet the weaknesses and sins, even of the best people. One of the great heros of the Old Testament, King David, is a case in point.

The repeated snafus heighten Old Testament expectation, aided and abetted by God's repeated promises that the day *will* come. True humanity will be found in a prophet who will be like Moses (Deut. 18:15), in an everlasting priest after the order of Melchizedek (Ps. 110) and in a just king who will come to Jerusalem (Zech. 9:9) as the descendant of David (2 Sam. 7:12–13).

All this will happen in the people of Israel, called to be a true son of God in the new Eden of the promised land (Exod. 19:3–6). The institutional representatives end up being 'false Adams' with the weaknesses of their strengths. The Old Testament is a story of *déjà vu* because of the repeated disobedience and persecutions inflicted on those who seek to be true to God (Luke 11:51). For one good king in Judah you find a dozen bad eggs and in Israel there were none.

In the end God had to take over himself. Jesus puts a stop to the eternal return of God's people to evil ways. He shows what it means to be a true man and a proper son of God. In him the hopes of Israel are made good at last.

THE LIVING REDEEMER. In this context of failure, Matthew announces that Jesus, the true Son of God 'called out of Egypt' is, at the same time, 'son of David, son of Abraham' (Matt. 2:15, 1:1). Luke also presents him as a descendant of David who is also the 'son of Adam, son of God' (3:38). Jesus comes as the promised redeemer, announced from the start of the story.

The story has a last battle against the old serpent, identified as an agent of Satan in Revelation 12:9 and 20:2. The victor will be a descendant of Abraham (Gen. 22:18), of the tribe of Judah (49:10) and a descendant of David (1 Sam. 7:12–13). The battle against evil involves Immanuel ('God with us'—Isaiah 9:7) going through suffering and death to bear the afflictions that dog humanity. He will be put to death for his people (Isa. 53). The Redeemer is also the Son of Man who comes with the power of his eternal reign, shown in signs and wonders that identify him as the Messiah (meaning anointed one, Christ) in the New Testament (John 3:14, 6:62).

As the conqueror of Satan, Jesus is the opposite of Adam. He resists temptation and lies and lives a true and just life. By his resurrection Jesus responds to Job's extravagant expectation—'I know that my Redeemer lives, and at the *last* he will stand upon the earth' (Job 19:25). The triumph of life over death is the motor that drives all the Old Testament onward and upward to Jesus.

The Old Testament saints had their unfolding story and played their part in it. They looked to the future. The promised salvation was expressed in the following hopes that were earnestly expected, in spite of the repeated failures:

- the coming of a Redeemer,
- the final establishment of God's rule of justice,
- a new *entente* between God and man,

- the outpouring of the Holy Spirit,
- the great day of Lord,
- and the new heavens and the new earth.

They had all the promises but they had to keep on keeping on till God himself intervened and made the promises good.

Conclusion

Jesus and the apostles never speak about God's story in an abstract way. Their teaching brings out the reality of all that human beings could hope for: love, joy and peace with authentic freedom and dignity.

This ongoing story of liberation from evil, sin and death focusses on the person of Jesus. It encourages us to lead a life of hope in serving God and our fellows. It implies a new way of living in the world: 'Do not love the world or the things in the world. If anyone loves the world, the love of the Father is not in him... the world is *passing away*...but whoever does the will of God abides *forever*' (1 John 2:15–17).

The Bible does not advocate escape from the world to chase after pie in the sky. It tells an earthy story in a heavenly perspective. Understood this way, the Bible story puts a spring in our step, a song on our lips and thankfulness in our heart. In this topsy-turvy world the best is for the last because that is the programme of God's creation. Our lives are re-formatted in newness of life as we look back to the past, because we look back to the future.

4

Divine Revelation

Is there, in the Bible, a revelation from God to human beings? Surprising though it may seem, that the Bible has a revelation has even been called into question recently by Christian theologians. The general public, on the other hand, would probably not even know nowadays what the question means, or why it is important.

As a book, the Bible can be admired as literature, appreciated for giving information about the teaching of one Jesus, or recognised as having a unique story. These things in themselves do not settle the question as to whether the Bible reveals God in ways not found elsewhere. Many people, even nominal Christians, have doubts that it is so.

However there are problems that go even deeper than this.

Nothing Is Revealed?

There is no shortage of pundits who think there is no God to be revealed anyway and that man just has to get on with it by himself. Some people who do believe in God in a vague sense might doubt that there are any divine truths revealed at all. Others think the

Bible, like other religious books, is just one possible source of the knowledge of God. Added to that, most people we meet have never given it a thought.

Despite these common attitudes we cannot doubt that this is an issue by which Christianity stands or falls. In fact, if religion is about knowing a God who is known in ways other than those made available by the things around us, no religion at all can exist without a claim to revelation. As someone said, there is no religion worth the name that does not claim to be 'revealed religion'.

There are two basic forms of revelation. One of these is natural and the other claims something special beyond the natural. The first is based on the fact that human beings, through their experiences, have some sense of God. Voltaire is supposed to have said looking at the sunset—I adore you O God, but as for 'that lady and her son', let's leave them out of it! With his compatriot Rousseau, he believed that something of God could be sensed naturally, without any supposed nearness of God or an appeal to a special revelation.

The second claim to revelation concerns what has come to man through extraordinary means. Inspired texts form a body of information recognised to be in some respect special by the religious group that adheres to them. The teachings of the Qu'ran, the Buddhist Scriptures, the I Ching, Confucius or the Bible claim to give knowledge of 'God' not available elsewhere.

For Christians, three questions must be answered: Is there a revelation from God? Where is it found? And is it unique? We will answer these in the present chapter and in the following one.

What Is Revelation?

When the apostle Paul defends the gospel in his letter to the Galatians he says that he 'did not receive it from any man, nor was I taught it, but I received it through a revelation of Jesus Christ' (Gal. 1:12). In Ephesians he adds 'the mystery was made known to me by revelation... When you read this, you can perceive my insight into the mystery of Christ, which was not made known to the sons of men in other generations as it has now been revealed to his holy apostles and prophets by the Spirit' (Eph. 3:3).

The apostle is echoing what Moses wrote a long time before: 'The secret things belong to the Lord our God, but the things revealed belong to us and to our children for ever, that we may do all the words of this law' (Deut. 29:29). The mystery of the gospel that was secret for a long time has now been made known, and because of this new revelation Jews and Gentiles become one in Jesus-Christ.

So what is Paul claiming about revelation? Three things, I think.

Revelation is something that is not known naturally, since Paul claims that he did not get it by human means. Moreover, it concerns something that was not known hitherto, either because it was a secret kept by God, or simply because it was not known before the revelation was made. Revelation makes a difference between before and after. To illustrate: information in the black box reveals the mystery of why a plane crashed; or again, only when a statue is unveiled can the public appreciate its significance and value.

A second factor is that revelation involves an intentional act by the person who is doing the revealing. The press officer makes known what has been discovered in the plane's black box and the Mayor says when he will unveil the statue. Revelations exist when someone decides that it is appropriate to make them. So they are different from simple acts of discovery when something that was there all along is found, like gravity or the movement of the planets.

Revelation means that God decided to do something so that men would know what he wants them to know. It involves a revealer, something revealed and a recipient. This means that revelation is a personal decision and a personal act. It leads to new relationships between the parties involved based on new knowledge. People are angry when the black box gives up its secret revealing the plane was badly serviced and lawsuits follow as a result. Or the Mayor gets praise for the fine statue he commissioned.

In the biblical context, when the 'revealed things' are made known, the Jews can follow the way of the law not made known to other peoples in this way. The apostle's readers can appreciate how much his words are more than any human teaching and consequently something unexpected happens: Jews and Gentiles can see that they are on a common footing because of the revealed gospel and become one people in Christ.

Finally, if these passages of Scripture imply that revelation needs to be received, reception is not of the essence of revelation. It will still be revelation whether it is appropriated or not. Returning to our illustrations: people may refuse to credit the information given by the press officer about the black box, and still believe human error caused the plane accident. Citizens may not bother to come to the unveiling of the statue and perhaps never notice it, despite the Mayor's efforts at promotion.

So in the Old Testament, we see that the Jews, who were entrusted with revealed truth, too often went their own way rather than following God's law. Paul writes what he does in his Galatian letter because people were turning aside from the revealed gospel to an imitation. Although revelation exists, people can reject it or remain in ignorance, like a blind person who cannot see in the full light of day or a deaf person who cannot hear the music at a concert.

People pretend 'nothing is revealed' athough a lot is revealed. They cannot or will not see and hear—a tragic situation indeed.

A Revealed Book

In the light of these three factors, that revelation brings new knowledge, that it is personal and that it involves people who may or may not receive it, what can be said about revelation and the Bible? Can we speak about the Bible as being a 'revealed book'?

Some people insist solely on the personal aspect of revelation. For them revelation, rightly so called, is found in the personal encounter of an 'I and thou', to use Martin Buber's expression. It is personal, living, existential and above all a life-changing experience. However, even though this aspect of revelation is important, that is not all there is to the matter, according to the apostle Paul. Revelation implies a new body of knowledge and brings the elucidation of a mystery that is now more fully understood. It is difficult to compress revelation into the straightjacket of a personal experience without content. There has to be revealed truth, which means understood facts.

Again, some other people say that revelation is an act of God found somewhere behind the reports that we have in the biblical witness. Something did happen, there were mighty acts of God, but we cannot be sure that what it says in our Bibles actually happened. Did the children of Israel come safe through the Red Sea and were the Egyptians drowned, did the walls of Jericho tumble down, or did Jesus really walk on the water and make a meal for five thousand out of a boy's picnic? Often such events are taken to be purely symbolic presentations of something else that took place.

People separate what 'really' happened from what the Bible says because they have difficulty believing in miracles. What the Bible says is incredible, just too much for modern individuals who believe only their eyes. However the Bible itself never drives a wedge between what happened, what is written down and what is to be believed. Together the three make up revelation.

When Paul says 'the righteousness of God is revealed from faith to faith' (Rom. 1:17) he means that the gospel is worthy of confidence from beginning to end, from where faith starts to where it leads. Faith, the experience of trust, and the gospel go together. 'The righteous shall live by faith' precisely because the gospel is trustworthy. The gospel is decidedly historical. It is what God 'promised beforehand through the prophets in the holy Scripture, concerning his Son, who was descended from David according to the flesh and was declared to be the Son of God in power according to the Spirit of holiness by his resurrection from the dead' (1:2–4). So faith in God's justice is not blind faith but is fleshed out by the content of the gospel.

Does this link between faith, the gospel and what happened mean that the Bible is a revealed book? If it is the case, it is not the same kind of claim to revelation that is found elsewhere, for example in the Qu'ran or the *Book of Mormon*. The first claims to be a transcription of a heavenly code, whereas the second came down to Joseph Smith inscribed on golden plates that were later withdrawn to heaven. The Bible is not in the same league as other claimants to revelation. Where does the difference lie?

Firstly, the claim that the Bible is revelation is not simply a formal one. It is made in light of what is revealed—its content or message, the gospel of salvation that makes its way through history from something promised to the fulfilment in the life, death and resurrection of Christ. Revelation is present in the truth that lies before us in the pages of Scripture. Secondly, there is, in the biblical texts we have referred to, a prominent human element that is absent from other holy texts, precisely to underline their sacred character. In the Bible, the truth of revelation is not in a sacred reserve separate from other truths, but comes down into the theatre of daily life though human beings. In Galatians Paul can even give his testimony by saying that 'God was pleased to reveal his Son in me, in order that I might preach among the Gentiles' (1:16). Revelation is not separated from the truth content of what God makes known.

These two ideas lead us to take a closer look at revelation as a form of knowledge.

Revelation and Knowing God

It would be incorrect to think that revelation is about accumulating factual knowledge. Already we have said that revelation is personal. To be more precise we must add that first and foremost revelation concerns knowledge of *God himself*. God does not communicate with us primarily to tell us about things, about what he has done, or even to tell us what we need as human beings. God's revelation is above all about God himself. All that God is and does is for his own glory.

When God reveals himself, he makes his name known, his own special identity. God is 'I am'. This is his eternal name, he is the one eternal God. His changelessness is his faithfulness (Exod. 3).

Revelation has what we may call active and passive dimensions, because God is on the acting end and man is on the receiving end.

In an active sense revelation indicates that God acts and speaks to make himself known. Acts and words are tied together in divine revelation. A case in point is Psalm 19, which begins:

> The heavens declare the glory of God,
> and the sky above proclaims his handiwork.
> Day to day pours out speech,
> and night to night reveals knowledge.

Note that the words declare, proclaim, pour out and reveal are all verbs of speech. God's creation is a form of speech. The psalmist adds in the following verse that revelation is universal and no nation exists where this 'declaration' is not heard. This knowledge leads up to, and is no doubt subordinate to the Word of God. In verse 7 we read:

> The law of the Lord is perfect, reviving the soul;
> the testimony of the Lord is sure, making wise the simple.

In theological discussions divine revelation is usually separated into 'general' and 'special', God's acts in creation and his words in Scripture. This rather artificial distinction makes the question of revelation more manageable. The contrast between the two might help, but biblically speaking God's words in creation and his words in Scripture go together. One cannot be separated from the other—the God who has created is also the God who speaks. Nor can one be understood apart from the other—we need the Bible to help us praise God the creator and we also need to understand creation to be able to put redemption and salvation into their proper context. When salvation is separated from a creational perspective it tends to be individualistic and subjective. It becomes a feeling about ourselves, lacking in the humanness that comes from an understanding that God is our creator and the Lord of human history.

God's acts and words convey truth about himself. Above all they tell us about him and how we relate to him. Just as our actions and words give people an impression of what kind of persons we are, so God's acts and words characterise God for who he is.

It is important in everyday life to be lucid about our fellow men and women. We could scarcely get on in the workplace or in other social networks without this insight. In the family it is important to be sensitive to the needs of our children or parents. Lucidity about others defines the expectations we have of those around us as well as our responsibilities toward them. Likewise, lucidity concerning God is vital for human beings without exception. If we do not grasp the truth of what God is like from his revelation we will have all sorts of false expectations about his love or his justice with regard to ourselves and to others. We might have a very nice idea about God that is disastrous because it is false. Or we might have an equally disastrous idea that God is cruel that totally alienates us. We can only be realistic about God when we are realistic about his revelation in deed and word.

The passive side of revelation is its receptive aspect. At the end of Psalm 19, after having meditated on the glory of God in creation and in his law, David concludes:

> Let the words of my mouth and the meditation of my heart
> be acceptable in your sight,
> O Lord, my rock and my redeemer.

How does the psalmist respond to revelation? In thought and attitude. People who believe that God has spoken to them will speak to God in return. Their prayer expressed openly in words and secretly in the heart, is that their life will be acceptable to God. As Calvin presented it in the opening of his *Institutes*, the knowledge of God and the knowledge of self are twins. The encounter of the two produces reverence, true piety and worship of God. This is why God is called 'rock' and 'redeemer'; God is faithful to his people and is continually active to save them.

This is not abstract knowledge but life-giving, saving knowledge.

How Does God Speak?

A Christian view of revelation and a Christian view of God stand or fall together. If you modify your ideas about one of them, the other will have to change to line up with it.

From the time of the eighteenth century Enlightenment, God was thought of as being distant. He is so far from the affairs of men as not to be revealed directly in a specific and personal way in our world. God does not speak in a supernatural way, even if it was allowed that the order of the natural realm showed that a great architect was out there somewhere. Man could get on with examining (and exploiting) this order without refering to anything taught in the Bible.

In the last fifty years things have swung in the other direction and these ideas have been turned on their head. In New-age thinking God is everywhere and everything is a part of God. Reality is endowed with a new form of mystery. It is not two (God *and* the world) but one. This is called monism or one-ism. The divine is in every form of life. Everything is invested with an aura of spirituality. Our contemporaries who often live regimented daily lives look for spirituality as an escape. Get beyond the surface through meditation, restore bodily balance through diet, look into the new forms of the occult, plan your future with astrology and something of the ultimate order will surface. God is not a speaking God, but the divine amniotic fluid nourishes life in the eternal womb.

How very different are these two forms of naturalism from biblical faith! In fact they are denials of how the Bible presents God in his revelation. The first supposes that God is nowhere around, certainly not in words or miracles, whereas the second sees the divine everywhere and everything is suffused with a sense of wonder. But the Bible says neither that God is absent, nor that we can find him everywhere.

One of the problems with these two world-views, whether they emphasise naturalism or mystery, is that they take the world we live in as being normal. They can recognise human weakness and failures but they have no sense that sin makes a mess out of God's good creation. If man is in dire straits he can achieve something to alleviate suffering either by his enormous technical know-how or by his experiences. It is hardly surprising that the world's third best-seller after the Bible and the Qur'an is the *Guinness Book of Records*. Man is proud of his ability to climb every mountain.

In the biblical view, the world is not normal nor is it 'just there'. In Genesis 1 God created by speaking and Psalm 33 sums up the creative act as being a word-act: 'By the word of the Lord the heavens were made, and by the breath of his mouth all their host' (33:6). Everyday events in the world are not just natural but come by God's word of command:

> He sends out his command to the earth;
> his word runs swiftly.
> He gives snow like wool...
> He sends out his word and melts them... (Ps. 147:15–18)

God's word governs comprehensively all that happens in the cosmos:

> Who has spoken and it came to pass
> unless the Lord commanded it?
> Is it not from the mouth of the Most High
> that good and bad come? (Lam. 3:37–8)

Joe Bloggs says if it snows it snows and if it snows it does so because of the weather system. He is a great believer in chance, good times and bad come, *que sera sera*. The Bible says these things reveal God's control and his control is exercised though his speaking. God's speech is the foundation of all things and together they reveal the grandeur and intelligence of the Creator.

Why can men not see it and why do so many people think we are here simply by chance because the watchmaker is blind? The Bible's answer to this concerns the second difference between naturalism and Christianity, the fact that man, as well as being finite, is blind and sinful. To deal with this condition, God makes a new move. To his word that orders the world he adds a word that saves the world. The saving speech of God is his word found in the Bible.

East of Eden

At the beginning of creation, presented in Genesis, God was present (Gen. 3:8) and man knew God and knew what he had to do. Because God was there with man there was no distinction between the supernatural and the natural. Nor were there any 'religions'. The religion of the creation was simply man knowing and loving God. Loving God and the neighbour was normal behaviour.

Then came the crash and man's stock plummeted. Man's rebellion led to a withdrawal of God's presence. Enmity came instead of love.

Man began to be afraid of God, as sin always makes us fearful of God. Soon there was the first murder. Many religions sprang up. They were pagan, *from the earth*, and were nature oriented. Man's life was cast east of Eden. Humanity's impossible project, whether expressed in the writings of Rousseau, in ideological visions of the new man, or in trips to Woodstock, has been to 'get back to the garden'.

What happened? At the gate of Eden, outside of God's presence, revelation ceased to be supernatural and became natural. This was not a failure of the revelation in creation, but was the result of the fact that men no longer 'saw fit to acknowledge God' (Rom. 1:28). The revelation was still there. It is even highlighted by signs that things are no longer normal in suffering, disorder and death. Because of man's rebellion, what was now needed was a new special revelation to heal the problems of sin.

This is a valid aspect of the complex distinction between general and special revelation. The general no longer hits the spot of human need. Something special from God is necessary. That the natural is no longer sufficient is shown indirectly in that paganism and religions in general have their priests, sacrifices, prophets, oracles and rites, all of which purport to be means of access to the divinity.

So what does the Bible say about the limits of general revelation and how is a remedy found in the Word of God as special revelation?

Revelation East of Eden

Revelation in a general sense is something revealed by God to man. General revelation is what can be known about God by all human beings through his acts of creation and providence. This category is broad enough to include what men see around them in the glories of nature, what they can observe through the regularities of history and also what their conscience tells them.

What does Scripture itself teach about this? The Bible tells us that there is an abundance of evidence to support the view that there is a general revelation of God in the world, a revelation that shows what the Creator is like. However, if it was sufficient for man before sin came into the world, it no longer allows him to know

God in a sinful world. General revelation does not lead to *natural theology*, the idea that things about God can be read directly from the book of nature. Looking at nature, history or our conscience does not allow us to claim you can't see God, but you *know* he's there. Could the eternity of God be read off from things temporal, or the righteousness of God from the injustices in history, or the love of God from a visit to the cancer ward? Not likely.

The abundance of evidence for general revelation is found in the Old Testament in the 'nature psalms' (Pss. 8, 19, 29, 93, 104, 147, etc.). All of these psalms bear witness to the Lord, affirming that he is great and so is his power. The New Testament builds on this perspective and indicates man's predicament.

Acts 17, Romans 1 and 2

In Acts 17:22–31 Paul speaks to the city fathers at Athens and attendant philosophers and says that God has so ordered things that men ought to be able to seek him and find him because 'in him we live and move and have our being', something that the Greek poet Aratus said falsely about Jupiter, rather than about the one true God. God is never far away.

In Romans 1, Paul again affirms the reality of general revelation. He even says that 'they knew him' (Rom. 1:21) and that 'what can be known about God is plain to men, because God has shown it to them. For his invisible attributes, namely, his eternal power and divine nature, have been clearly perceived, ever since the creation of the world, in the things that have been made' (1:19–20).

Romans 2 extends the principle of general revelation to the human conscience and the case of those who know nothing of the Word of God:

> When the Gentiles, who do not have the law, by nature do what the law requires, they are by nature a law to themselves, even though they do not have the law. They show that the work of the law is written on their hearts, while their consciences also bear witness, and their conflicting thoughts accuse them or even excuse them... (Rom. 2:14–15)

What these two texts add up to is that there is a revelation in the world which should allow the Gentiles to have immediate recognition of God as the eternal creator of the universe and to know right and wrong by his standards. What the apostle seems to be saying is you can see God, but you *don't know* he's there.

However, despite the reality and clarity of the revelation of God out there in the world, although it is totally sufficient because God has revealed his invisible power and glory and despite its authority to excuse or accuse our behaviour, we draw a blank when it comes to recognising God for who he is. Instead of following the road that leads to the knowledge of God, man, according to Paul, turns off into all sorts of blind alleys. Here is what he says about it to counterbalance what he says positively about the knowledge of God in Acts 17 and Romans 1:

- It is a folly to worship an unknown God in the light of creation (Acts 17:23).
- If man is 'God's offspring' and 'has his being in him' idolatry is totally unwarranted (28–9).
- God makes himself known clearly in creation and hence we are without excuse (Rom 1:20).
- Men know God but fail to honour or thank him (1:21).
- They exchange the glory of God for senseless idolatry (1:23).
- They exchange the truth of God for a lie (1:25).
- They serve the creature not the Creator (1:25).
- They exchange what is natural for what is contrary to nature (1:26–7).
- Not seeing fit to recognise God for what he is, their behaviour goes from bad to worse (1:28–30).
- They know God's decree of judgment against sin, but they wallow in it (1:32).

That adds up to quite an indictment.

There is a difference of accent in Acts 17 and Romans 1, not because the apostle changed his mind, but probably because of his way of handling a different context and audience. However, there is a common thread that runs through the two passages. What the apostle says positively about general revelation is consistently minimalised by counter references. Man disastrously abuses what he knows. He suppresses, replaces or rejects it and becomes a slave to idolatry and degradation. This is because the Gentiles do not want to recognise the general manifestation of God's power and glory. Every sign of the divinity is traded for counterfeit ideas and filthiness. Sin exchanges the palace for the pigsty.

Human Inability

Inability to profit from what can be known of God lies in man's unwillingness to recognise God and in his desire to protect his supposed liberty by going his own way. Man consistently rejects God and does not want to know about him.

Of course materialistic punters will never realise this and will never accept the apostle's analysis. And this is logical, because Paul reaches these conclusions from the standpoint of special revelation. Man is inexcusably faulted by his rejection of what can be known about God from the creational revelation. That is why he needs a new revelation, one that is specially adapted to deliver him from this predicament. Otherwise he will remain clamped by his sin.

It is precisely for that reason that after chiding the Athenians for the folly of their idolatry, Paul swings abruptly to the resurrection as a demonstration of timely deliverance from the judgment of sin. Mockery, dilly-dallying or faith are the only possible outcomes in response to this challenge (Acts 17:31–4).

Inexcusable

The reality of revelation that surrounds every human being and extends down into the inner depths of the conscience provides a rope that is short enough for hanging but not long enough to lower man to safety.

Everything our eyes see, every thought, every creative effort, every faculty that sinks its roots into the depths of our being, bespeak the glory of God and the wantonness of the sinful dilapidation of God's gifts. Every minute that passes provides fresh opportunities to accept the obvious. The broad road draws man on and the multitude of missed opportunities of giving glory to God only equals the depth of the degradation of the human heart.

C.S Lewis said that one of Satan's most successful ploys is to make people believe that he does not exist. Convincing us that the abnormal is normal and that all is well in this troubled world must be a close runner-up.

5

God's Special Revelation

Believing God as Creator and believing revelation go together. When you study a famous painting of a French café at night it's obvious that there was a painter. If you know a bit about the subject you recognise the style of Van Gogh. The canvas tells something about its creator. If you perceived that he was a troubled soul, you would not be wrong.

Similarly, the creation reveals something about God and his character. That is why the image of the designer or the watchmaker has often been used as an image for the work of God.

Special Revelation

We have seen previously that general revelation tells us something about God and that it has its limits. It became insufficient because of the blindness of sinful humanity, but God did not wipe his hands of the situation. He acted in another way so as not to leave himself without a clear witness. This is what we call special revelation.

Over against general revelation, the word 'special' tells us something about the nature of this revelation. It describes a certain kind of action that is limited to specific times and places. Only a few important letters are sent special delivery, not everyday correspondence. Special revelation also indicates that specific words or actions are the result of a precise decision and action on God's part. 'I am the Lord your God' is different from any other series of words; the miracle of the exodus from Egypt is no ordinary sea crossing. Extraordinary divine intervention seems implausible to many people, as they have never heard such a word or actually witnessed it themselves. Finally, whereas in general revelation things putter on as normal in the world, special revelation implies an event that breaks with the regularity. Mail may be delivered at regular times twice a day, but a special delivery can arrive unexpectedly any time, even while you are out.

God's special acts and words in the world are limited, extraordinary and occasional. They convey things no one could ever deduce from looking at the creation or in the human heart. They mark times when God decides to act for a specific purpose. Some people think God is speaking to them today in a special way. Others think that God never speaks. However, no one can imagine what hearing a special word of God would be like since no one today has ever heard one. In both cases it has been forgotten that God only ever acts to achieve certain ends that he has decided upon, so it is vital to know what God's purpose is before thinking about what is possible, or what is not, as far as our expectations are concerned.

The content of the Bible is rather surprising on this score. Firstly, in contrast with the general revelation that is literally everywhere, special revelation is in short supply. It is limited to some people God had dealings with of old, like Abraham, Isaac and Jacob, Moses and the people of Israel. These folk received the word given by God. It was also given to prophets whose job it was to recall God's covenant when Israel was forgetful. Later revelation was associated with Jesus and his apostles. After this, revelation ceased, although the Roman Catholic church pretended to keep it alive in an indirect form in developing traditions. However, it is obvious that God was not speaking in Indonesia at the time of Abraham, in South America at the time of Isaiah or in the Isle of Man in the first century. It is also apparent that he is not speaking today like he did during the apostles' lifetime. If it were so, we would logically add texts to the Bible and make it longer and longer with lots of additions, with the problem of authenticity raising its ugly head.

Claims to special revelation today, like claims to extra-bodily experiences, are often defeated by their witnesses. I once went to a retreat centre in France and was struck by a 'revelation' concerning the place, framed and hung in the dining room, in place of honour. When I returned a couple of years later, it had disappeared. Someone had found that this particular 'revelation' had fallen short.

Secondly, in the Bible's history-line, drawn from Adam to Jesus Christ by Matthew (1:1–17), Luke (3:23–38) and Paul (Rom. 5:12–20), revelation is found unevenly spread. This irregularity is another surprising aspect of special revelation. God's words and works tend to be found in clusters at times when God is acting in a specific way to save his people. There are long periods when nothing happens. In one instance, at the time of Eli (1 Sam. 3:1), when God had been silent for a while, the writer remarks that 'the word of the Lord was rare in those days; there was no frequent vision'. Revelation was not on tap then, nor is it now. It is special!

So why did God act in this selective fashion?

The Purpose of Special Revelation

A common misunderstanding is that God started to speak to man only after the fall. However, God spoke and acted before it was necessary for him to speak to man about his problems. After man had rebelled against God, his speaking to man had a different aim. It was no longer simply for communion but also for correction and reorientation.

The speaking was always there. All God's works of creation and providence are related to his word of speech (Gen. 1:3, Ps. 33:6, 9, 29:3–9, Isa. 30:31, 66:6, for example). God is a personal, self-conscious being and speaking or saying are the ways in which he brings his thoughts into existence and communicates with his creatures. God speaks and man can discern the mind of God although not like he can understand other human beings.

When man rebelled against God, his sinfulness blinded him to this revelation. God's special revelation became necessary not because what he had already done was vague or insufficient in itself but because humanity now needed something more to be able to understand the general revelation. Without special revelation, men have strange ideas and reach many false conclusions in their scientific activity or in their religious search for God. Superstitions are spawned in response to general revelation. Why in some religions is an animal like a cow thought to be holy, why does voodoo exercise such a hold over whole tribes, or why can the spirits of ancestors be considered guides for decision-making? Special revelation in act and word is needed to exorcise the errors from human religion and culture and to help men understand their ecosphere correctly.

Because of sin, new revelation became indispensable to any understanding of God. It was necessary not only because man had to have it to keep alive, but also because of God's purpose for the created world. In this perspective, special revelation is an act of God's grace, it is free and undeserved. In his goodness God speaks and acts to restore a sin-devastated world and to renew humans in his image. The ultimate purpose, in line with the principle of grace, is life and salvation for creation. Everything in special revelation contributes progressively to that end.

Jesus spoke often about the 'kingdom of God', nowhere more so than in the parables in Matthew 13. The story of the sower, the good seed and the weeds, the mustard seed and the leaven, the hidden treasure, the pearl of great worth, the net and the different types of fishes all express two principles. Firstly, the continuing process, the growth toward a final situation is capital. In a sense, the outcome is inevitable. The second idea is that in an ongoing situation there might seem to be no development, but there is secret growth. Jesus describes how the word of God acts, secretly, towards an end when the whole process comes to fruition.

God's kingdom grows out of the mysterious action of his word in the world. Its finale is not earthly but heavenly, but it grows to that end in an earthly way. That is why God calls a special people, the family of Abraham and his descendants, but promises to bless all the nations of the earth through this one family (Gen. 17:4). It is why God makes a covenant with a people and gives a promise that runs all through the Bible, 'I will be your God and you will be my people'. The end will come when all things are made new because the purposes of God have been fulfilled. God dwells again with his people 'and God himself will be with them as their God' (Rev. 21:3).

The words and deeds of special revelation are like Lego building blocks fitting together. The completed construction of a heavenly city will replace the garden that was lost to man at the start. God's word is kingdom building.

How does God bring about this special revelation?

How God Works in Special Revelation

A common misconception is that God's special revelation is found in the Bible and is limited to it. This is only half the story.

The words we read on opening the Bible are only the final touches on God's special revelation. A great deal of divine activity preceded the production of these words, and without it the words themselves would not exist. This activity includes God's general providence in history, acts by which he saves his people, miracles, the giving of promises and their fulfilment, the preparation and calling of witnesses, the work of the Holy Spirit with regard to them, verbal proclamation, the leading of the Spirit in writing down their message and finally, the transmission of the written word to others. Special revelation includes a whole series of different actions on the part of God, the greater part of which are hidden and are known only by what Scripture itself tells us about them.

Because of this, a biblical view of the inspiration of Scripture requires a biblical view of the providence of God and a doctrine of God who personally rules over and supervises history. A worldview rooted in modern rationalism with a universe closed to divine activity makes such a view impossible. If God does not have access everywhere, he can intervene nowhere. So for a good many nominal Christians the inspiration of Scripture is nothing more than the literary genius of special people, its witness is nothing other than relative to a bygone moment and its message is culturally landlocked. If it is referred to as the 'word of God' this expression is only used metaphorically. The Bible is called *holy* not because of any of its inherent features but because of the effects it may produce in us.

Let us take a case in point to illustrate how broad God's activity is in revelation by referring to Paul's epistle to the Galatians. What goes into this text is not just a matter of the apostle sitting down and writing his letter, like I decided to have another go at this book today. His penning it was the end point of a production line. A multitude of factors influenced what he wrote. Some of the more obvious ones are found in the following ten points. Points 1–4 form the background, 5–6 the situation and 7–10 the capacities of the author of Galatians for the task:

1. Paul's education as a Jew and his in-depth knowledge of Judaism;
2. his meeting with the risen Jesus and miraculous conversion on the Damascus road;
3. his theological training in the Syrian desert where he had unutterable visions;
4. his conviction about the newness of the gospel and his showdown with Peter and the other apostles about their compromises;
5. the dangers he saw for the Galatian church;
6. his authority as an apostle and the need to intervene to sort things out;
7. his understanding of how the relation between the law and the gospel applies to a practical problem in the infant church;
8. his pastoral concern for people;
9. his God-given genetic heritage and psychological make-up;
10. finally, his literary mastery, including the use of the rhetorical forms common in ancient literature to make his point.

Given all these and many other factors, at some point Paul decided to take emergency measures and write his letter. So perhaps around 49 AD (dating Galatians is a complicated question, according to whether one adopts the 'north or south Galatian theory'), perhaps at Antioch, the apostle sat down and for a couple of days wrote 'large letters with his own hand' (Gal. 6:11) to these churches in distress. This meant buying parchment and ink, making a plan of what he wanted to write, as he had no 'undo typing' key, paying for a copy to be made and then the transport costs for sending the letter.

Overall, this amounted to a considerable investment of energy and cash. Why go to all this trouble? Paul was conscious of writing under the leading of the Spirit to transmit his 'gospel' which was not of human origin, but 'through a revelation of Jesus Christ' (1:12). This was his life and a matter of life and death for him.

The amount of ingredients that go into producing the epistle to the Galatians is amazing. When we are reading Galatians we tend to forget these factors and just look at the final form of the text in front of us. Before the actual writing and the attendant inspiration, the number of preliminaries God oversaw is impressive. This is a forgotten aspect of special revelation and the more's the pity, as it highlights the nature of the God with whom we have to do.

Because of these considerations, the *manner* in which special revelation is accomplished can be approached from two angles, either from its objective and external perspective or from the subjective and internal one. We will briefly consider these before looking at the *content* of special revelation.

Acts of God in Revelation

The point we have made is borne out in an important way by the major event of the Bible. The central focus in special revelation is an external act of God that is miraculous in nature. The person of Jesus is a miracle in his origin, his nature and in his words and works. Jesus himself is the miracle of world history.

Jesus did many miracles that showed his power over nature, his compassion in healing by defeating the consequences of sin and death and finally his power over sin itself and its originator, Satan. Jesus has the power to forgive sins, which is miraculous, as only God can forgive sin. Jesus does the work of his heavenly Father, not his own work. He is miraculously active as God's priest, prophet and king and he sums it up in the terse phrase 'I am the way, the truth and the life'. He is also a unique revelation: 'no one comes to the Father but by me' (John 14:6). These miracles of Jesus are all less than the miracle that *he himself is* in the incarnation, God in human flesh.

The author of the Hebrews sums it up in his opening verses:

> Long ago, at many times and in many ways, God spoke to our fathers by the prophets, but in these last days he has spoken to us by his Son, whom he appointed the heir of all things… After making purification for sins, he sat down at the right hand of the Majesty on high.

What exemplifies the high point of revelation is typical of what we find throughout. God acts and speaks to his people. There are many acts of God in the history of salvation, 'many times and many ways' and miracles are of the essence of revelation, not something tacked on. In fact it can be said that at every point at which God touches the ways of this world with his presence we encounter something mysterious and miraculous, inexplicable in human terms.

God calls Abraham from paganism, Sarah miraculously has a son, who is saved from death by God's provision on Mount Moriah, Jacob is blessed instead of his more extravert brother Esau, he wrestles with the messenger of God and is renamed Israel. Joseph saves his brothers in Egypt because unlike the soothsayers he can interpret Pharaoh's dream. God delivers his people after a series of signs and wonders, leads them to the land of the promise by many instructive acts in the desert, delivers them from the Philistines when he appears to faithful judges, establishes David on the throne, exiles his people for their unfaithfulness and restores them, promises them salvation through a son of David who will be a deliverer and keeps the hopes of a remnant alive until Jesus appears.

If many of God's acts are done through natural processes, when the extraordinary appears, the miraculous brings with it salvation and judgment at the same time. If in his special appearances God comes to save his people, his presence also brings holy judgment when he encounters sin. Miracles always imply judgment of godless idolatry and unexpected salvation. Therefore, God's covenant in Deuteronomy includes blessings for obedience and curses for unfaithfulness. That God is God is unmistakable: 'See now that I, even I, am he, and beside me there is no god; I kill and I make alive; I wound and I heal and there is none that can deliver out of my hand' (Deut. 32:39).

When Jesus appears, however, God's acts of revelation rise to a new level of intensity, for three reasons. Firstly, the incarnation of God's son goes beyond any Old Testament expectations of the coming of a Messiah because God himself appears and acts in human form. Secondly, the miracle of the incarnation includes blessings and judgments pronounced on God's people. As the true Israel, the Son of God called out of Egypt, Jesus is the blessed one spoken of truly in all the statements of the Beatitudes, but who also bears the curse of death and the ignominy of sin for and in the place of his people. 'Crucified for our transgression and raised for our justification' presents the two-sided miracle of salvation. Finally, the resurrection is the concluding miracle not because a cadaver is resuscitated (which it is), but because the Son enters into the final victory and the glory of life eternal. Such things are unknown in ancient mythology even if corpses coming to life again have appeared in mythical imagination. The resurrection attested by the appearances of the living Jesus (1 Cor. 15) finds its conclusion in the appearance of Christ at the end of the age (Acts 1).

The dual aspect of special revelation in act and word has its own logic about it. If God intervened to do great things in salvation, it's hardly astonishing that he himself should tell us what they meant. Moreover, revelation in word does not simply recount some unique acts of God; it is *true*. The acts and the witness go together. No one will ever believe in special revelation in the Bible unless they believe in it outside the Bible, and to do that we need to believe what Jesus said: 'your word is truth' (John 17:17).

So what then can be said about the word that we have received textually in Scripture? This question brings us to the second aspect, the manner of revelation and its internal or subjective perspectives.

Word-Acts of God in Revelation

Imagine that God did many things to save his people without adding his word to his acts. In a good many cases the human witnesses could have given a fair account of what happened. However, more often than not, because of lack of understanding, confused accounts would have been the result. For this reason, God not only acts, but also explains the significance of his actions.

A good illustration is when Moses met God at the burning bush. When the bush didn't burn up Moses said, let's take a minute to see this great sight (Exod. 3:3). The bush doesn't burn just to catch Moses' attention, it provides a means by which God explains to Moses who he is. God is changeless in his purposes, like an inextinguishable flame. He also answers Moses' question about how he can explain this to the Israelites. Another case is on the Damascus road when Jesus meets Saul. His companions hear a loud noise, but Saul falls to the ground and hears Jesus speaking (Acts 9:4).

When God acts to reveal himself to his servants he adds words to make his purposes clear. Acts are mute without words to interpret them. The basic form of special revelation in the Bible is an account of divine actions and the divine interpretations that go with them. Other aspects of biblical revelation—laws, poetry, wisdom and worship, are built on the infrastructure of the divine acts of salvation.

Another illustration. The two who met Jesus on the Emmaus road received a lecture from the Old Testament about his death and resurrection, yet only when he broke bread with them did they get the message. They had the facts, but they needed the interpretation that came with his presence to understand that he was alive.

So to be fully understood, the external side of revelation needs completing with internal illumination. Acts of God are revelation in so far as they produce knowledge. For this reason, revelation includes internal understanding aided by the Holy Spirit. What would we know about what Jesus came to accomplish had he not also taught his followers? And what would we know if he had not sent the Holy Spirit to lead his disciples into all truth about the understanding of salvation (John 14:15–31)? Probably precious little.

Prophetic Revelation

By what process are the acts of God complemented by verbal revelation and eventually transmitted on the written page? The external act is internally appropriated; through this process history becomes prophetic history. It is interpreted in the light of a whole, completing what has gone before and announcing what will come later. To return to the burning bush: God interprets this event to

Moses and the bush takes on prophetic significance. It points to the holiness of God (Exod. 3:5), indicates that God is the God of the fathers (6), and that God has seen oppression and comes to save (9, 10), that the people will be saved to worship God (12) and that this is God's memorial, as his name will always be the same (15). The future is also predicted—Pharaoh will resist but the Israelites will plunder Egypt before they leave.

The role of Moses in Old Testament revelation is emblematic. It is summed up in Numbers 12:6, a passage that provides a key for the way revelation works:

> (The Lord) said: If there is a prophet among you, I the Lord will make myself known to him in a vision; I speak with him in a dream. Not so with my servant Moses... with him I speak mouth to mouth, clearly and not in riddles, and he beholds the form of the Lord.

The prophetic word often stems from visions and dreams, but with Moses, God speaks to him face to face. Moses stands out as exceptional. Only Christ surpasses him in terms of the directness of revelation. Moses alone knew God in this special way (Deut. 34:10), but throughout the prophetic age of the Old Testament, God fulfilled his promise by putting his words into the mouths of prophets and speaking to his people through them (18:15, 18, 20).

Israel's prophets, when they were true prophets, spoke the words of God and no others, just as Moses had done, although they received the message internally, in a different way, through dreams and visions. The method was different, but the result was not inferior by comparison with Moses. The words were not theirs, but the Lord's, as in the case of Jeremiah (1:9), Isaiah (6:9, 51:16, 59:21), Ezekiel (3:4), or Amos (7:15). The prophets, like Moses, present the word of God received in visions, what they had 'seen' as divine communication, often pretexted with 'Thus says the Lord'.

Prophecy is therefore primarily a word that results from God 'touching the mouth' and teaching it what to say (Exod. 4:12). A whole succession of prophetic witnesses are to be expected because of the Lord's promise. This form of revelation is different from external manifestation because of God's internal action on the prophets. It is also different from a form of ecstatic trance-like state where the person is totally unconscious. The prophet was a man of the Spirit, moved by the power of God to speak God's word through visions and dreams: 'it was borne by the Holy Spirit that men spoke from God' (2 Pet. 1:21).

So when the prophets spoke God's word they transmitted it in their own way, according to their own psychological make-up, intelligence and linguistic ability, but the word they spoke was God's word received by internal suggestion. As persons they were not passive in this process, because, being moved by the Spirit, they passed on in their own personal way what they had received. God did not over-rule the human personality of his servants, but he adapted himself to it in order to communicate his word.

God manifested himself in external acts to save his people but he also suggested his words internally so that they could be communicated to them via prophetic utterances resulting from visions, dreams and communications. As revelation developed and particularly in the New Testament revelation, the personalities of the witnesses occupied a more prominent place. The divine influence and the human factors became more of a piece in revelation, the Holy Spirit working to inspire the authors of the written witness in inspiration. More will be said about this later in chapters 8 and 9.

The Content of Special Revelation

What is the message of special revelation and how can its specific content be described?

Most people no doubt think the Bible is some kind of random collection of stories that are edifying because the good guys invariably are sorted out from the bad. Even among Christians there is probably a low level of understanding of what makes the content of the Bible specific. Children in Sunday school often answer 'Jesus' to any question you ask them; many adults will not do otherwise if you ask them what the content of the Bible is. The development of revelation throughout Scripture remains a vague notion to them and they can make little of the Old Testament.

The key to special revelation is found right after the fall, in the opposition that God promised to put between the offspring of the serpent and the offspring of the woman, resulting in a bruised head and a bruised heel (Gen. 3:15). The offspring of the children of Satan will be mortally wounded by the offspring of the woman, who will be injured though not mortally. God promises that in spite of sin, history will continue and that good will eventually defeat evil. The content of special revelation is in this promise, the promise of God to save human beings through one of their own descendants.

In the New Testament the apostle Paul stated in Romans 4:13 that God's promise was the essence of faith in God in the Old Testament. He refers to Genesis 15:6: 'the promise to Abraham and his offspring that he would be heir of the world did not come though the law but through the righteousness of faith.' Abraham trusted in God and that was 'counted to him as righteousness'. He was saved by faith that God would keep all his promises of salvation for his offspring.

When the law came with Moses, it did not change the principle of salvation by grace through faith for humanity given in God's promise: 'the law was added because of transgressions, until the offspring should come to whom the promise had been made' (Gal. 3:19). The promise is the foundation of the covenant God made with Abraham and the fulfilment of the covenant could only be achieved via the promise. The law of Moses made the promise all the more important for the covenant. God will save his people through what he does for them.

The fundamental 'I will be your God and the God of your people' is deepened in all God does throughout the older Testament. The promise of God, maintained in spite of the disobedience of his people, concerns first and foremost not the 'descendants' of Abraham, but the one descendant who will fulfil the covenant. 'The promises were made to Abraham and to his offspring. It does not say "offsprings", referring to many, but referring to one "and to your offspring", who is Christ' (Gal. 3:16). Paul ties together the whole of the history of special revelation as being a promise concerning Jesus Christ and salvation by faith in him. This is the substance of God's purposes: his promise and the faith it calls for.

The Final Revelation

Revelation made to man meanders and deepens as it runs through the history of the Old Testament to Jesus Christ. In him the promise of Genesis 3 and the promises of the covenant made to Abraham find their destination. He comes to keep the promise and to accomplish salvation. He is the end point of God's revelation and the New Testament itself is nothing more and nothing less than an explanation of the completion of the covenant by him.

In this sense, the content of special revelation is the promise of salvation and faith in this promise is faith in God's salvation in the Old and the New Testament. Nothing can be added or is to be added to the final revelation in Christ.

6

Word Revelation

The Bible is a book with a particular written form, because it is the book of *God's covenant*.

The biblical covenant is a special relationship that binds God and man together with a shared interest and mutual love. It provides the form that underlines the script of the Bible.

The action of the covenant drama is a tragedy with a happy ending. The plot unfolds in the lavishly equipped theatre of God's glory, the creation, a place owned by a generous benefactor. There was no reason for God to build this theatre other than his own philanthropic activity, but once he had done so he was intimately involved with it and its personnel. He intervenes repeatedly in their interest. As the owner he is the main figure of the unfolding story.

The other actor is man, humanity in general, constantly making a mess of things. If this wasn't in itself tragic, it would be a comedy. God views the situation with a mixture of reactions: anger, because his theatre is used for bad plays; irony, because he sometimes chides man because of his stupidity; and compassion, because he wants to help him find a way out. But man is irremediably off-track.

And yes, behind the scenes there is the off-stage figure of a prompter providing the cues. This is of course Satan, who does all in his power to make a take-over bid and run the productions. He influences many of the powerful actors inciting them to make havoc and vie for control. Many terrible things happen because of the foolishness of the actors, aided and abetted by Satan. The theatre gets totally run down. It even seems at times that God's project is destined to fail and that evil will triumph in the end.

However, in the last act of the play, a long-expected hero appears. He sets things right, kicks Satan out, rescues the other actors and begins to renovate the theatre so that it will be restored to its original function. The ending of this continuing drama will be a happy one. Because of the rescuer, God's glory begins to shine out again. Only those who have taken sides with Satan against the hero will be excluded from the grand finale.

The Script

The Bible is the script of the ongoing history of the covenant of God and the creation. Not everything that happens is written down. Even the major events on the world stage are only recorded as they touch the precise purposes of God to save his people. For instance, the Bible says almost nothing about the Pharaohs, the great empires of Babylon, Greece or Rome which form the backdrop of biblical history, and nothing at all about the Aztec civilisation, the Chinese dynasties, or other parts of the ancient world.

It seems surprising that it should be so, but the Bible only tells us about when and how God specially intervened. He didn't do so in southern Africa, south-east Asia or the Americas before the coming of Christ. God overlooked the 'times of ignorance' and left men to be 'a law unto themselves' (Acts 17:30, Rom 2:14–15). God acted to reveal himself and save humanity through the family of Abraham and gave the promise to bless all the nations of the earth through him (Gen. 12:3). When this promise was fulfilled in Jesus-Christ, salvation was made known universally and men everywhere are called to repent.

God's Way

We can ask why God chose to act this way, not showing himself to all people, everywhere and at all times. It's a legitimate question. The apparent lack of equality of opportunity shown in the Bible story line seems unacceptable to most people today. However, it is all part of a divine logic that is different from our logic. God never acts as we would if we were in his place. In fact, he even acts in a way that is contradictory to what might seem right by our standards. This is part of God's way of surprising us, choosing the things that are nothing to confound the way of the world.

God chose to make salvation known to all men by working through a family, Abraham, Isaac and Jacob and their descendants, and through the recalcitrant people of Israel down to Jesus-Christ; this way of acting may seem strange. It is even worse for Muslims, who have replaced the line of Isaac by that of Ishmael. But the message of the Bible, as Paul states in Romans, is that salvation comes to the world from the Jews' (Rom. 11:11). Though we may want to know why, we will never be able to answer. It is a scandalous question, part of the scandal of salvation, the fact that God has chosen to save humanity by his own Son's death on the cross. All we can say is that it is God's choice and that God declares: 'Israel is saved by the Lord with an everlasting salvation; you will not be put to shame to all eternity' (Isa. 45:17).

God saves human beings because he has a plan. The events of history are not like unexpected volcanic eruptions. God acted according to plan along a projected line of salvation. Whenever he intervened in history a record of his word was made. There is an inherent logic in this procedure, for two reasons.

Firstly, what happens in history does so according to divine plan. What comes to expression in the written word of the Bible does so because there is an eternal and secret plan behind it all. When Islam claims that the Qur'an is a written transcript of a celestial text, or Mormonism says that the plaques of the *Book of Mormon* were brought from heaven by an angel and copied by Joseph Smith, there is an element of truth in the falsehood. Divine truth expressed in human words must in some way mirror eternal truth, truth in God, to be truth at all.

This kind of resemblance is found in the biblical notion that God declares his truth. Particularly in the writings of the prophets, God sets forth his truth in order to interpret history. Isaiah provides a case in point:

> I did not speak in secret,
> in a land of darkness;
> I did not say to the offspring of Jacob,
> Seek me in vain.
> I the Lord speak the truth;
> I declare what is right. (Isa. 45:18)

A biblical link exists between what God decided in his plan, formulated in his inscrutable wisdom in eternity, and what he has done and does in our world to enact it. His word records the outcome of his eternal decisions. It is the mediating link between our understanding and God's. God's plan engenders his acts and his acts engender his word. Without the divinely inspired word and the Holy Spirit who accompanies it, we remain in ignorance of everything about God, even if we might feel that a god exists.

We accept by faith that God 'works all things according to the counsel of his will' (Eph. 1:11). What God, contrary to all false gods, has *decided*, he *does* and he *declares* it to be his work. As Isaiah says, once again:

> Behold the former things have come to pass
> and the new things I now declare;
> before they spring forth
> I tell you of them. (Isa. 42:9)

> Before me no god was formed,
> nor shall there be any after me
> I, I am the Lord
> and beside me there is no saviour,
> I declared and saved and proclaimed. (Isa. 43:11–12)

> I am God and there is none like me,
> declaring the end from the beginning
> and from the ancient times things not yet done,
> saying, My counsel shall stand,
> and I will accomplish all my purpose...
> I have spoken and I will bring it to pass;
> I have purposed and I will do it. (Isa. 46:10–11)

If God 'declares the end from the beginning', if he 'declares and saves and proclaims', is it not obvious that this is a God who has a coherent plan? He acts according to his 'counsel' and then interprets what it means in our language. God's secret will becomes his revealed will when he makes it known, and when he makes it known it is recorded for our instruction.

Many people think that this is impossible and that it constitutes a denial of historical contingency and of human freedom. On the contrary. The God of the Bible doesn't have to negotiate with men over what he has determined to do. God is sovereignly free. On the other hand, he does not act in such a way that an impersonal fatalism might. His decisions are personal ones. God is big enough, because he is all-powerful, to accomplish exactly what *he has decided* to do though secondary means, and in particular through *the free acts* of his creatures. The world may look as though no one is in control but as Martin Luther said, God controls everything in such a way that it seems like no one is in control. God knows the picture in the tapestry of history right side up; from our perspective from the back of the tapestry we see only a confusion of colours and ragged ends of thread.

Secondly, if God has acted in history, why is his word necessary? The answer to this is found in the function of language. Whereas events come and go, and are often soon forgotten, language distils what is essential out of fleeting experiences. It conveys meaning and provides a guide for thinking. A fan at a football match might momentarily be looking the other way and miss a bad foul, but when the crowd shouts 'Foul!' his attention will be brought back to what is happening. The word 'foul' indicates the rules have been broken and that a free kick will be given. God's word is a record to convey what has happened. It is like an action replay of what has happened. It also sets the scene for what is to follow.

Man was created in the image of God with the ability to communicate with words. Moreover, language has a certain authority to convey truth about reality. Look at how man named the animals according to their nature in Genesis 2:19–23. If our way of using language has limitations as shown by 'communication problems' à la Basil Fawlty, this in no way detracts from our ability to use linguistic symbols properly and meaningfully. If it were not the case would I bother wasting time writing this on a sunny afternoon or would you trouble yourself to read it?

Now if God created man with a tongue, can he himself not speak, or the eye and not see, or the ear and not hear? It is unimaginable that God does not see, hear and speak. We must conclude that the God who creates and acts is also a God who speaks, a God who can communicate with us without causing misunderstandings. If we do not have complete understanding of what God says and if our knowledge is not exhaustive, it does mean that we cannot know enough of God's intentions and know them truly. I have never toured the whole of Canada but I have been to New Brunswick and Quebec, so I truly know something about Canada.

God can both act according to his plan to save his creatures and speak to inform us of his intentions. God's truth, like his glory, is inexhaustible but precisely because this is so, he speaks to us in such a way as to give us real knowledge of himself.

He Stoops to Communicate

No miracle or marvel, no wonder of nature, can be more stupendous than the way God has chosen to communicate with his creatures.

In the Old Testament, at Sinai, the people asked Moses to stop the voice of God speaking from the mountain and just let him speak to Moses as they could not bear it any longer (Exod. 20:19). When God's only Son came among men, his appearance was characterised by a remarkable veiling of his glory with human flesh and blood. John underlines the contrast in the first chapter of his gospel. It was not the ineffable Word of creation that appeared 'nakedly' when Jesus Christ came, but the Word made flesh. The Word was with God and the Word was God from before the beginning of creation (John 1:1). The very same Word, says John: 'became flesh and dwelt among us, and we have seen his glory, glory as of the only Son from the Father, full of grace and truth... No one has ever seen God; the only God who is at the Father's side, he has made him known' (1:14, 18).

What did the disciples see? Just a first-century male Jew. Nothing out of the ordinary. What was remarkable was that the human form embodied the grace and truth of divinity in such a way that Jesus was still God in heaven while being a person with a human nature on earth. Precisely this allowed Jesus to say to his disciples 'I am in the Father and the Father is in me' and 'whoever has seen me has seen the Father' (John 14:9–10).

The apostle Paul in Philippians 2:5–8 speaks about what we call the 'incarnation', the coming of Jesus among humans, as having a double form: 'He made himself nothing, taking the form of a servant, being born in the likeness of men. And being found in human form, he humbled himself by becoming obedient to the point of death, even death on a cross.'

Jesus became nothing, akin to a mere slave of the time. He went further, to the point of death, and even further again to the worst death, that of the cross. This was total abnegation, but this was not a mere man, this was the God-man, God incarnate.

This provides the model for the divine written word. God stoops to our depths to communicate with us. God's acts are mighty and marvellous and his miracles are stupendous and wonderful. He can spread the heavens like jam on a slice of bread, make sterile women conceive, divide the waters, bring the dead to life, make axe-heads float as if they were wood, make the sun stand still and the walls of Jericho tumble down. We have no difficulty believing that, because God is God. But when God speaks, as in the incarnate Word made flesh, God humbles himself to our level. He speaks to us in human words that are susceptible to misunderstanding. When God speaks, his words, like the person of his Son, have a servant form. They seem to be enslaved to the here and now of our world and yet, at the same time, like the Son, they are full of grace and truth.

So we can speak, with John Calvin, of God *accommodating* himself to us, of his condescending to our weakness when he lowers himself in such a way that he actually takes on our way of speaking to help us understand him. God babbles baby-talk to us just like a mother does when she soothes her baby. That is why the Bible is a homely book and doesn't have a title like *Being and nothingness*.

God even goes so far as to describe himself as having a human bodily form and human-like emotions. God has thoughts like humans do, eyes to see, ears to hear and hands and arms to act. He has emotions that are like human love, pity, compassion or anger.

These human ways of speaking serve a purpose. They help us to understand that God is a covenantal God. Relationship with him is what ultimately defines who we are and what we are as human beings. God's accommodation to us in our language is not incidental. It is part of the action that is necessary for there to be a relationship between God and man and for the revelation that defines that relationship. God stoops to our level so that we can understand who we are and what we are for. The greatest blessing of all is to see in the condescension of God a necessary movement that alone allows us to know that God is a God of love.

The words of divine revelation, for this reason, are the words of a love letter. This will help us to see why from the earliest times the words of God took on the form of a covenant, linking God to man with a promise of salvation. The written words are not a step down from the living presence of God, but a step up, in which God's presence is encoded.

Covenantal Words

God did not leave man at the exit from Eden. He began a series of saving acts that together are known as 'the history of redemption'. How long after the Fall these saving acts began is difficult to say, but we have a trace of them in Genesis. God's people were never left without witness. God acted to save his people, he spoke words to men to underline the presence of salvation. God's acts and words together make up a covenant relationship between God and man. We can sum it up like this: when there was a Scripture, there was a people of God to whom it was given; when there was a covenant people they had a Scripture.

The book of Genesis is made up of several books of 'generations' following on from the first reference in chapter 2 verse 4: 'these are the generations of the heavens and the earth when they were created' (Gen. 5:1, 6:9, 10:1, 11:27, 25:19, 36:9, 37:2). In chapter 5 the generations and the book go together: 'this is the book of the generations of Adam'. So although we cannot be totally sure, the 'generations' may well refer to the titles of books that were incorporated into the whole of Genesis by Moses. We do not know who wrote these texts or exactly when they were written before the time of Moses. However, we do know that a line of written texts recorded God's dealings with men.

Another pointer is the ancient practice of marking places where divine events took place. Inscribed stones or memorials preserved a record of what God had done. These pillars were covenant markers to indicate that a bond existed between the Lord and his people. Take, for instance, the outcome of Jacob's wrestling with the angel (which was probably a covenant test) at Bethel: 'this stone, says Jacob, which I have set up for a pillar, shall be God's house' (Gen. 28:18, 22).

The books of the generations and the memorials are witnesses to the fact that God came to save his people and that he is their LORD. God made a covenant with his people and the written markers to attest that fact. There is a treaty between God and his people, a law governing their relations. In the literary forms of the book of Exodus we find expressions of the covenant in writing. God is the author of the treaty and he establishes its conditions.

God identifies himself, who he is, what he has done and what he demands as service: 'I am the Lord your God, who brought you out of the land of Egypt… you shall have no other gods before me' (Exod. 20:2–3). There is a written testimony: 'The Lord said to Moses, Come up to me on the mountain and wait there, that I may give you the tablets of stone, with the laws and the commandment, which I have written for their instruction' (24:12). Some scholars think that the two tables of the law represent the two parties in the covenant—one is for God's record and the other is the people's copy. So God inscribes his words with his finger on the tables of stone (31:18). The people swear allegiance: 'all the words that the Lord has spoken we will do' (24:3). Their representatives eat a solemn communion meal to seal the covenant (11).

Later, when 'Moses had finished writing the words of this law in a book to the very end' this inspired re-edition of the Decalogue was put in the ark of the covenant, 'that it may be a witness against you' (Deut. 31:24, 26). The written word becomes a text with the authority of God himself. It signifies at one and the same time the will of God as Lord, his faithfulness to the promises made to his people and their obligation to obey the word and its commands. On the one hand, God is a faithful Lord who keeps his word of covenant, and on the other hand, his people must love him and keep his commandments (Exod. 20:6, Deut. 7:9).

At this point, we can see that the word of God is the historical inauguration of the people of God, a people with a witness and a calling, a people with a holy Scripture, the text of the covenant. Additions were made to this basic text to record the development of the covenant relationship, to remind the people of their obligations, to express their praise, or to mark when the covenant itself was renewed. So, at the end of Joshua's life, we find an exemplary case of recommitment:

> The people said to Joshua, 'The Lord our God we will serve and his voice we will obey'. Joshua made a covenant with the people that day, and put in place statutes and rules for them at Shechem. And Joshua wrote these words in the Book of the law of God. And he took a large stone and set it up there under the terebinth that was by the sanctuary of the Lord. And Joshua said to all the people, 'Behold, this stone shall be a witness against us, for it has heard all the words of the Lord that he spoke to us. Therefore, it shall be a witness against you, lest you deal falsely with your God. (Josh. 24:24–7)

The stone does not hear of course, but it is a personification. God is represented and hears, being present as a witness before his people. In the book of Numbers the tabernacle, the sanctuary where God dwells, is called the 'tabernacle of witness' (Num. 17:7, 8, 18:2).

There is written revelation because God witnesses to his covenant in Scripture and does so from generation to generation in order to preserve his people: 'The words of the Lord are pure words… you, O Lord, will keep them; you will guard us from this generation (the unfaithful) for ever' (Ps. 12:6, 7).

So biblical witnessing concerns, first and foremost, not man's witness about God, but God's bearing witness to himself in his revelation. What Scripture says, God says. Our witness as human beings is only ever secondary and is of no use unless it is anchored in the witness of the God of the covenant and faithful to it.

Throughout the Old Testament God sends prophets to be his witnesses. Their preaching is prefaced with 'Thus saith the Lord', but they also write prophecy as God's witness to his covenant. When John the Baptist appears as the last prophet of the old dispensation, he was not the light but was 'sent from God… to bear witness to the light' (John 1:6–8). Jesus himself is called 'the faithful and true witness' and his works bear witness to who he is, because he does them for the Father (10:25). Jesus promises to send his Holy Spirit of truth, the 'Comforter' to enable the disciples to 'bear witness, because you have been with me from the beginning' (15:26–7).

Of these trained messengers Jesus says, 'you will be my witnesses… to the end of the earth' (Acts 1:8). The hearing and proclaiming that constitute the prophetic ministry of the apostles and which serve to lay the foundation for the new people of God (Eph. 2:20) do not exclude but include a written word, as is the case with the Old Testament prophets. After speaking at length about the witness to the Son of God, John the evangelist says: 'I write these things to you who believe in the name of the Son of God, so that you may know that you have eternal life' (1 John 5:13).

Coming as it does from prophetic witnesses, the word of Scripture itself is God's covenant witness to the salvation he has accomplished. It is given to establish his people as the people of the covenant, the people of God. We can see the logic behind the divine way of acting. The revelation of God to his people comes with divine authority. His word is recorded within its historical circumstances; when new divine revelation occurs, further records are kept to complete the existing texts. So Scripture grows, providing a continuing record of

God's covenant dealings. It has canonical status, because it is the testimony to the divine presence. We will say more about the canon (the norm or rule) of Scripture in a later chapter.

So the writers of the New Testament can look back to the Old and stand on the shoulders of the Old as God's word. They recognise its authority. This explains why they can quote from it as part of a unified word of God using expressions like 'God or the Holy Scripture says', or refer to it as 'the oracles of God', or affirm that 'Scripture cannot be broken' (John 10:35).

Jesus and the apostles quote almost every book of the Old Testament as having authority, but never do they quote anything else, apocryphal writings or pagan wisdom, as being the word of God. This does not imply that human wisdom cannot take its place in God's word in the book of Proverbs, that Paul cannot quote a pagan poet as having said something true about God in his sermon at Athens, or that it is out of line for Jude to illustrate his message from the apocryphal book of Enoch. There is no problem with these cases because *all* of Scripture draws on a common linguistic stock, words and phrases that are part of common usage.

However, we can never forget that when we refer to the practice of Jesus or his apostles as being our authority, we cannot expect that their authority will be recognised by the authorities of the world, the talking heads, the boffins, the intelligentsia or religious leaders. Jesus had the authority of someone who was excommunicated and crucified. The authority of his apostles was that of a group of intolerant sectarians who were hounded out of the public view and fed to lions. So we should not be in the least surprised or offended when our attachment to the authority of Scripture as God's word, his written revelation, is ridiculed. In fact, there is something wrong with us as witnesses if the contrary is true, whether it be in our family, the work place or academia.

Propositional Revelation?

Some people get all hot under the collar when divine revelation is seen as reaching down into the text of Scripture. Old chestnuts like *errare human est* (error is human) are used to justify the claim that a revelation in human language cannot be revelation. Or it is held that if God is a personal God, he cannot be tied to an impersonal reality like a text. Or it is said that there is no such thing as timeless truths or that it is dangerous to think God has revealed truth. Such an attitude puts us in possession of truth—an attitude bound to end up in intellectual terrorism.

These things are just hot air and have little to do with what the Scripture actually says about itself. They are all rationalisations that seek to dodge the obvious. Many good arguments for propositional revelation have been made in recent years by people like James Packer, Paul Helm or Wayne Grudem and here is not the place to go into great detail.

What does propositional revelation really mean? Well, it does not mean that the things 'proposed' by Scripture are no more than the impersonal and esoteric truths we might find in a textbook on an obscure subject. Propositional revelation can fundamentally be said to mean two things:

Firstly, there is no opposition between personal and textual revelation when the text is considered to be that of a person expressing truths. 'Everton is a grand old team' is a proposition expressed personally by Paul as being something he considers incontestably true. A Liverpudlian of course will not agree, but an unbeliever will also contest that John 3:16 is true, and this is a proposition of God's word. So 'Everton is a grand old team' is something affirmed to be true by someone called Paul. When Scripture proposes certain things as being true, then it is God himself who is putting them forward as his revealed truth.

Secondly, the propositional truth of biblical revelation is above all covenantal truth. This means two things. First, in the different forms of biblical language the truths expressed are covenantal truths. The historical truths of Scripture belong to covenant history and the prophetic truths foretell future history that will come to pass. Even covenant praise offered to God and poetry contain expressions that describe God's holiness and justice in a fitting way.

The images of Scripture convey truth about God too. For people living in an arid desert who see nothing but hard immovable rock, to say 'God is a rock' is much more vivid than 'God is changeless' or 'God is faithful', but that is what it means! Even the blessings and curses of the covenant found in Deuteronomy 28 and 29 are revealed propositions that are true, because they are not just vain threats or empty promises, but things that actually come true when the people of God act in certain ways. Jesus made a promise 'I will come again'. Certain scoffers don't believe it for a minute and say, 'where is the promise of his coming'. Peter reminds us of two things: a day with the Lord is like a thousand years and God is not slow to fulfil his promises (2 Pet. 3:8).

The fact that the propositional truth of biblical revelation is above all covenantal truth also means that it is relation-defining truth. Accepting or rejecting the truths of Scripture determine what kind of relationship we have with God. We cannot reject his truth and know his love, just as we cannot embrace errors and love God. Error is the enemy of God as it is the enemy of truth. On this issue Christians have to learn that they cannot run with the hare and the hounds, no more than they can love God and money at the same time.

If we have really understood what is implied by God's revelation in the words of Scripture then we will know how important it is to live according to the truth in order to please God, and this will make us people who are serious about truth.

A Reality Check

The important thing about the special revelation of God being made verbally is that it will allow us to separate truth from error in different realms: about God, about ourselves or about the world around us. Doing so will free us from the slavery of our illusions, of false ideas about ourselves. The propositional truth of Scripture is not a 'religious belief' in the upper mystical storey of human experience that allows us to go on living our life as we wish on the ground floor. The truth of Scripture provides us with a reality check—seeing whether or not we are lined up with God's reality.

As Christians we have feelings that are more or less the same as those experienced by the people around us—happiness, fear, depression, anger or warm appreciation. What makes us different from them are our thoughts, the renewed intelligence described by the apostle in Romans 12:2: "Do not be conformed to this world, but be transformed by the renewal of your mind, that by testing you may discern what is the will of God, what is good and acceptable and perfect." If there is no propositional revelation of truth in Scripture there can be no transformation, no renewal of the mind, no testing, as there is no criteria to test by. There remains only flat-earth relativism that makes everything horribly banal and removes the tragedy from life.

With the revealed truth of Scripture, here is what we can do as Christians:

- We can test our *motivations*—do we really desire to please God above all and seek to do so by conforming our thoughts to his?
- We can test our *orientations*—do we really know the living God and rather than pushing him away, make the covenant God the Lord of our lives?
- We can examine our *perspectives*—does God decide what is good for us, do we approve what he approves and reject what he rejects, knowing that he rejects what is spiritually bad for us?
- We can ask if we exercise *discernment* because we understand the antithesis between truth and error—do we have a healthily critical attitude to the fashions and fads that enslave the poor souls around us and make obsessive monkeys out of them?

Finally and most serious, if God had not told us any truths, we could never know about him either. If we know his truth, it will cut an ever-deeper incision in our life. This is the condition for freedom in this life and hope for tomorrow.

7

Revelation and Inspiration

The Bible is a book whose authors are not only inspired but *divinely* inspired. This means that when God acted to reveal himself he also took appropriate measures to make sure that a correct understanding of what he had done was preserved in the text of Scripture. Divine revelation was completed by the inspiration of the holy Scriptures, the final act of God that ensures we know his truth.

But what is *inspiration*? The word comes from the Latin and is used in the Bible translated by Jerome in the fourth century, called the *Vulgate*. It describes the breathing of the Spirit, referred to in various biblical texts:

- Genesis 2:7, the Lord God breathed into his nostrils the breath of life;
- 2 Samuel 22:16, the foundations of the world were laid bare… at the blast of breath of his nostrils;
- Job 32:8, the spirit in man, the breath of the Almighty makes him understand;
- Psalm 33:6, by the breath of his mouth the Lord made all the host (of the heavens);
- Acts 17:25, (God) gives life and breath and everything;
- 2 Timothy 3:16, all Scripture is inspired.

Is this divine inspiration 'breathing in' man or 'breathing out' by God? That we will attempt to determine.

Sometimes it is said that the idea of the inspiration of Scripture relies on a few isolated texts. This is not the case. It's not surprising that there are some texts in the Bible that are central to the issue. Some texts are more important than others for establishing any biblical doctrine. If we want to know what the Bible teaches about the new birth, it's most natural to review the writings of John and in particular his gospel, chapter 3. But the whole of Scripture will bear out, directly or indirectly, what John says specifically. Likewise, concerning inspiration it is only natural to go to 'exemplary' texts on the subject.

Walking in the mountains you could maybe dodge a couple of falling rocks, but if the rocks were part of an avalanche your chances would be slim. The texts we review in this chapter are like two rocks, but they are underpinned by the whole weight of Scripture. 2 Timothy 3:16 and 2 Peter 1:21 are supported by several other passages that corroborate their evidence.

Prophetic Apostles

While he was on earth, did Jesus envisage the period after his departure? Did he make any provision for the transmission of his teaching and the sound interpretation of the meaning of his death and resurrection? Even humanly speaking it would be strange if it were not so—but Jesus was also acting on commission from God.

Before his death, he spoke explicitly about his resurrection. He predicted several events that would precede his return in glory including the destruction of the Jerusalem temple, the dispersion of the Jews and the preaching of the gospel to all nations. The disciples will be persecuted and Peter will live to a ripe old age before dying a martyr's death. From this prophetic perspective the disciples of the four Gospels received their call from Jesus to become his apostles, or the ones he sends, after his departure. Before and after the resurrection, Jesus spoke about the church.

Jesus called his disciples, he instructed them to be apostles, promised them the Holy Spirit to make them fearless in proclaiming his truth, ordered them to make disciples of the nations and to call forth his people from among the Jews who believed and from paganism. Looking back on this work of reconciliation, Paul describes God's new people in this way: 'You are no longer strangers and aliens, but you are fellow citizens with the saints and members of the household of God, but on the foundation of the apostles and prophets [an alternative translation is 'prophetic apostles'], Christ Jesus being himself the cornerstone' (Eph. 2:20–21).

Given these conditions, it would have been unlikely if new Scriptures had not been formed to complete revelation and provide, via the apostles, a foundation for the people of God. This is the background of the inspiration of the New Testament Scriptures; the texts found there are simply a reflection of this reality. Inspiration is a divine act that needs to be considered not as something isolated but in the broader context of the purpose of God in salvation.

2 Timothy 3:15–17

This is the major text referred to in the debate about inspiration; it speaks not only about the act of inspiration but also about a corpus of inspired texts and their usefulness. Paul writes to Timothy as his mentor:

> From childhood you have been acquainted with the sacred writings, which are able to make you wise for salvation through faith in Christ Jesus. All Scripture is breathed out by God and profitable for teaching, for reproof, for correction, and for training in righteousness that the man of God may be competent, equipped for every good work.

In this passage Scripture is said to be 'God breathed' (*theopneustos* in Greek) which is not exactly the same in meaning as the word 'inspired'. *Theopneustos* does not express the sense of an action of God *in* the human authors of Scripture (*in*-spiration). The text says simply that the word of Scripture itself is a divine out-breathing. The biblical word indicates the powerful outgoing of breath from God's mouth. Scripture was formed not by some inner inspiration in men but it was the result of the creative action of the Spirit. The word of God in the Scriptures is 'breathed out by God'. It concerns primarily the text itself and not inspired individuals.

What this expression conveys is that the Scriptures are the work of God, without defining how God's Spirit operated with regard to men as they produced a written record. 2 Timothy 3:16 says nothing about the role of the human authors. This is surprising because with our 'how to do it' mentality we want to know how things work. What Paul tells us is that the Scriptures are the result of a powerful action by God's Spirit, similar to the work of the Spirit in forming the heavens, in creation or in making man. The texts (*graphe*, Greek for writings) are the result of a divine creative act.

'God-breathed' is a good deal more explicit than 'inspiration'. Rather than an action within the speakers or a reference to the content of their thought, it states that the elaboration of the very texts of Scripture happened by the breathing of the Spirit. So Scripture was formed and so it remains. There is a permanency in the result of the Spirit's work that is quite different from a passing influence on the thought of a writer.

The immediate context of this statement is also interesting. Paul says Timothy has benefited from childhood from the 'sacred writings' (Greek, *hiera grammata*), an expression only used here in the New Testament. It refers to the Old Testament Scriptures from which Timothy received instruction. From this we can at least conclude that Paul considered the whole of the corpus of writing known to pious Jews to be the result of divine inspiration—the *Tanakh*, a name formed from the initial Hebrew letters of Old Testament's three subdivisions: the *Torah* ('teaching', the five Books of Moses), the *Nevi'im* ('prophets') and the *Ketuvim* ('writings').

However, is that all that Paul is getting at? I think there may be more, even at the expense of stepping outside the bounds of traditional interpretation that tends to limit 'sacred writings' to the Old Testament. To paraphrase: what the apostle seems to say is: 'Timothy, you have known the sacred writings from childhood and it's true that these writings lead to Christ and to salvation, but *all* Scripture given by God-breathing is equally profitable'. Paul proceeds by way of a limited contrast—'this is true but also that…'

Is it too much to think that the apostle is referring in this statement not only to the Old Testament but also to the apostolic writings? Additions are at least anticipated.

This interpretation fits the context well. Paul is talking about Christians being competent and 'equipped for every good work' (3:17). Can this be the case in the church age thanks to the Old Testament alone? No, and this is precisely why Paul, as Timothy's mentor, goes on to give the following advice: 'I charge you in the presence of God and of Christ Jesus... and by the appearing of his kingdom to preach the word... for a time is coming when people will not endure sound teaching' (4:1–4). The charge cannot be fulfilled with only Old Testament truth, but needs the addition of apostolic truth about the revelation of the kingdom of Christ. Paul gives his exhortation in the name of *Christ*. God-breathed revelation concerns the coming of Christ, his revelation and the present and future kingdom. What the apostle describes corresponds to the function of the New Testament in the Christian church.

To be sure, Paul's crisp statement includes no precisions or list of the books that fall into this category. He states that the human writing of Scripture is the outcome of the powerful, creative action of the Spirit. This is the reason for the truth of Scripture and for its edifying character. Because of its character, it is profitable for building up a Christian life-style through the quadruple action of instruction, exhortation, amendment and training in uprightness. These are the ingredients that go into 'every good work'.

To resume: God-breathing, *theopneustia*, is the effective link between the Holy Spirit and the written word. This is what makes the confession 'Holy Scripture is the word of God' legitimate. Faith in the written word is the prerequisite of gospel preaching with its double function: preparing the coming of the kingdom and warding off heresy.

2 Peter 1:19–21

2 Timothy 3:16 is, for most people, the classic text about biblical inspiration, mainly because the word 'inspiration' is found there. It tends to eclipse the more complete statement found in 2 Peter.

If the Timothy text places the accent on the divine origin of the sacred writings, the one in 2 Peter develops the relation between the divine action and human instrumentality in the prophetic word:

> We have something more sure [than the voice on the holy mountain], the prophetic word, to which you will do well to pay attention as a lamp shining in a dark place, until the day dawns and the morning star rises in your hearts, knowing this first of all, that no prophecy of Scripture comes from someone's own interpretation. For no prophecy was ever produced by the will of man, but men spoke from God and were carried along by the Holy Spirit.

The apostolic message is neither fable nor myth (2 Pet. 1:16); rather the power of the coming of Jesus is attested by the objective experience and testimony of the witnesses who had seen Christ transfigured on the mountain. They heard the holy voice saying 'This is my beloved Son, in whom I am well pleased' (17, recorded in Matthew, Mark and Luke).

Peter had been an eyewitness and heard the voice, but the prophetic word that attests this event is even more certain than what was actually heard on the mountain. This is a surprising statement, but there are situations when we do wonder whether we have really heard something! A spoken word takes a second, but a written one is a perpetual witness. The prophetic word is the witness of the apostles, the light in the dark that makes the morning star, Christ, rise in believer's hearts to bring a new day.

What is the function of the prophetic word that Peter speaks about? Contrary to fabulous hype or imaginative myths, it is the divine promise by which we wait for the 'new heavens and new earth' (2 Pet. 3:13). Because of this promise, Peter writes a memo to believers to 'remember the predictions of the holy prophets and the commandment of the Lord and Saviour through your apostles' (3:2). And he refers specifically to Paul as one of these apostles who penned prophetic Scripture equal to the Old Testament scriptures:

> And count the patience of our Lord as salvation, just as our beloved brother Paul also wrote to you according to the wisdom given him, as he does in all his letters when he speaks in them of these matters. There are some things in them that are hard to understand, which the ignorant and unstable twist to their own destruction, as they do the other Scriptures (3:15–16).

This is astonishing. Peter recognises that Paul spoke prophetically about the divine promise. He knew 'all his writings' and admits that Paul was sometimes hard to understand. Who will contest that? Not the modern scholars who write books with titles like *Wrestling with Paul*! Moreover, Peter recognised Paul's writings to be on the level of 'other Scriptures', perhaps referring to those of the Old Testament. Peter certainly claims that Paul had written holy Scripture thanks to his gift of divine wisdom. The prophetic word was given to bear witness to Christ and his promise because believers need to persevere in the faith.

What then can be said from Peter's text about the nature of the prophetic word? It is 'sure' and certain, being founded on the promise of God himself. Verse 21 defines it negatively and positively. It doesn't come into being by someone deciding to sit down and write a chapter or two, like I did after lunch today. Nor does it come from the mental constructions of a human being, like the interpretation of Peter's text given here, which might well be contested by someone else. Negatively, the prophetic word does not arise from a personal initiative and its content is not made up of human ideas. Scripture does not come out of 'someone's own interpretation'. Positively, the prophecy of Scripture exists because of the initiative of the Holy Spirit. The source of Scripture is in God himself—the prophets are God's servants—and it comes to us through the instrumentality of the Spirit.

The description of the work of the Spirit, although brief, is more complete than that of 1 Timothy 3:16. Peter says that men were 'carried along' by the Spirit. They were not just guided or lead as they wrote. The precise sense of the word 'carried along' indicates they were picked up, transported and brought to their destination by the lifting power of the Spirit. The same word in Greek is used in Acts 27:15 and 17 of the ship Paul was on going to Rome and how the wind drove it along. Through this sort of powerful action men 'spoke from God'. God had an end in view, the transmission of a prophetic word. The Holy Spirit 'drove' men along to his divinely-willed destination. However, in this procedure men spoke and the human words recorded were at the same time words from God.

Finally, notice that Peter makes a general statement. What he says concerns prophetic Scripture and its writing; it applies whenever this kind of activity takes place. Since Peter states that Paul wrote prophetic Scripture, it is legitimate to say that Paul spoke from God, being carried along by the Spirit and that all the inspired writing of the corpus of Scripture came into being in this manner.

Both of these prime texts can be applied to all the Bible as the inspired word of God.

The Origin of Scripture and Its Authenticity

2 Timothy 3:16 informs us that the word of Scripture is God-breathed. As God's word, it continues to have a God-breathed function when we receive its message. It is living and active as God's word when we open it and hear it. 2 Peter 1:21 illuminates the role of men as intermediaries in the transmission of the prophetic word. The initiative comes from God not from men; to be prophetic the word must depend on the initiative of the Spirit. This fact establishes the authenticity of Scripture. It is God's word. Special attributes, to which we shall return later, belong to it as God's word: it has authority, truthfulness and clarity, and forms a unity. The origin of the divine word is the foundation for our assurance about the truth of the message of salvation contained in the Scriptures.

The words of men are here, and here alone, words of God; God speaks in human language. The Scriptures are characterised by an organic unity in which the divine and human factors join to form one word, a word that is divine and human. The prophetic word is neither an untouchable extra-terrestrial reality landed on earth, nor simply a human word like all others, to be read like any book. The

Scripture has a mysterious duality of form in which the divine and the human are inseparable. It is not half divine and half human. It is 100% divine and 100% human without distinction between the two.

Of course many questions are bound to remain unanswered, as with all divine actions that touch human reality. When we think of the person of Christ, Son of God and man, or about conversion, which is the work of the Holy Spirit and also a real human decision, or about divine predestination and human freedom, we have to maintain a 'two-factor' theology. Anything else is a half-truth.

How was the unity of the divine and the human attained in Scripture? How were men kept from error? How could almighty God limit himself to time-bound human language? How could the eternal word become temporal? These and other questions remain in the realm of mystery that belongs to all divine acts.

God has not chosen to answer these questions, and others, even though we would like answers. We do not know and we will never know *how* Scripture is the word of God; but we do know *that* Scripture is God's word, because that is the witness of the word itself. That should be sufficient, unless we set up mental or sentimental roadblocks as a barrier to what the Bible says about itself.

Some Illustrations

These two texts don't tell us everything about inspiration. Scripture contains much more evidence, even if not in the form of direct statements, that lines up behind these two cases and illustrates their teaching. Our aim here is to put a few more products on the shelf.

We saw in chapter 3 how Jesus authorised the testimony of the apostles. It is genuine because it was based directly on the authority of Christ and does not lean on other outside sources. Although Paul had a different background from the others his testimony, like theirs, relied directly on Jesus. His gospel was not man's but God's, and for this reason he declared other gospels to be fraudulent.

He explained in Galatians what he meant by his gospel not being of human origin: he was 'called by grace'; the Son of God was 'revealed in him' so that he could preach the word. He took the initiative without relying on a nod from the twelve (Gal. 1:11, 15, 17).

His letters to the Corinthians provide a telling example of how he viewed his apostolic mission. He received God's word by inspiration and texted it to others. Let's look at a few instances of this. In *1 Corinthians 2:11–16* Paul says this:

> No one comprehends the thoughts of God except the Spirit of God. Now we have received…the Spirit who is from God, that we might understand the things freely given us by God. And we impart this in words not taught by human wisdom but taught by the Spirit…For who has understood the mind of the Lord to instruct him? But we have the mind of Christ.

This following illustration shows how Paul's thought develops in the first two chapters of his epistle, where it is essential for him to establish his legitimacy against his Corinthian critics:

Jesus and the message of the cross (1 Cor. 1:23–4)
is foolish and scandalous for Greeks and Jews
but power and wisdom for those saved by faith

↓

Because they are revealed by the Spirit who knows the depths of God (2:10–12)
the Spirit knows the deep intentions of God
the Spirit reveals the will of God
the Spirit reveals the truth of the scandal of the cross

↓

The Spirit is given by Christ to the apostles (2:13–16)
they speak, being taught by the Spirit
they are witnesses of Christ
their words are a result of the action of the Spirit
they have 'the mind of Christ'

↓

Consequence: the apostles and inspiration
the content of the New Testament is the written witness of the apostles
inspiration concerns not only thoughts but words (2:13)
the words express the mind of Christ
the mind of Christ is the revelation of the will of God in Christ
inspiration brings us the truth through apostolic writings
there is 'no other gospel' (Gal. 1:6–9).

It beggars belief to think that Paul, or anyone else for that matter, could say something like 'we have the mind of Christ' unless he did so by special revelation. And how is anyone's mind expressed other than in words? And here these precise words are being addressed to the Corinthian sceptics. Although the apostle is not making any direct statements about the doctrine of inspiration in this text, it is impossible to construe his claims other than by presupposing a belief in the teaching of inspiration we find elsewhere.

A little later on in *1 Corinthians 7* he deals with the perennial issue of marrying or not marrying, and in a particular situation, because persecution is rearing its ugly head. It's not what he says about marriage that concerns us here, but how he backs it up:

> To the married, I give this charge, (not I, but the Lord): the wife should not separate from her husband...To the rest I say (I, not the Lord) that if any brother has a wife who is an unbeliever, he should not divorce her...I think that I too have the Spirit of God (1 Cor. 7:10, 12, 40).

Some bright sparks invariably bring up a red herring in discussions about the authority of the apostles (particularly Paul!) and inspiration: 'You see, they say, Paul recognises that he has not the same authority as Jesus, but a lesser kind. Paul is only speaking humanly; Jesus is our reference.'

But is it the case? I think not. In verse 10 Paul is repeating something Jesus taught during his earthly ministry (found in Matthew 19:6). Subsequently he deals with a new situation that has arisen, about which Jesus knew or said nothing. Paul adds his own teaching on the subject, something not broached by Jesus, in verse 12: 'I say to you'. This is not a lessening of authority, but on the contrary, he puts his word on the same level as Jesus' teaching. In fact, he verbally echoes the expressions of Jesus in the Sermon on the Mount 'you have heard it said, but I say to you...' (Matt. 5:22, 28, 32, 34, 39, 46). Just as Jesus completed the Old Testament law with his teaching, by not abolishing but fulfilling it (Matt. 5:17), Paul does likewise with respect to Jesus. He has the same teaching authority as the Master because he received it from the Master himself, as verse 40 states: 'I think I have the Spirit of God', which is a way of saying 'Of course I do'. A mighty claim indeed!

Verse 40 is conveniently avoided by the red herring merchants, as is the corroborative statement in *1 Corinthians 14:36–40*. People shrug off what the apostle says here about women and ministry on the grounds that it is obscure, unimportant or culturally conditioned and they pass over how he follows it up:

> Was it from you the word of God came? Or are you the only ones it has reached? If anyone thinks he is a prophet, or spiritual, he should acknowledge that the things I am writing to you are a command of the Lord. If anyone does not recognise this, he is not recognised. (14:36–8)

Unless we indulge in mental gymnastics to avoid the clarity of this statement, we are obliged to conclude that Paul was claiming that:

- he is bringing the word of God to this situation;
- it has a universal and binding character;
- it is an unavoidable command;
- the Lord is speaking to the church through him;
- not receiving it implies not being approved by God's standards.

The 'command' is what he has written and since it expresses the word of God, it can only have come by divine inspiration. God has no other vehicle of communication to the church universal than that.

Moving to *2 Corinthians*, we find an important autobiographical comment on the ministry of the apostle, which includes a parallel with that of Moses in the old covenant, in chapter 3:

> Our sufficiency comes from God who has made us competent to be ministers of a new covenant, not of the letter but of the Spirit. For the letter kills, but the Spirit gives life... If the ministry of death, carved in letters on stone came with such glory... will not the ministry of the Spirit have even more glory?... For if what came to an end came with glory, much more will what is permanent. (2 Cor. 3:5–11)

Back to the red herring diet, with the letter that kills and the Spirit that gives life! 'Oh yes, its clear isn't it, that the text of Scripture can't be divinely revealed. It's just a dead letter. The Spirit, not the letter is what gives life, so get the Spirit, brother!' This misses the apostle's point. After all, if the letter kills, it is surely very much alive.

The apostle is not making a contrast between a dead text and a living dynamic Spirit. The contrast is between the letter read without the Spirit, with 'minds that are hardened' and the letter read with the Spirit of Christ that 'removes the veil' (14, 16). The Spirit opens the understanding of the letter, but doesn't replace it with a different principle. The Spirit does not dispense with the letter but gives it the dynamic power of its own truth by applying it to the heart. In the new covenant the law is planted in the heart, as Jeremiah 31:33 and Ezekiel 36:26–7 prophesied. 'When one turns to the Lord, the veil is removed. Now the Lord is the Spirit and where the Spirit of the Lord is there is freedom' (16–17). This means that at the present moment, a moment of 'permanence', the risen Lord is present in the form and person of his Spirit, bringing freedom. What freedom? The liberty of the spiritually appropriated letter, that does not kill but gives life to the heart. And how is the word given, after all? By the same Spirit!

At first glance, what 2 Corinthians 3 says does not seem to have a lot to do with the subject of Bible inspiration. But on closer inspection, it turns out to have a good deal of relevance. Paul aligns himself with Moses, none other. Moses formally founded the old covenant people in fulfilment of the promise given to Abraham. Paul with his permanent 'ministry of righteousness' lays the foundation stone of the new covenant people, fulfilling the promise to the Old Testament prophets. Moses wrote on tablets of stone, but Paul writes his letter on the hearts of God's people, 'not with ink but with the Spirit of the living God…on tablets of human hearts' (3). Paul's ministry is of divine origin like that of Moses. It seems not unlikely that Paul's function will be aided and abetted by inspired epistolary productions. The writing of inspired Scripture, as in 2 Timothy 3:16, is part of the package.

In addition to the Corinthian letters, a remarkable thing that serves to nail down our point is found in *1 Timothy 5:18*: 'For the

Scripture says, "You shall not muzzle an ox when it treads out the grain" and "the labourer deserves his wages".' The apostle is giving an exhortation to pay a living wage to those who are elders in the church and who teach. If you don't feed your ox, your grain won't get ground; labourers cannot work on fresh air.

The first illustration about the ox comes from Deuteronomy 25:4. The second about the 'labourer and his hire' is not to be found in the Old Testament even if things are said there about not withholding wages. It is a verbatim quote of Jesus in Luke 10:7 and is almost the same as Matthew 10:10 (apart from the word 'wages' that replaces 'food'). Both expressions are bracketed under the category of 'Scripture' (*he graphe*). Just as Peter could quote Paul (2 Pet. 3:14) as being 'Scripture', Paul could also quote Luke. New Testament scholar, John Wenham, dates Luke to 54 AD and 1 Timothy was written toward the end of Paul's life in 57–9. It is therefore possible that Paul could have known Luke's gospel, even more so because Luke documented Paul's work in the Acts of the Apostles.

Finally, there is one more case outside the Pauline corpus parallel to 1 Corinthians 2 and 2 Corinthians 3. In *1 Peter 1:10–12* we read:

> Concerning this salvation, the prophets who prophesied about the grace that was to be yours searched carefully, enquiring what person or time the Spirit of Christ in them was indicating when he predicted the suffering of Christ and the subsequent glories. It was revealed to them that they were serving not themselves but you, in the things that have now been announced to you through those who preached the good news to you by the Holy Spirit sent from heaven...

The messengers of the new covenant are the evangelists who preach by the action of the Spirit, bearing the gospel of Christ. Their activity corresponds to that of the prophets of the Old Testament who were messengers of the covenant. They were writing prophets who wrote under the action of the Spirit. So will the new covenant prophets be, by the special inspiration of the same Spirit. The New Testament will bring more clarity, more truth, more certainty and not less; in the doxology at the end of his letter to the Romans

Paul says: 'the mystery that was kept secret for long ages but has now been disclosed through the prophetic writing and has been made known to all nations' (16:26). You only have to flip through the New Testament texts to realise how much the apostles used the Old Testament prophets with greater clarity to back up all they said about salvation in what they wrote. Would their inspiration be less than that of their enquiring forerunners?

'Scripture Says' and 'God Says'

It has long been recognised that 'Scripture says' and 'God says' are synonymous terms. If when Scripture says something God is saying it, the text of Scripture and the word of God spoken are identified. The link between the two is verbal in nature and is made by God who inspired what is written. Several different texts may be identified to show this is the case.

Certain biblical texts identify the Scripture as a word spoken by God himself. Two illustrations:

- Galatians 3:8 says 'Scripture, foreseeing that God would justify the Gentiles by faith, preached the gospel beforehand to Abraham saying, "In you shall all the nations of the earth be blessed".' This quotes Genesis 12:3. There it is God who said it to Abraham, as the Scripture did not yet exist;
- Romans 9:17 uses the same procedure with reference to Exodus 9:16. God spoke to Pharaoh directly through Moses and Scripture itself is identified with the divine word.

The text of Scripture in both cases reproduces the word or act of God and is therefore his word. 'Scripture says' is shorthand for 'God, recorded in Scripture, says'.

Secondly, looking at the same issue from the other angle, there are texts where the words of men in the Bible are said to be God's words. Two illustrations again:

- Acts 13:34–5 introduce quotations of words from two Psalms by 'God has spoken in this way';

- Hebrews 1:6–8 reproduces passages quoted from Psalms 97:7, 104:4 and 45:7 which are human words of praise spoken about God as words that God himself says. Acts 4:24–5 does the same, quoting words of David, with this prefix: 'God who through the mouth of our father David said by the Holy Spirit…'

In the Old Testament passages referred to in the New we find the words of men spoken of or to God. They are quoted in the New as being words of God himself. It would be blasphemous to take a human word as being divine, unless the written word itself was understood to have come from God. This alone would permit the association between the human word and the word of God. In this sense, it is natural to use the abbreviated form 'God said' instead of saying 'Scripture, the word of God, said'.

Thirdly, we find cases where the New Testament gives an exhortation as coming from God, using words from the Old Testament. This is the case in 2 Corinthians 6:16 and Hebrews 3:7, the latter introducing the quotation with 'The Holy Spirit says…' So the words for and from a former generation have a direct application. They are words of the living God who speaks through them in the present.

The apostles invented none of these practices. They followed the operative model they had seen in the teaching of Jesus. Jesus recognised full well the human aspect of the Old Testament as being the witness of Moses, David and the prophets. However, the human element is eclipsed by the primacy of the divine word. When Christ refers to 'the Scriptures' he means that God is their author. This is the case in Matthew 21:42, John 5:39 and 10:35. This is true not only of the Scriptures in general but also of their individual words. 'Have you not read?' implies 'do you not know that God said?'. A good example is Matthew 22:32, where Jesus asked his hearers: 'have you not read what was said to you by God: "I am the God of the living".'

One final example, taken from Matthew 19:4–5. Jesus answers the trick questions of the Pharisees on divorce in the following way: 'Have you not read that he who created them from the beginning made them male and female, and said "Therefore a man shall leave his father and his mother and hold fast to his wife and they shall become one flesh"?'

When we look up the text in Genesis 2:24 we see that what Jesus quotes as being a word of God is a comment by the inspired author in that context, not something spoken directly by God. Paul quotes the same Genesis text in Ephesians 5:31 as being a generally recognised truth of Scripture to which he can appeal.

Conclusion

These rather intricate illustrations may give the impression of being nit-picking. They are significant, however, as they function as part of a common mentality with regard to the text of Scripture and its divine authority. They are important as are all small rivers that flow to the sea.

Even reputed liberal theologians can be objective enough to admit this. Jesus and the apostles thought the Scriptures were divinely inspired not only as a whole, but also in their individual words. This is what they thought about it. Then they go on to say, of course, that in the twenty-first century, with our more sophisticated knowledge, we can have another take on the subject and consider inspiration as being something more flexible! The ultimate question is whether the practice of Jesus and his messengers is binding for us, and that involves our presuppositions and the nature of our faith in Christ.

To look at the issue from another angle: if we do not wish to accept that the Scriptures are inspired in a plenary, verbal and organic way, what are we left with? Only vague ideas about inspiration as a special disposition to piety attributed to some individuals or groups of people. But this 'inspiration' is just another human function, and it can tell us nothing about God's truth as coming from God.

Without biblical inspiration we are shut up in a closed human universe without any truth about God. That may be fine for some punters, as it leaves them large margins of liberty as to what they believe and do. But it is hardly a Christian viewpoint.

If it is argued that Jesus is truth and truth is always personal, how do we know that? Surely we can only know it from Scripture;

if Scripture is not reliable, we cannot know it at all. We are stuck in a vicious circle.

The witness of Jesus and the apostles is invariably neglected because an idea of inspiration influenced by romanticism is assumed to be the only plausible one. Inspiration must be non-rational, mystical and therefore non-objective and non-verbal. But the witness of the New Testament attributes inspiration not to people but to writings and to texts that take form in words. It is therefore impossible to eliminate the verbal aspect of inspiration and to refer to it simply as being the illumination of the writer.

8

Inspiration: What it Isn't, What it Is

The word inspiration conjures up pictures of romantic poets in Parisian garrets, painters struggling to get the right texture or songwriters hoping the mood will come.

Adding 'divine' to 'inspiration' makes all the difference. It indicates the special contact between God and the authors of Scripture and its consequences for what they wrote. If we claim inspiration is the result of this contact, it is not satisfying to leave things there. We must attempt to say something about the nuts and bolts of inspiration. What tools do we have to describe what theologians call the *mode* of inspiration?

We will look at this in a negative and positive sense to see how the human and the divine aspects of Scripture are complementary.

What Divine Insipration Isn't

Because so many false ideas orbit around the notion of inspiration it's not bad to start with what it isn't.

One current take on the question is that God did something special when he acted to call a people. Inspiration describes a sense of his presence in their group consciousness. God made a motley crew into a community. From among them came some witnesses who told what God had done. A religious tradition was born in a body of writings. However there was no *direct* relation between God and the Scriptures. The Bible is simply a growing human tradition about God and his presence, not a divine Word. It has all the limitations of any other human word. This is essentially a modern reinterpretation of what inspiration could be and the Bible itself, as we have seen, does not speak in these terms.

Another idea about inspiration that allows more room for the writers refers to artistic inspiration. Inspiration is an aspect of cultural creation, something that sets the gifted apart from common mortals. Inspiration in the best cases is the source of great works of music, painting and literature, even if in the worst it is an excuse for a lot of junk that finds its way into museums. The work itself takes second place to the artist, who is sometimes considered with semi-religious veneration. That is why artists get away with murder for bizarre behaviour. They are, after all, *artists*. Inspiration is a hidden reservoir and a poem or a song only taps a little of the artist's potential. That paintings never get finished or that some music fails to hit the high spots does not detract from the potential of the creator. Inspiration is above all the creative gift of an individual. Some of the biblical writers had this kind of charisma, but biblical inspiration is something much more than flair.

When the Bible speaks about inspiration we find an altogether different perspective. Even if its authors were not anonymous pen-pushers they are less in view than their writings. They were ordinary folk, not celebrities lining up for awards. In the Bible, inspiration is the special gift of God that happens during 'inscripturation'—the putting of the message into the words of Scripture by the writers. At other times they were as uninspired as we are. More of this later.

A Variety of Methods, One Result

Again we can ask, if the writings of the Bible are all inspired, why are they not all of equal value, quality and style? Why are there ups and downs, uplifting parts and flat bits?

An illustration might help. Look at planet earth. God created a multi-environment: oceans and rivers, plains and mountains, forests and deserts, hot and cold climates. It would be monotonous if the world were all Siberian waste! Perhaps you prefer the mountains, but you can also fancy an occasional trip to the coast. Just as God made all types of landscape for us enjoy, he also made the Bible a rich diversity. Liking Deuteronomy doesn't mean that you can't appreciate Jude too. Some places we like better than others, perhaps because of our temperaments, perhaps because they have helped us in time of great need. Recently, some intellectual agnostics have made a great deal of Ecclesiastes and Job, and interpreting Jonah as a parable makes it interesting literature.

The Bible was inspired in such a way that the character of the authors and their subject matter are credible. When the Holy Spirit was at work inspiring Scripture, he did not ride roughshod over the personality of Amos, Isaiah, Mark, John or Paul. The Spirit works in such a way that their words express their human capacities.

Nor is the content equally important in different parts of Scripture, even though all of it is inspired. It's obvious that the content of John's Gospel is more significant than Philemon, or Exodus than Esther. The authority of the Bible is not equal in all parts, even if it is all equally inspired. Authority depends on what is being said and some parts of the Bible speak more naturally about the 'big issues' than others. Some subjects are nearer to the central message of the Bible. There are things primary and secondary, which doesn't mean that the secondary things are unimportant or uninspired. Even second fiddles in an orchestra have a part to play; without the journeymen tennis players there would not be many tournaments, only exhibition matches.

Different Ways of Inspiration

When we look at the different parts of Scripture, it is also clear that they were not all produced in the same way or with the same intention. Scripture itself indicates the way in which its various texts were inspired.

A wide variety of processes are involved in inspiration: poetry writing, historical narrative depending on author-recall, letters, personal experiences, prayers, genealogies, prophecies and proverbial wisdom all find their place. There are also some cases where a sort of dictation is found and the words of God were transmitted directly. God himself inscribed the Ten Commandments on stone tablets. God's word was also spoken directly through prophets like Isaiah, who received an order such as the following: 'Go and say to Hezekiah, Thus says the Lord…' (Isa. 38:4–6). Jesus spoke directly from heaven to the evangelist John on Patmos and said 'write this to the angel of the church of Ephesus, Smyrna or Pergamum' (Rev. 2:1, 8, 12).

This does not mean that dictation is the exclusive model of inspiration. Much of Scripture is the result of other methods than the kind of dictation a boss might do using a Dictaphone. The Holy Spirit worked in revelation in many ways (Heb. 1:1) as the wide variety of practices shows. The nature of human participation in the process of inspiration was variable. When Luke wrote his gospel he did so by 'undertaking to compile a narrative of the things which have been accomplished among us' (Luke 1:1–3).

An interesting case, perhaps unique in Scripture, illustrates one way the word of God was reported and preserved. In Jeremiah 36:2 we read that 'this word came to Jeremiah from the Lord: "Take a scroll and write on it all the words that I have spoken to you against Israel and Judah and all the nations, from the day I spoke to you, from the days of Josiah until today".' Jeremiah had been prophesying for about twenty-three years at this time. Now he wrote down in one book a readers' digest of his messages, which had always had the same thrust. He spoke constantly on the same subjects—the sins of the people and their danger, threats of punishment and the promises of God.

The resulting scroll with its prophetic words was destroyed by king Jehoiakim. He didn't like it a bit, cut it up with a penknife, burned it in the grate in his winter quarters and ordered Jeremiah's arrest. What a disaster when the king destroyed the scroll, as bad as some of today's computer accidents! This, however, did not stop God speaking to his people. Another scroll was produced, with many more words. Man cannot avoid God's word when God's intention is to give it and to preserve it: 'Then Jeremiah took another scroll and gave it to Baruch the scribe who wrote on it at the dictation of Jeremiah all the words of the scroll that Jehoiakim had burned in the fire. And many similar words were added to them' (36:32).

Lots can be learned about Scripture from reading Jeremiah 36. Something we might forget is the amazing patience of God with regard to human beings. Before taking action, God had Jeremiah preach for a quarter of a century, providing multiple chances for people to have a change of heart. When his judgment finally came, it was no knee-jerk reaction. God had his special messengers to bring his word (36:1) and they faithfully transmitted it all (4). There is a line of transmission: from God to Jeremiah to Baruch, who wrote it down in a manuscript. This is inspired Scripture, substantially the same text as the book of Jeremiah we have before us today. God also preserves his word. It cannot be destroyed, although men might try, but it is *God's* word; it is restored and even amplified.

Another thing we do well to recognise is that the word of God is never particularly agreeable for human beings. The king didn't appreciate it at all, although some of his servants were upset when he burned it. Our natural reaction to God's word and its teaching is not one of thankfulness. God's word tells us, as Martin Luther ofttimes said, that God is opposed to us. We are not on good terms with him, or his word, because we want things our own way. The consequences of refusing the word of God are dramatic, for a nation or an individual. The king burned the scroll and was destitute for his pains. Hearing and obeying God's word is a life and death issue. How we respond leads to weal or to woe.

Inspiration and the Covenant Context

Speaking of the inspiration of Scripture in a positive way requires placing inspiration, which is a special and final act of revelation, in the context of God's dealings with his people. What was his aim when he called them to be his witness in the world?

As we have already said, the Bible is a text formed in the context of the covenant that unites God and his people. In this arrangement God is the Lord and man is his servant as a citizen of the world. Human responses and actions have their meaning within the covenant context. This is also true of the inspiration of Scripture and its mediation through God's servants.

As the Lord of the covenant, God is also Father of his people. He follows their growth, guiding them, knowing their intimate thoughts and problems and dealing with their wandering away when necessary. The end of this process is when God reveals himself in the perfect sonship of Jesus Christ. In this context, it is natural that as Father, God leads his children to verbalise their thoughts, joys, fears and the expectations that arise in their experiences. When they do so, God himself inspires their words in specific cases to express the nature of his Lordship.

God's role in inspiration mirrors his function as Lord of the covenant. He takes the initiative to reveal himself, he guides human beings associated in the act of revelation, forms them for the task, inspires their very words and exercises a quality control on the inspired writings. The result is Holy Scripture, which is not only human, but in its form and content the word of God too. The Bible has a dual nature that reflects what the covenant between God and man is like, both divine and human.

How can we understand the respective and complementary roles of the divine and the human in the inspiration of Scripture? Let's look at one and the other.

The Role of God in Inspiration

God inspires Holy Scripture as his word through the presence and influence of the Holy Spirit. His thoughts reach our minds through some specific procedures:

- God himself is the author of the Scriptures which are *his* word—what God wanted to communicate to man begins in the divine mind;
- as his word it was correctly transmitted via his chosen servants;
- God commented on what he had done in his revealing acts with words that say how he wants them to be understood;

- as author, God superintended the whole process by 'suggesting' to the human authors *in situ* the things to retain;
- what he globally proposed to the human writers through suggestion, makes up the content of the revealed word;
- the content corresponds to what God wishes to make known: events, doctrines, prayers, praise, rules of conduct or preaching, as well as many other ideas.

The Bible came into being by the leading of the Holy Spirit. This underlines the fact that God is the author of the Bible's words. The lead role was not that of the human writers, but Scripture found its origin in God's will, as we have seen in 2 Peter 1:21. Christ sent his apostles to preach; bearing witness in word and writing are two of a kind. According to the apostle Peter, the apostles were chosen to be this kind of witness: 'he commanded us to preach to the people and to testify that he is the one appointed by God to be the judge of the living and the dead. To him all the prophets bear witness that everyone who believes in him receives forgiveness of sins through his name.'

An illustration of what is called 'suggestion' could be found in the way a dramatist writes a play, with actors following their respective parts. He creates a plausible situation with characters who act as expected. When we watch the play the words and actions of the actors seem realistic and natural in their given situation. Their acts and words are credible, but all the time they are acting out the author's plot in the script. This illustration is of limited value; it would be wrong to think of inspired authors like manipulated puppets. It serves to show how placed in certain situations, suggested actions and words arise naturally. Inspiration does not violate the freedom and personality of the writers of Scripture but gives them full reign.

Is God the Author of Scripture?

It is plain that the Bible is a human document; for this reason, it seems like overkill to claim that God is *the author* of Scripture. Is this idea sustainable?

Over the last century so much has been learned and said about the human side of the Bible that the sense of its divinity has waned. The divine character of Scripture has become so neglected that it is important not only to see that it is part of the church's heritage, but also that it belongs to the Scripture's own witness. It is necessary not to neglect the divine character in order to have a kosher attitude toward the Bible. If God is the ultimate author of Scripture, man does not hold the copyright and cannot consider himself the originator or the owner of the text. Furthermore, he is not the final custodian of its meaning either.

Across large swathes of the modern church, the Bible is considered to be an expression of man's growing spiritual awareness. It is taken for granted that its value lies in showing progress from something primitive to a refined form of religion and ethics in the teaching of the Beatitudes or the Golden Rule. God's involvement in the process is discreet, to say the least. He has the patience to let man get on with it, and the outcome depends largely on man. What the Bible tells us about God, on this understanding, is that when men suffer, he suffers too. This can encourage us to be better human beings. God is the Father of all created beings, all men are equal in his sight and human life has significance because the message of the Bible includes everyone in God's love.

No one will deny that in the Bible there is progress and development in man's understanding of God. However, this does not mean that it is totally conditioned by its cultural setting or that it is a product of human progress. Inspiration is not the development of insights because human beings become better every day and in every way.

The Role of Divine Sovereignty

From an evangelical perspective, the main thing about God is that he is sovereign over anything else that exists. We don't believe this because we need a security blanket, but because it's the biblical truth about the nature of God. Sovereignty is misunderstood if it is equated with dictatorial power or as implying the shredding of human responsibility. It must be seen in harmony with other divine attributes, for instance the love, justice, holiness and truth of God. When we look at it this way, it cannot be a threat; God's power is always a wise and loving power, a power that is just and holy and in conformity with the truth. Divine sovereignty is good—the opposite of the arbitrary human power that traumatises us. No doubt reticence about an all-powerful God stems from the many dramatic abuses of human power in the last century.

As the author of Scripture, God is behind the Bible. Like the author of any book, he has chosen its form and its contents and has even selected the words used. By the inspiration of the Holy Spirit he has communicated what he wants to be revealed through the human writers and via what they write. To put it bluntly, what God wants to say goes into writing in their manuscripts and so is transmitted to us.

There are not many options open as to the origin of Scripture. Either God is the author of Scripture, behind the human activity involved in its making, or man is. In the first case, this tallies with the Christian belief that God is Lord over all and that only God can truly speak of God. In the second case, if man speaks for God, he may give a good account of himself, but can he give a good account of God? The next step down this road is to wonder whether any God exists other than one that is buried in the human psyche.

Of course theologians try to concoct all sorts of halfway houses between what they consider to be two extremes, divine or human. Their constructions invariably implode unilaterally into a Bible that is just another human production. Ultimately nothing is known about God's truth.

The Human Witness in the Bible

At this point someone will remark that all the witnesses in the Bible are human beings and that there is no direct speaking by God. If that is the case, to claim that God is the author of Scripture is contradictory. Better to settle for a good human witness, accepting the fact that God has done some real but mysterious things to save man. However, what value is a witness if its testimony is not true, precise and objective? How can we be assured that it's the case?

The Bible has a dual aspect. The covenant between God as Lord and man exists in a real communion between the two partners. Both parties are united and speak in the same document. The inspiration of Scripture is divine verbal inspiration in which God speaks through and with his human partners who bear witness as they are led by the Holy Spirit.

This can be illustrated by the way the word witness is used in John's Gospel. The witness of the Holy Spirit and the witness of the apostles are not separate things, but one witness. The witness of the Spirit finds expression in the words of the apostles. This does not mean that despite human weaknesses and errors the Holy Spirit uses human words as well as he can. On the contrary, the Holy Spirit makes men apt to bear his witness to Christ. God has spoken in Christ and through his servants inspired by the Holy Spirit. This is how Jesus repeatedly presents it in John's Gospel:

- The Father that sent me has borne witness to me (5:37, 8:18);
- The works I do in my Father's name bear witness to me (10:25);
- The Spirit of truth who proceeds from the Father will bear witness about me (15:26);
- You (the disciples) also will bear witness (15:27);
- If we receive the witness of men, the witness of God is greater, because it is the witness he has borne to his Son (1 John 5:9).

The word 'witness' in these examples has the sense of a legal testimony made before a court of law. It is a claim to truth. The divine and the human are complementary witnesses. The Holy Spirit makes one witness out of the two. They are joined together in such a way that the words of men become, through the inspiration of the Spirit, the evidence deposed by God concerning his own truth. God bears witness to himself in Scripture as the author of truth.

Human Witness and Spirit Recall

Witness in the context of a binding covenant between God and his people is a true, precise and binding expression of God's dealing with his people in creation, judgment and salvation.

When God's only begotten Son came in human form, the Father bore witness to his unique nature at the moment of his baptism and the transfiguration with words from heaven. The Son only bears witness to himself as the Father has given him the occasion and the words to do so. His unique witness was transmitted to his apostles who received the licence to testify from the Holy Spirit. They give the authorised version. In the light of this, John can say at the end of his gospel: 'this is the disciple who is bearing witness about these things, and who has written these things, and we know that his testimony is true' (John 21:24).

It is because of the truth-nature of the human witnesses, inspired by the Spirit, that the Old and New Testament draw a hard and fast line between true and false prophets (see Ezek. 13:2–3, Jer. 14:14, 23:16, Gal. 1:1, 6–11). Real prophets bear the divine word that is true and, in the case of prediction, will come true. Their word is sealed by the witness of God himself through his Spirit.

However, when they speak, inspired by the Spirit as they are, the witnesses loose none of their humanness, only the errors and incapacities that plague sinful understanding of God and his ways. John speaks as John, Luke as Luke and Paul as Paul. Though they are led by the Spirit, there is no violation of their personal make-up. Mark does not write the sophisticated Greek of the epistle to the Hebrews, but in a popular way. Amos does not quit being a shepherd taken from behind the flock when he prophesies for a few months. The human writers of the Bible are not inspired in such a way that their capacities are superseded. Four gospels are better than one, contrary to what some people might think. This is so because the Holy Spirit unites their witness into one witness to the truth.

The Human and the Divine, One Witness

Revelation comes to the inspired writers from the outside. It is God's truth revealed to them. That's logical, as there is nothing in man that can reveal God. The Holy Spirit works with this disclosed truth so that it is appropriated mentally and then spoken by the authors of Scripture. God is the author of the content and substance of his revealed truth as his Spirit witnesses through the instrumentality of human understanding. The result is that the human word written is the word of God.

How does this mysterious action take place? Obviously we know little about it. This, however, we can say: by revelation God brings things spontaneously into the minds of those to whom he is suggesting his truth. The writers of Holy Scripture speak the truth with the same spontaneity in their writing. How is this so? Here we touch the mystery of God and we can go no further because this, like all God's acts, is incomprehensible to our limited human intelligence.

The result is that the human words of the writers are the words of God who is their divine author. God's word comes to us in human form, the word of God in the words of men through the instrumentality of the Spirit. The Spirit of God and the human letter are not two separate entities. Like two strands of thread, they are wound together into one rope because inspiration makes one entity out of two. The Scriptures are the result of verbal inspiration; God can be called their author since the word of God, in this case, is found in men's words.

Words in Communion

Some further comments about the human aspect of Scripture can be added to this broad perspective.

Firstly, the biblical writers wrote freely and spontaneously. They did everything that writers normally do when producing a text. The Bible is the product of their choices. They chose when to write and to whom. They planned it, decided its content, made choices about literary style, used different forms of language, no doubt made corrections while writing and decided when they had said all they wanted to. The personalities of the human authors are everywhere transparent in Scripture, as well as their limitations. Even their weaknesses are not brushed under the carpet when they write; they lay themselves bare. We learn about Moses' lack of confidence, David's adultery, Jeremiah's depression, Job's doubts, Peter's failings and Paul's face-off with the other apostles or with Barnabas.

Secondly, the Holy Spirit works in inspiration through two actions we can call *concursus* and *confluence*, which indicate that humanity is not sidelined but accompanied in its work. *Concursus*, or 'running together', is like one athlete pacing another when an attempt is made to break a record. Having another runner alongside helps the record breaker and improves his performance. This illustrates that in the production of Scripture the Holy Spirit is right alongside the human author, prompting and encouraging him. Without his action there would be no *holy* Scripture.

Confluence is like two rivers joining, as happens near St Louis in the USA, where the Missouri and the Mississippi meet. From that point, the river is no longer one or the other (although it is still called the Mississippi in this case) but a combination of both, swelled by water from two tributaries. Scripture has a dual origin, with the full force of both its sources, divine and human. When rivers join, we can no longer say this water here is from the Missouri and that over there is from the Mississippi. They are mixed together to make a mega-river. Likewise, we cannot say of the Bible, this is human and that is divine, because the human is Spirit-inspired and the divine has taken on human garb. The writers of Scipture in their penmanship act in harmony with God and through his Spirit, God is one with them in their message. This reflects, in inspiration, the spiritual communion between God and man in the covenant. Without it there is no word *of God*.

Finally, the one witness is constituted of the divine and human factors *at the time of writing*. This is achieved through the literary formation of the text at the point where the words go on the tablet, parchment or paper. Inspiration is not something that comes upon an already extant text to 'inspire' what is otherwise simply human. Nor is it something that pre-exists the text in the writers. Inspiration is special work of the Spirit. It belongs to a specific moment, place and person; it is unique to the situation where holy Scripture is being formed. Inspiration crystallises God's word in Scripture in human language, where it is preserved in inspired form.

To sum up: inspiration is a form of special supernatural guidance that bears actively on the writers when they are writing Scripture through the influence of the Holy Spirit. Passively, inspiration is the result of that influence. Because of inspiration the writers' words become the words of God in the Bible. For this reason they are true and are clothed with divine authority.

The Bible is authoritative because it is the word of God; it is intelligible to us because it is the word of man. This is why believing that the Bible is the word of God is so important; a divine word we could not understand and a human word would not rise above what we find elsewhere in great literature. Only God's truth can meet our needs, heal us and reply to our deepest expectations and aspirations.

Conclusion

What we have said has profound consequences for what we do with the Bible and what we expect from it.

We cannot make light of the fact that God is the ultimate author of Scripture through the work of his Spirit. If we forget it, we will not read the Bible aright, not expect it either to be true or to have a message that holds together. It will sink in our expectations to the level of any other book. We will not think that all of it is important or has something to say to us. Probably we will end up having our favourite places of pilgrimage to which we return every now and then for a spiritual top-up.

At the same time the human character of the Bible cannot be neglected. It has the same features as other books, with chapters, sentences and words. Our access to the meaning of the text, God's meaning, is through what we read. If people find the Bible to be a dead letter, they have not progressed from the form of the words to an understanding of what God is saying. We need to learn to listen to God in Scripture.

The message of Scripture must be taken seriously, because we won't hear this message elsewhere. One of our big problems is that we often know what God says to us, but we take rearguard action to protect our own agendas by watering down the meaning of Scripture. One of the aggravating things about a good deal of Bible study or preaching is it seems to be a spin off from the text and fails to deal with what it actually says. The sharp focus of Scripture is lost.

Finally, because of inspiration, holy Scripture is our principle means of receiving God's grace and an aid to spiritual growth. The word received, meditated and taken to heart is sanctifying and life-changing. It encourages spiritual rearmament. For this reason the psalmist says:

> I have stored up your word in my heart,
> that I might not sin against you…
> The unfolding of your words gives light;
> it imparts understanding to the simple. (Ps. 119:11, 130)

Over and above the diversity of operations in inspiration, the outcome is the same, gifting us with God's own word. The result of inspiration is that God spoke and continues to speak via a text mediated through human persons and means.

From the Bible's witness we can understand *that* it has a special quality of inspiration, even if we will never understand the mechanism of *how* this result was achieved. The result was obtained in different ways, with different people and at different times, but the mechanics of how it was accomplished are beyond our ken.

9

The Word of God

There is a good deal of disagreement over what is meant when the Bible is called the word of God. Some brief introductory remarks will illustrate that discussing this problem is like walking through a minefield.

Sometimes the expression word of God is simply a sign of respect for the book's venerable character, like when we call someone sir or madam. It is often construed in a metaphorical way and there has been much discussion about the content of the metaphor.

From the time of the early church in the second century, Marcion and others attempted to define which parts of Scripture were authoritative. With the advent of post-Enlightenment criticism, similar distinctions were made between the form and the content of Scripture to separate the wheat from the chaff. The distinctions were almost endless: the New Testament was accepted but not the Old, or the teaching of Jesus but not that of Paul, or the fundamental message (the *kerygma*) and not secondary 'mythical' teachings, or the ethical but not the factual content of the word.

More recently, increasing consciousness of the human aspects of Scripture have caused some interpreters to consider that the word of God itself was not in Scripture. Because of the closeness of the acts and words of God, the real content of Scripture was to be found in the acts of God behind the human text. It was often said that the Bible contained a human witness to the word of God that always lies beyond it. I once heard a preacher introduce the Scripture reading with the phrase: 'Let us listen for the word of God', substituting 'for' for 'to'.

Karl Barth, the leading Protestant theologian of the last century, was typical of this approach. For Barth there are three forms of the word of God, the living Christ, the written word and the preached word, but only the first is the real McCoy. The other two are human instruments that are not in and of themselves God's word, although they *become* it when we encounter the living Christ through them. Barth's position raised many questions not least of which was how something can become what it isn't to begin with. The Reformers made a distinction between the witness of the Holy Spirit in the inscripturated word and the internal witness of the Spirit to the truth of the word in our hearts. Barth jettisoned the first and kept the second in modified form and truth became subjective.

The unfortunate thing about all this high-faluting discussion is that it adds up to rationalisation on rationalisation. The main aim of the critics is to avoid what they call 'abstraction' or 'impersonal truths'. It has, however, little to do with what the Bible says about itself. If we want to know what the word of God is, our lines must be drawn from the Bible.

A Strange Expression

We have to admit that 'word of God' is something of a strange expression. After all, we would not call Churchill's history of the Second world war 'the word of Winston'. In and of itself 'word of ...' leads us to expect some kind of oral communication in a solemn context, something like the Queen's New Year message or a State of the Union speech.

When it refers of the Bible, 'word of God' is not used in this sense. If some of the writers of Scripture did hear an oral message, most didn't, and no one alive today has received a direct word spoken by

God, as when the disciples heard the voice of God on the mount of transfiguration or the apostle Paul was stopped dead by it on the Damascus road. We can't imagine what such a word would be like.

When the expression 'word of God' is used it is primarily by way of contrast with the words of men. In Psalm 12 for instance, 'the words of the Lord are pure words' (6) is contrasted with the lies, flattering lips, speaking deceitfully and boasting tongues spoken of in the previous verses (2–3). In particular, the word of God refers to its ultimate origin, as a word that comes to us from God, over against any number of human speech acts. It is not equivalent to human communications for the simple reason that it has qualities that belong only to the nature of its author. Some of the same attributes we use to refer to God also describe his word—in Psalm 12, sovereignty, purity, faithfulness and power to save. Such things cannot be ascribed to human beings as the Psalm makes amply clear.

When we hear and read the word of God we ought to expect to be impressed by its character and divine origin, just as whenever I speak in French people can hardly miss my roots in 'perfidious Albion' as they refer to it here in France.

That God uses human means to communicate with us does not imply that it is less his word, or that it is only half his word, or that he ceases to be sovereign when he speaks to us. In fact, the humanity of Scripture, as we have already seen, does not exclude its divinity. God's glory resides precisely in the fact that he uses human means to transmit his truth to us, just as the beauty of nature paints his invisible glory in the visible world.

We propose then to look a little further into how the expression 'word of God' is related to its origin in the divine nature.

God's Person and His Word

The Bible makes a link between the fact that God is personal and that he speaks, just as there is a link between our personality and the way we speak and act.

What I am writing in this book unveils who I am as a person. People in the know about such things could conclude from my style that I am not young and I live in France. Almost everyone could stick a theological label on me. However, these things are far from exhausting my personality. There are a great many aspects that go beyond anything that can be inferred from my writing. You do not know whether I like to eat Indian or what I am planning for my summer holidays.

This illustration helps us understand how God and his word are identical in some ways and how they differ in others. The word *depends* on God: it issues from him and cannot be detached from the broader reality of his divine wisdom. In some respect, we may go as far as to say that the word of God is an attribute of his divine person. It conveys something of the identity of God. However, as an expression of God's person, the word does not mirror all that could be said about the reality of God. The word expresses in a limited way something about the whole of God's person, but there are many things about God that escape our knowledge.

On the other hand, if my words express what I am as a person, they are also distinct and separate from whom I am. They can be recorded on an MP3 or written in a book and have a life of their own. Similarly, if there is continuity between God and his word, there is also a certain difference between them.

The word of God became flesh in the incarnate Son and it became Scripture in the written word. Although both of these depend on and exist in communion with God, they are to some measure distinct from God. The Son is divine, but is not the Father. If Scripture is God's word, 'Holy Scripture', it is not the object of bibliolatry, because God has spoken in words that are part of our own human language. To describe the word of God properly, we have to observe the continuity and discontinuity, the identity and difference between the person of God and his word. This is important. If theological modernism sees only the differences, some forms of fundamentalism go to the other extreme and forget that in Scripture God adapts his expression to our humanity.

When we say that we can consider the word as being an attribute of God we are indicating that this word depends on God for its existence and that it reflects the divine nature in certain ways. We propose to develop two aspects of this idea.

The Word of God and Salvation History

Something is known about the attributes of God not because man has an intuitive knowledge of them, but because they are revealed in a covenant context, when God intervenes to save his people.

All the things we call 'biblical doctrines' in some way or other are related to divine acts. Redemption is God's act on the cross to save, justification is God's act declaring us to be accepted by him, the second coming of Christ is his appearing in glory, and so on. The attributes of God are mirrored in his acts and we come to know him by his actions. An attribute of God is a perfection 'attributed' to him without which he would not be God. God's attributes define his nature and tell us about his character. A mute, inactive God would be as unknown in a personal sense as a statue of the Buddah in the lotus position 'sitting quietly doing nothing'.

God's attributes correspond to his names and are markers of the divine nature. The Holy one is holy, the only God is one, the Ancient of days is eternal. The church fathers often saw the attributes and names of God as synonyms. Augustine counted more than fifty. In his *Institutes* John Calvin did not make a classification of the attributes as found in other theologians following the example of John of Damascus in his book *The Orthodox Faith* from the eighth century. He tends to see all the attributes of God in the light of divine independence and underlines the fact that they are not shared with humanity, but are unique to God.

When the attributes used to speak about God are also used to describe the word of God, this shows that his word is different from ours. It is a dynamic and living word. The word of God lines up with his other attributes because God is known via his word as the God who speaks and addresses us. God is essentially the living God, *infinite* in nature, but also *personal* in his capacity to communicate.

Several examples illustrate how the word of God is described in a way similar to God himself, underlying the fact that God's word carries with it the marks of his personhood.

GOD'S WORD IS POWERFUL. God is the sovereign Master of the universe and his word is similarly powerful and authoritative. It may be hidden, as is the case of secret divine providence, but it never lacks effectiveness. It may appear weak and derisory, but it never lacks in compelling meaningfulness. It accomplishes exactly what God intends. Isaiah 55:8–11 describes this and calls God's people to make his word their nourishment and their foundation:

> My thoughts are not your thoughts,
> neither are your ways my ways, declares the Lord.
> For as the heavens are higher than the earth,
> so are my ways higher than your ways
> and my thoughts than your thoughts,
> For as the rain and the snow come down from heaven
> and do not return there but water the earth,
> making it bring forth and sprout,
> giving seed to the sower and bread to the eater,
> so shall my word be that goes out from my mouth;
> it shall not return to me empty
> but it shall accomplish that which I purpose,
> and shall succeed in the thing for which I sent it.

There is something close to a personification of the word of God in this oracle. The word of God works with the same mysterious effectiveness as God does himself. It accomplishes the will of God mysteriously, just as God's thoughts and plans are way beyond man's understanding. Similarly in a parallel text in Hebrews 4:12–13:

> The word of God is living and active, sharper than any two-edged sword, piercing to the division of soul and of spirit, of joints and of marrow, and discerning the thoughts and intentions of the heart. And no creature is hidden from its sight, but all are naked and exposed to the eyes of him to whom we must give account.

The word of God and the 'eyes' of God work together and evaluate human conduct. The statement in this text serves to answer the question that could be raised after reading Isaiah 55—what about those who make little of God's word? Doesn't that make it *de facto* ineffective and nullify Isaiah's claim?

God, however, is a covenant-keeping God and his word is a covenant word. The effectiveness of its action does not depend on human response or human belief. It is powerful and always attains its goal, either in blessing or in condemnation, as it is like a *double-edged* sword. The language of Hebrews 4 is judicial, not military, and the sword referred to is the sword of judgment. Faith enters the promised rest of God (9), but disobedience brings man into a situation where he has to give account. The word of God is powerful as the criteria of judgment, as Jesus himself understood: 'The one who rejects me and does not receive my words has a judge, the word that I have spoken will judge him on the last day' (John 12:48). Jesus explains that his word is judge because it is the Father himself who has ordered what he, Jesus, should say and speak. The word of God is a word of judgement because God is the judge through the words of the Son.

THE WORD IS MEANINGFUL AND WISE. The power of the word of God is associated with its meaning. It brings to light the reality of things and interprets their fundamental direction and end. As meaningful and wise, the word of God is creative and gives substance to reality:

> By the word of the Lord the heavens were made
> and by the breath of his mouth all their host…
> For he spoke and it came to be;
> he commanded and it stood firm. (Ps. 33:6–9).

Just a couple of verses previously we are told that 'the word of the Lord is upright and all his work is done in faithfulness… he loves righteousness and justice and the earth is full of the steadfast love of the Lord' (4–5). As with God, as with his word, which in creation is an edict of loving faithfulness, justice and kindness. This gives ultimate meaning to life.

The error of pagans, explained by Paul in Romans 1, lies in their ungodliness because they do not receive wisdom from the word of God in creation. Even though 'what can be known about God is plain to them, because God has shown it to them… they exchanged the truth of God for a lie' (Rom. 1:19, 25). Just as the presence of God brings light, so his word is enlightening and gives meaning to human experience. Without it our understanding becomes darkened (21).

THE WORD IS THE PRESENCE OF GOD. Human words, we have said, reveal something of the speaker. Words can be faithful in promises, weasel words in deception or the binding words of oaths; human language always tells us something about human nature.

Communication problems lie at the heart of social ills and make growing up difficult for many children. As creatures of God, human beings are not lacking in divine communication, because God is by nature a God who speaks. Our problem comes because we do not listen to God's word, and even when we do, all too often we do not take it seriously.

In Scripture, the word of God is said to reveal God because he is present with his word. In Genesis 1:1–3 we already find a model that sets the pattern for what follows. God creates, the Spirit is on the face of the water and God speaks. In Psalm 33:6, as already seen, the word goes together with the 'breath of his mouth', a reference to the out-breathing of the Spirit of God. In John's Gospel, Jesus says to the disciples who are finding his teaching tough going: 'It is the Spirit who gives life; the flesh is of no avail. The words that I have spoken to you are spirit and life' (6:63). The apostle Paul says that when he preached the gospel in Thessalonika, it 'came to you not only in word, but also in power and in the Holy Spirit and with full conviction' (1 Thess. 1:6).

In Scripture, God is always present and active with his word, whether it be in verbal pronunciation or in written record. This is underlined by two passages in Deuteronomy. God's law was given to Moses in the form of written statutes or directions. They will make the people of God stand out if they follow them. Others will say: 'Surely this great nation is a wise and understanding people. For what great nation is there that has a god so near to it as the Lord our God is to us whenever we call on him?' (Deut. 4:6–8). God is near his people and lives among them because his word dwells with them and tells them concretely what obedience means. Further on in Deuteronomy, in chapter 30, the same themes reappear: 'This commandment that I command you today is not far off... But the word is very near you. It is in your mouth and your heart so that you can do it' (30:11–14).

The word of God is the life that God gives, his living presence, and it produces salvation. Paul takes up the theme in Romans 10:6–8 when he exhorts the Jews by saying that the message of Christ, the way of salvation for all, is there to be believed:

> the righteousness based on faith says... 'the word is near you, in your mouth and in your heart', that is the word of faith that we proclaim; because if you confess with your mouth that Jesus is Lord and believe in your heart that God raised him from the dead, you will be saved.'

Having the divine word written in the heart means to have God for God and to live as belonging to him, in his presence (Jer. 31:33). Just as with the case of the law in the Old Testament, God stands among his new covenant people as risen Lord through the word of the gospel. Jesus reigns and is present through the word that announces salvation by faith in him.

ATTRIBUTES BELONGING ONLY TO GOD ARE ALSO USED FOR HIS WORD. The word of God is also presented in parallel to other descriptions of God's character. In the Bible several attributes that are applicable to God alone are also used to describe God's word, the most obvious being 'holy'. The major illustration of this is found in Psalm 119, which is a hymn of praise to the word-law of God. Read it though picking out the following references!

The laws of God, his commands, statutes, ordinances, rules, testimonies, or put simply, his written word, are described as being:

- righteous (7, 62, 75, 106, 123, 138, 144, 160, 164),
- wonderful (18, 129),
- good (39),
- true (43, 140, 142, 151, 160),
- faithful or sure (86),

- eternal (89, 152, 160),
- life-giving (93),
- perfect (96),
- sweet (103),
- light (109),
- right (128, 137f, 172).

These adjectives usually describe the nature of God, but here they apply to a material reality, the written testimony of God. 'Righteous' tops the list as the attribute of God par excellence in salvation.

The psalm illustrates that when the word takes written form it does not limit God, no more than ice or steam are limitations of water. The word maintains its character as being superior to all other words because it is the word of God.

GOD IS THANKED BECAUSE OF HIS WORD. Some churches, such as the eastern Orthodox, observe a ceremony of the veneration of the word. This holds certain dangers in spite of good intent. The immediate object can always run the risk of replacing the real object of worship—God himself.

The saints of the Old Testament showed a respect for the word of God that is at the antipodes of the criticism found in modern rationalism and humanism. The written word is a reason for praising God. He is worshipped for having given his revelation in this form. In Psalm 119 again, the psalmist 'loves' God's law 'exceedingly' and makes it a subject of delight (167). Seven times a day he 'praises God for his righteous rules' and finds true peace in loving God's law (164). David adores God with his word and for his word.

If you had to choose between fearing persecution and hardship and fearing being found out by God's word, which would worry you? The psalmist has no doubts: 'Princes persecute me without cause, but my heart stands in awe of your words' (161). It was holy fear of God's word that reinforced Christ's resolution when he said 'they have persecuted me without cause' (Ps. 69:4, John 15:25). It is this fear that is the beginning of wisdom, as David repeats in Psalm 56:5: 'In God whose word I praise, in God I trust; I shall not be afraid. What can flesh do to me?'

Trusting in God is achieved by trusting in his word, which has great and precious promises for the believer, because God is faithful and true.

The Word of God Is a Trinitarian Word

According to Scripture, God's word exists mysteriously in God before being spoken to men. The God of the Bible is a trinitarian God. The first century Jew Philo of Alexandria pointed out from his reading of Genesis 1 that diversity exists within the one God. The trinitarian nature of God is vital; if God is three in one and an intelligent being, communication must exist naturally among the three persons for them to be in communion.

The big difference between God and false gods is that the latter are dumb and cannot speak. Having no capacity of communication they can neither be known or useful, as they cannot hear prayer or save human beings. The classic passage on the subject of worshipping false gods is in Isaiah 44:9–20, but Habbakuk 2:18–20 is almost its equal:

> What profit is an idol…
> for its maker trusts in his own creation
> Woe to him who says to a silent stone, Arise!
> Can this teach?
> And there is no breath in it
> But the Lord is in his holy temple;
> let all the earth keep silence before him.

By contrast, the God of the Bible is wisdom itself and a God of communication. Speech belongs to the God who is one in three. The second person of the Trinity, the Son, is the Logos-Word of God, in whom the Father and the Spirit communicate. This intra-divine communication is secret and hidden within God. It lies in the depths of his intelligence and finds one expression that we know of in his plan or eternal purpose (Deut. 29:29).

Even if this plan is beyond human knowledge, Scripture indicates the reality of its existence. God is a God of communication in truth and love, not only with relation to his creatures, but firstly in himself. If rational creatures can express their thoughts and feelings in words, it is because human beings are made in the image of God, and verbal communication is part of that image.

Communication is an essential feature of God's being; without this characteristic God would not be God. Within the Trinity each of the distinct persons has some special relation to the divine word. Biblical revelation witnesses to this:

- God the Father exercises his sovereignty by his word, as described in Psalm 29, Isaiah 40:26, 43:1, 62:2, or Ephesians 3:14.
- The Son in his incarnation receives and fulfils the word and is himself the Word made flesh as we read in the gospel of John and his first epistle (1.1, 1 John 1.1–3).
- The Spirit is the 'breath' of God, the power by which the divine word is efficient in creation and in inspired revelation, as in 2 Timothy 3:16 and 2 Peter 1:19–21.

We have argued that the communicated word is a determining attribute for God. However, as is the case for divine love or justice, attributes are not simply synonymous with God. If we can say God is love, we cannot inverse this order and say love is God. Similarly, if God is a God of communication and speaking belongs to his being, there is also a distinction between God and his word. As with the Trinity there exists unity and distinction, so also between God and his attributes there is a oneness and a difference. Love belongs to God as does his divine word, but a distinction is to be observed. These are features of the divine being that are distinguished from God himself. They are expressed outside himself in a way that is different from the realities existing within his divine being.

Jesus' high-priestly prayer in John 17 gives insight into the divine fellowship and how the word functions in that context. The Son receives the word from the Father; they have their oneness and communion in and through it. The Son manifests himself and gives the word to his disciples. They keep the word, making communion with the Son possible and, in him, with the Father. The word of truth sanctifies the disciples in the truth and unites them with the Father:

> I have manifested your name to the people whom you gave me out of the world...I have given them the words that you gave me, and they have received them and have come to know in truth that I came from you; and they have believed that you sent me...Sanctify them in the truth; your word is truth...for their sake I consecrate myself, that they also may be sanctified in truth. (6–8, 17–19)

The word is the point of unity between the Father and the Son, and between the Son and the disciples who receive it. This shows how vital the word of God is for knowing God. The word makes us one with God and expresses profound unity in and with him. However, the word is distinct from God's person; it is 'manifested' and 'given' and 'known' as something that comes from God and leads us to him. The word is at once one with him, yet different from his person.

Word belongs to God and touches the depths of intra-trinitarian relations. The existence of the word, of communication in God, is necessary for God to be God. By the word, God communicates within himself and forms his plan, the counsel of his will. By his word also God communicates freely with his creatures. As with all God's acts in creation, the giving of his word is an act of divine freedom that is rooted deeply in the eternal person of God. His word to his creatures is a free exercise of a power that makes God God. His speaking to us is rooted in his speaking in and to himself. Speaking to us is an act of freedom, as God condescends to us. The revealed word is rooted in what God is in and of himself, a God of communication and of word in truth, wisdom and love.

God freely reveals his word to his creatures. It expresses a capacity that belongs to him in a unique way. When God speaks to man orally or in written words, the word remains *his* word.

What This Means for God's Revealed Word

If there is an intra-divine capacity for communication and if biblical revelation is a free external expression of that attribute, certain consequences exist for divine revelation. At this point we will indicate just four.

HEARING SCRIPTURE IS HEARING GOD SPEAKING TO US. Firstly, when we hear and understand the word in revelation we are privileged with a gift that expresses something essential to God's nature. The word of God that comes to us is not tacked on to the divine make-up, but it transmits a message rooted in God's own truth and intelligence. The word mediates between God's nature and our rational human natures. It gives us the possibility of seeing objectively what pleases God, what we need to know about him and what we must do behaviour-wise to walk on the sunny side of the street. The word of God provides objective criteria that limit the tyranny of our feelings.

LISTEN UP... When we hear God's word, we are in the presence of the living God. This insight will prevent our reading the Bible being a game in a hermeneutical playground. It will also transform preaching from being a weekly sleeping pill to something dynamic and practical in our lives. The biblical word is living and powerful and we must always expect God to act through it to direct our ways. Scripture has meaning and God as its author is its unifying centre. God, through his word, interprets reality before we do. We are challenged to respect his word and to begin seeing things from his perspective. This fosters true worship, which is essentially doing everything for God's glory. How could we know how to do this without the leading of his word?

...AND LEARN THE VALUE OF HIS WORD... Worshipping God by receiving and obeying his word means valuing the word without any taint of bibliolatry or superstition. We do not adore the love of God, but the God of love, and similarly the word of God sends us to the God of the word. James Packer once said, I believe, that nobody actually practices bibliolatry like people pray to statues. When we make the distinction between the word *in* God and the word *of* God given to us we are respecting a mystery; our knowledge is limited to the parameters of the revealed word. This is important. It will stop us going beyond what the word says to create our own laws by adding tradition upon tradition. It will also discourage us from removing anything that ought to be received and obeyed by subtraction from the word of God.

... BY RECOGNISING THE LORD AND THE SERVANT. In analogy with Jesus Christ, the living Word, the word of Scripture is characterised at one and the same time by its lordship and its servant form. God's word is to be received, believed and obeyed simply because it is God's word. However, this can be a challenge. The Bible is characterised by its lowly style, its historical character and limitations because God has spoken to us using our language and in particular cultural situations. The word is not abstract, general or timeless truth and must be understood in the light of these conditions.

God is the Lord of the word and he alone understands it entirely. We understand it differently; because of its servant form our understanding is partial, secondary and incomplete. This fosters humility and will help us to avoid the voices of the sirens that lure us to use Scripture and our understanding of it to lord it over others. Because of the specific nature of the word of God, which is at one and the same time transcendent and immanent, the order of the day is as follows: 'If anyone imagines that he knows something, he does not yet know as he ought to know. But if anyone loves God, he is known by God' (1 Cor. 8:2–3).

The Word of God and Its Verbal Aspect

The notion 'word of God' describes a precise linguistic concept. God reveals himself in a personal way through words in Scripture. The testimony provided by these words in sentences, paragraphs, chapters and books, through the human authors, is his own witness. What the Bible says, clearly and directly, without any gerrymandering, is God's word to us.

This means firstly that what we read, hear read or explained to us is his truth for us. It doesn't have to become the truth, nor does it have to be understood or accepted to correspond to what God requires of us. He has made himself clear to us. 'No one can say

"Jesus is Lord" except in the Holy Spirit' (1 Cor. 12:3) is a divine truth. The opposite is false. 'God was in Christ reconciling the world to himself' (2 Cor. 5:19) is God's truth for ever after the incarnation. What then if there are disagreements over what reconciliation means? We look at how Scripture defines reconciliation to clear things up so we know what to think on the subject.

When we receive the word of God with heartfelt trust, placing our confidence in it, nothing changes in the content of the word itself. It is not the word that becomes meaningful, it always has been. We become different because it has become meaningful for us. Maybe things we already knew but were off the radar of our interests now become terrifically meaningful. The penny drops.

Secondly, God has done more than act to save human beings. The word is not an appendix tacked on to revelation. It is an integral part of it, without which revelation would be incomplete. God tells us what his intentions were when he acted. Imagine that Christ had suffered, died and risen again without any word revelation. Nobody at all would make any sense of what the passion of Christ meant. It would be like watching a film on television without any sound and with the picture out of focus. To understand what God means, we need a Bible whose propositions are guaranteed by God himself.

Without any word from God there could be precious little knowledge of the Son of God. That is why those who claim to have a high esteem for Christ but a low view of Scripture are cutting the branch they are sitting on. Their position is rather uncomfortable.

Conclusion

The word of God has many aspects because any human ideas that seek to present something about almighty God always run into complexity. To resume, we can say that the biblical idea of the word of God includes several complementary perspectives.

The word of God involves:

- the powerful person of God who makes a plan for all things. He acts to bring it into reality in the history of his creation. He makes himself powerfully known;

- the meaningful word of God spoken to men so that they know his law and gospel and recognise his divine lordship;
- the divine presence of the Holy Spirit. The inspired message of truth is given through prophets and apostles. It makes God's grace known and forms his people according to divine truth.

Fundamentally, the word of God is not inaccessible or unknowable. Biblical truth is not a labyrinth. 'Every word of God is true; he is a shield for those who take refuge in him' (Prov. 30:5).

The problem with biblical truth is not that people can't get what it means, but that they do whatever they can to avoid its meaning because they're not willing to accept it. They think that recognising the truth of God about our sin and salvation might mean losing too much else. That is what people are afraid of.

However when our eyes are opened to see 'wonderful things in God's word' then we exclaim with the blind man who received his sight: 'Once I was blind but now I see' (John 9:25). We see because the word 'is a lamp to our feet and a light to our path' (Ps. 119:105).

10

The Human Word

The debacle of the twentieth century shredded human dignity and raised questions about what human nature is. Michel Foucault, a well-known French philosopher, said that the tide of time will sweep man away like sand on a beach. Fears about the future inevitably foster a tragic view of human nature and destiny, offset by the flight of the First-world masses in the West into the 'no-tomorrow' culture of spending, leisure and pleasure, while others are hungry in many parts of the world.

It is hardly surprising that the idea of the humanity of Scripture also comes under fresh scrutiny. Is this *the* story, is it the *true* story and does the story concern *me*? Questions about Scripture nowadays centre on the effects its message would have if we accepted it. Would we become intolerant fundamentalists and lose our lives into the bargain? Today many people are in the game of drifting; permanent anchorage is thought to restrict freedom.

When the Bible's message seems irrelevant, or even problematic, it appears superfluous. An agnostic I know told me that humanity needs spiritual renewal, but not according to Christian values. That is why this question of the humanity of Scripture is important.

Humanity and Scripture

The human character of the Bible is more prominent than its claim to be the written word of God. As B.B. Warfield said over a century ago, the Scriptures are 'human writings, written by men and bearing the traces of their human origin on their very face'. Establishing the teaching of the Bible about its revelation, inspiration, authority or truth requires detailed examination of the relevant texts and seems irrelevant to many people. All they see are its human features. In this category they include historical and cultural aspects, errors or limitations and moral blemishes that make it unsuitable either for children or for those with a politically correct mentality. As a recent critic said, the Old Testament is bad, but the New gets worse! The Bible has all the features of a barbaric bygone age and it seems further in the historic past by the year.

This is why people have their own *Reader's Digest* 'bible' featuring Psalm 23 or the Beatitudes. If it is hard work to demonstrate the 'divinity' of the Bible, its humanity seems to jump off every page, sometimes in a disconcerting way. Reading the Bible with my family some time ago we came to 'Samson went to Gaza, and there he saw a prostitute and went in to her' (Judg. 16:1). My son, quite young at the time, gulped and said, 'This story begins badly'!

There is a multitude of books on the Bible as the word of God but relatively few about its humanity. Evangelicals tend to be coy about it, unless they are making the humanity of Scripture a pretext for a change of theological orientation. A recent commentator affirmed that 'classical' Christians almost instinctively shy away from too close an examination of the human aspects of the Bible. They feel in their bones the danger of the human devouring the divine. Its alleged imperfections make it difficult to believe that it is the word of God at all. For this reason, modernistic theologians have made strenuous efforts to have their cake and eat it too by redefining the word of God so as not to identify it too closely with Scripture. To make more room for its humanity some theologians have coined the idea of a partial or limited inspiration.

Even the fact that this chapter is about the humanity of Scripture underlines something rather unusual. One would not necessarily discuss the humanity of Shakespeare or Dickens, no doubt because it is taken for granted. Speaking about the humanity of Scripture is justified in the light of its divinity. Without that, there wouldn't be much cause for talking about it at all; only in the context of its divinity is it meaningful to speak about its humanity. This fact raises the question of the stereophonic authorship of Scripture.

In what follows we will look at the notion of dual authorship, the idea of the analogy between Christ and the Bible, how God accommodates himself to human beings in his revelation, and the sticky issue of errors in Scripture. Finally, we will propose that the humanity of Scripture has a special function in God's purposes.

Dual Authorship

The evangelical doctrine of Scripture stands out from modernistic views because it maintains that the Bible has two authors, God and man; the humanity of Scripture is only correctly understood in the light of its being the word of God. What does this imply for our understanding of the humanity of Scripture?

Dual authorship means each text of the Bible is simultaneously co-authored. To understand it, we must see that each individual portion, each chapter, book, section, and the whole book, carry the hallmark of God and men.

Dual authorship gives rise to many of the hallmarks of the Bible's teaching: Scripture is divine, but it has a human form; its commands are absolute, yet they are given in relative situations; its message is coherent, but many things remain paradoxical for us because we cannot take them in; Scripture itself is clear, but needs the illumination of the Holy Spirit to be read meaningfully. These special features indicate that we have little understanding of how God's Spirit works not only in relation to its inscripturation but also in the way Scripture continues to speak.

What is involved in the idea of dual authorship? Firstly, God speaks through human witnesses in such a way that they speak God's words when they use their own language. The Bible gives us the words God wanted to communicate, not some approximations. For example, the well-known text John 3:16 (in the context of 16–21) is probably not a word for word reproduction of what Jesus said to Nicodemus, but a commentary, or gloss, that the apostle John made on Jesus' teaching on this point. It gives us John's understanding of the person and work of Jesus and at the same time it is exactly what God wished to tell us about his only Son.

Secondly, the biblical writers had a special relationship with God: the divine author in the Bible speaks through the human authors and they in turn bear witness to the divine. God makes himself known by telling us things in his word. When the human writers speak they are telling us the things of God, not their own ideas. Revelation is personal *and* propositional. The writer of Genesis 1 knew nothing about modern cosmological ideas. The divine act of creation, however, is recounted in majestic fashion. Scientific knowledge was not required to say that God was the originator of all things in heaven and on earth.

A third point about the dual authorship of Scripture is that we know something of how the mind of God works *via* the human minds of the authors, including their thought-processes and intentions. There are not two different meanings to its texts, one divine and one human. There is a unity of the divine and the human in a single word, even if the mind of God infinitely surpasses what was formulated in the writers' human minds or what we grasp today. What God revealed is never less but always more than what the prophets and apostles understood. For example, the 'suffering servant' of Isaiah 53 existed in the divine mind long before it was transmitted through the mind of the prophet in words that predicted what the future would hold.

Implications of Dual Authorship

Four implications can be drawn from this unique self-witness for what we understand about the Bible.

1. Getting to the mind of God through the mind of the human writer underlines the importance of taking it at face value (or to use technical language, of a grammatical and historical understanding of the text of Scripture). Attention is to be given to human situations, factors and nuances, and to the logic of the text. The Scriptures are

open to textual analysis and the propositions distilled from them are windows into the heart of God. We know that Jesus really did 'suffer under Pontius Pilate' at a given moment in history.

2. Some people think that the unity of the Bible comes from God and its diversity from human factors. This is not so. The diversity is divine as much as the unity and both are human as well. There is a real unity in Scripture because of its divine authorship; no diversity ever destroys the fundamental unity of the biblical message. It would be the case only if we were to think that human divergences undermine the unifying aspect of revelation. The diversity of Scripture is as much a part of God's intention in revelation as its unity. We enjoy the fourfold diversity of the gospels; our understanding would be much shallower if we only had Mark's Gospel. It seems pedantic to say that we need not believe in the virgin birth, for instance, because it is only found in Matthew and Luke. The fact God put it there is sufficient witness to this doctrine.

3. When we ascertain, by serious reading of a text, what God is communicating through his human witnesses, we can expect that a general application of this principle or teaching will be legitimate in other cases. God will always react in the same way to similar problems, despite different situations. His truth in one place will never be contradicted in another, either in theory or in practice.

4. The Scriptures are fundamentally clear because of their self-witness. Through the work of the Holy Spirit, some lay-people have a more biblical understanding of what Scripture teaches than some highly qualified theologians who read it through critical-tinted glasses. After all, the New Testament writers did not need modern critical methods to understand the Old Testament. Harmonisation is an approach much maligned by critical theology, but it is fundamental to how we view the different aspects of reality that make up daily experience. As a matter of principle, what the Bible says should not be set against itself.

Two Models

There are two common ways of looking at the humanity of Scripture in the context of divine revelation. Both do justice to the complementary character of the Bible as the word of God in the words of men. The first is the parallel drawn between Christ and the Bible and the second is called divine accommodation.

Concerning the first, a neat parallel called the Christological analogy is sometimes made between Christ and the Bible. Just as Christ is at one and the same time divine and human, so also is the Bible. The neatness of the parallel is both its strength and its weakness. The divinity of Christ and Scripture is real divinity and the humanity of both is real humanity. As a human being Jesus was without sin and Scripture in a similar way is without error.

This link between Christ and the Bible is not simply a convenient theological construction. Texts such as John 1 and Hebrews 1 speak of the personal revelation and the written revelation of God in almost the same breath. In divine revelation, the word is both incarnated and inscripturated. However, there is no equal measure between the two, as Scripture is by nature subsidiary to Christ. The Word becoming flesh is primary. It is the template of all divine action in and through creaturely reality.

The advantage of the Christological analogy is that it illustrates how real humanity is possible without implying sin, fallibility or error. Without this, all that remains is a purely human book that is somehow used by God to communicate a message, which in its written form is not his message in any direct sense.

The disadvantage of the Christological parallel is that there is a difference between the person of Jesus and the character of the Bible. The first is a personal incarnation, the Word made flesh; but the analogy breaks down if we say 'God was made word in Scripture', which seems to devalue God. In the case of the Bible, there is no incarnation. The human words of the Bible remain human words, even though God speaks his truth through them. The mystery of the personal union of the two natures in Christ does not shed light on the nature of the union in the divine-human word of Scripture[1].

---

1 Christ and Scripture are not equivalent realities as there is only one hypostatic union between God and man, that of the person of Christ. With Christ's incarnation there is one person with two natures, divine and human. With Scripture there are two persons at work (God and human prophets) and one nature (the one scriptural speech act).

For this reason, perhaps, the parallel between Christ and the Bible does not tell us much about the human character of the Bible. In fact, apart from the link between without sin and without error, we do not find out much about the particular nature of its humanity. The best way of becoming aware of the humanity of Scripture is looking at the text itself and its features, not looking at the person of Christ. Perhaps it is useful to be content with a simple statement such as: the Logos indwelt the person of Jesus and God's communication to us dwells in the text of Scripture.

The second of the two models mentioned above is accommodation. When God gave his inspired word, he accommodated or adapted himself to man's humanity. This idea has a fine theological pedigree, going back to Reformation times with Calvin as the great theologian of accommodation. The basic ideas of the Reformer have been developed in three directions:

DIVINE LOVE. Accommodation is an act of divine love in which God adapts to 'men with all their weaknesses, gifts, talents and abilities'. A later Reformed theologian even exaggerated this to the point of saying that God did not choose the great as his witnesses but 'ignoramuses and illiterates, who learned nothing in the schools of men which they passed on to others.'! Accommodation indicates the way God lovingly adapts to human beings and situations and makes his truth known in a way that is understandable for us with our human limitations. When God speaks in Scripture, the things necessary for salvation come through in a down-to-earth word.

PARTNERSHIP. Accommodation is an act of partnership. It points to the ultimate divine accommodation, the incarnation of our Lord. Understood in this way, it illustrates how human beings are privileged to be partakers in the knowledge of God's truth. Divine accommodation is the vehicle by which truth is delivered to our doorstep. Without it, nothing of divine truth could be discovered. God did what was necessary in our favour by making his truth known. He comes down to our level and in doing so lifts us up to his.

ORGANIC INSPIRATION. Finally, accommodation indicates the vital role of humanity in revelation. God's enters the arena of human history to convey his truth by speaking through men's thoughts and words. The word 'organic' is used to indicate that in the act of inspiration God strengthened the activity of human beings so that their words could be his word. Human nature is important; the words of men in their concrete humanity are divine revelation. They were shaped and prepared by the Spirit and summoned to serve God. They wrote without any coercion, because they were lead to speak God's truth naturally.

This does not mean that the biblical writers were 'time bound' or 'culturally conditioned' to the extent that their message is not universally understandable or true. It does mean that God's truth comes to us with the marks of the time, place and cultural situation in which it was given. God enabled the writers of Scripture via the activity of their conscious minds to express thoughts and words appropriate to communicating divine truth for every nation and time. They spoke from their own perspective with their own language, cultural particularities, natural and historical perspectives and limitations. Yet there was much more to it because when they 'spoke from God' they spoke to us as well.

It is often said that the divine word organically inspired has the 'form of a servant' and partakes in the lowly and humble appearance of Christ. This is true. It is part of the scandal of the gospel. *God's Son* appeared as a servant and *his word* assumed a self-effacing and modest exterior. A hand is not visible in a glove, but it fills the glove and flexes it.

Fallibility and Errors

Today the humanity of Scripture comes under scrutiny in two ways. Firstly, it is generally accepted that humanity means fallibility and that there are mistakes in the realm of facts in the Bible as elsewhere. In addition, modernism has challenged the morality of the Bible and claims that many of its teachings are unacceptable because they are not humanistic.

Concerning the first argument, modern theology has often made an equation between humanity and fallibility in the realm of Scripture. Since error is human, there are, so it is said, undisputed errors in the Bible. One reads in much theological literature things such as 'the Bible is human and therefore not an infallible witness to divine revelation' or that the writers of Scripture can also bear false witness through their 'capacity for error'. Sometimes it is even said that the Bible is verbally inspired but it remains fallible and it is not inerrant. The language of Scripture is said to be the 'earthen vessel' whereby the hidden treasure of grace is received. It is not revelation itself, but a 'channel' and a 'medium'; it is 'provisional' and 'relative', its true humanity involves a 'vulnerability to error and a limited cultural horizon'. It is characterized by 'historical inaccuracies' and 'internal contradictions'. You will find more accuracy on a cornflakes box.

All of the above statements can be discussed, but these generalisations tend to be a liability. When such ideas are put forward, they reveal that a very limited view of humanity has been adopted. It is doubtful that those who make these statements about Scripture would make the same value judgments about the quality of their own writings. The question is whether or not the humanity of Scripture is identical to all other expressions of humanity. We think not. In the case of Scripture the inspiring Sprit of God has taken humanity into his service. Real humanity it certainly is, but erring humanity it is not.

The question of fallibility was often taken in the past to imply the presence of factual errors in Scripture[2]. It consisted in pointing out supposed errors one by one and concluding that Scripture could not be fully inspired or true. Most of these alleged errors in Scripture have been known for a long time, and possible solutions to them have been suggested in many places, including in books like Gleason Archer's *Encyclopaedia of Bible Difficulties* (1982). Solutions to many problems can be found, sometimes even from new archaeological information.

---

2 See also chapter 12 on the question of inerrancy and errors.

Some Difficulties

Four Gospels not one
Even if some of the details in the Gospels are difficult to harmonise and subject to discussion, there are no major discrepancies regarding the high points of the life and death of Jesus. Perspectives sometimes differ according to the writers' intention and aims, but the four narratives complement each other in remarkable fashion. There is little reason to think that the Sermon on the Mount (Matthew) and the Sermon on the Plain (Luke) are not different events, or that Jesus could not have cleansed the Temple twice. John is not 'unhistorical' as some theologians claim. Nor should the Gospels be treated as 'faith' texts and not essentially historical.

Contradictions in the genealogies of Matthew and Luke
Matthew gives the lineage of Joseph the 'legal father' of Jesus, whereas Luke traces that of Mary, in the light of the miraculous conception. Both go back to David. This interpretation has been current since the 5th century.

How many angels were at the garden tomb after the resurrection?
A comparison of the texts allows us to conclude that two angels were there, replying to the juridical conditions for valid testimony. If, in Matthew and Mark, there is only one angel and in Luke two 'men' in dazzling apparel, no doubt in the first case one of the two was prominently active in rolling the stone and frightening the guards and this retained the attention of Mark. If there were two there was necessarily one!

Matthew got it wrong (27:9) by attributing to Jeremiah a text that is found in the prophet Zechariah (11:13)
Matthew combines quotes from both prophets and attributes the ensemble to Jeremiah who was the most known, and particularly because Jeremiah was persecuted and rejected and is thus a type of Christ. Mark does the same in 1:2–3 when he quotes Isaiah and Malachi and attributes the whole to the first.

Gerasenes, Gadarenes or Gergesenes (Matt. 8:28, Mark 5:1, Luke 8:26)
Who got it right? For all three Gospels there are ancient manuscripts that offer the three different names. So was it at Gerasa, Gadara or Gergesa that the demoniac was healed? The manuscript evidence is inconclusive and there have evidently been errors of copying. Origen, in the third century, concluded that Gerasa was not possible as a geographical location and since Gadara was not important in his day he plumped for Gergesa and even invented his own etymology to back up his idea. Archaeology indicates

Gadara as the likely place where Jesus did a miracle that targeted non-Jews in the Hellenised Decapolis region. All the manuscripts probably read Gadara at some point.

In Peter's denial, how many times did the cock crow, once or twice?

Mark (14:30) says twice although Matthew and Luke only refer to one without giving a count. This fulfils Jesus' prophetic word which refers to the cock crowing and Peter's three denials. The lack of precision is neither an error nor a contradiction. The crow of the cock is a technical term in Greek (*alektrophonia*) for a watch in the night and it can be thought that Peter's second denial was at the beginning of the third watch, 3 a.m.

The Bible quotes non-inspired authors

Proverbs uses ancient wisdom and Paul quotes philosophers known in the Greek world in Acts 17. 'Bad company ruins good morals' in 1 Corinthians 15:33 is from a play by Euripides. Truth can be a function of common grace and can be recognised as such. Although they are sinners men can formulate true opinions, sometimes even about God. These human judgments take on another form when incorporated into the divine word. The most surprising example is perhaps the word to Paul on the Damascus road, 'It is hard to kick against the goads' (Acts 26:14) which is taken from Aeschylus (*Agamemnon*, 1624). What Jesus said to Paul was in Aramaic but translating it into Greek the apostle used an expression known to Festus, from his cultural world.

How can the words of satanic temptation be counted as the word of God?

They are the words of God according to their function in the context of the whole of the text of Scripture. They are historically authentic. All that is the opposite of God's truth and all other moral error referred to in Scripture exists as a warning. Similarly, the reference to the prophecy of Enoch in Jude 14 can only be considered to be an error if it is shown to be inauthentic, or if the writer quoted Enoch as being inspired Scripture, which is not the case.

Did Saul hear a voice on the Damascus road or not? (Acts 9:7, 22:9)

There seems to be a contradiction between the two presentations of Saul's conversion. However, it's ill advised to jump to this conclusion, because both narratives come from Luke who was careful and who knew better than to contradict himself. Exegetical study of the Greek permits a distinction between hearing a loud noise and hearing a voice with intelligible content. All those present heard the noise but Saul alone heard in it a message from the risen Lord. See also John 12:29 where the voice of God is perceived by the crowd as being thunder.

Fallibility and Ethical Questions

A good while ago a pundit made the comment if anyone is in hell, they don't want to be in heaven. This implies that the teaching of Scripture is inhuman and morally unacceptable.

The factual difficulties presented above may be less worrying to most people than they were in the past. What troubles people today is more likely to be related to the content of the Bible's message and its alleged moral imperfections. How can so much bloodshed be accepted? What does this say about the God of the Bible?

There are no easy answers to these questions. Rather than theoretical considerations maybe a concrete example like the conquest of Jericho is more useful. In a prior generation, gospel songs were written in a triumphalistic spirit because God intervened in favour of his people. The falling of the walls of Jericho was a subject for praise and gratitude to an almighty God. When we read the book of Joshua today we are less likely to make the story into a song of praise and more likely to worry about its ethical implications. Why did God 'devote the town for destruction' and only save Rahab the prostitute and her family (6:17). Such a story seems only appealing in the context of a superior culture with a 'God on our side mentality' crushing an inferior one.

It is hard to take and perhaps that is why so many people have tried hard to find a satisfying explanation. Liberal theology wriggles away from the problem by saying it's all legendary anyway, even though the problem of why the legend should be there at all remains. Another approach proposes that this happened in primitive times and such things were current fare. We can't expect the ancient Israelites to have been non-violent postmodern humanists. God adapted his way of doing to the time. That is hardly reassuring as it makes for a God conditioned by external factors. Or it is said that the Canaanites were extremely wicked and God was purifying the land for his people and the judgment was in fact a liberation, but this looks rather like a case of ethnic cleansing. Yet another suggestion is that the judgment of the Canaanites was a type of the final judgment against all human sin 'intruded' into the Decalogue. If this may be more theologically satisfying as a possible interpretation, it does not make what happened at Jericho any more ethically palatable. Finally, some commentators say that the Canaanites knew the rules of war and that when Joshua's band walked around the walls seven times, there was plenty of time for them to surrender and avoid catastrophe. This however does not deal with the major problem which concerns why God gave the order to kill the inhabitants of the town who did not surrender.

It is difficult to see any straightforward way round the ethical problems in this text without engaging in some mental gymnastics that attempt to justify God with our own criteria. This is always a risky procedure, as God justifies us, not vice versa. Job found out about the dodginess of trying to find satisfactory explanations for divine behaviour. He had to learn to hold his tongue and admit that he was not up to it.

Perhaps three remarks can serve to put things into perspective concerning Jericho and other similar problems.

Firstly, it is obviously wrong to think that we can understand the reasons for God's doing one thing and not another. The reasons he acted in this way with the Canaanites are ultimately beyond our understanding and we have to leave it at that.

Secondly, the story of Jericho is part of a package. God is a God of love and justice and his actions work out his plan of salvation. The dark parts of the picture only serve to emphasize the light of the whole. After all, you don't look at one corner of a Rembrandt or a Vermeer and conclude that it's a sombre painting. If we cannot see the whole picture at present, what the Bible does tell us about the love and the purposes of God in salvation is sufficient reason to trust in God precisely when we do not understand.

Finally, we do not believe in the innate goodness of man as a standpoint from which we can pass judgment on God. When we read the biblical accounts of divine judgments our tendency is to recognize that we are sinners and we ourselves deserve nothing better than God's just judgment against our sin.

These three considerations can be summed up in the following way. What we do know, understand and believe about the character of God as the only true God leads us to say what the apostle Paul said when he presented God's righteousness over against man's sinfulness: 'let God be true though every man is a liar' (Rom. 3:4). The downsides arising from our lack of understanding fade into the background when our overall perspective is correctly adjusted to focus on the love and truth of God. The goodness of God is *a priori* and cannot be doubted by anyone who believes in him. Of course someone will say that it's not much consolation for the Canaanites, and that is correct. But at least we can thank God that by his mercy he has saved us from being in the same position under divine judgment. There is no human explanation for this amazing grace, no more than a human explanation for judgment.

Something Old, Something New

What is the purpose of the humanity of Scripture in the context of God's actions taken as a whole? Why did God not give revelation in a Qur'anic kind of transcript or on golden sheets brought down from heaven? Why does Scripture have its specific and challenging human form?

As we have seen, when the question of the humanity of Scripture is discussed, negative factors tend to come to the fore—its fallibility, limitations, errors, weaknesses and moral blemishes. But these descriptions belong very definitely to the fallen and sinful realm and fail to do justice to the kind of humanity we find in Scripture. Few of us would want to define our humanity by our mistakes or our limitations.

From another angle, how can the humanity of Scripture be viewed positively? From a biblical perspective the basic thing about humanity is that man is the image of God, created, fallen, renewed and glorified. In other words, to borrow Thomas Boston's classic description, human nature exists not in one but in a fourfold state. From this point of view humanity is:

1. Created
2. Created and fallen into sin
3. Created, fallen into sin, but renewed by the Holy Spirit in the likeness of Christ

4. Created, fallen into sin, renewed by the Holy Spirit and finally glorified with a new resurrected body like Christ himself.

Where does the humanity of the Bible fit into this fourfold analysis? Does it line up with the sinful and fallen humanity of category 2? This would certainly account for the negative factors mentioned above. Or is it more appropriately considered as belonging to category 3?

The good news of the Christian message is that since man's ruinous fall into sin, God's Holy Spirit has been at work to renew the fallen creation. The humanity of the Bible itself fits into this process of renewal. The context of divine revelation is one of renewal in which God touches both the humanity of man and that of Scripture. Three comments can be made along these lines.

Firstly, the background of the human aspect of Scripture is that of a new humanity which is being fashioned in the old. The primary feature of verbal communication is not that it is fallen but that it is created. After man's fall, the goal of divine revelation is redemptive and restorative. It is not simply aligned with the conditions of fallen existence but brings something new into the context of lostness. God does not accommodate himself to human fallenness and leave it intact; rather his presence and word redeem and renew it. Christ assumed human nature in a fallen and sinful world and yet in the incarnation the Holy Spirit fashioned a sinless humanity.

Through the act of inspiration, God-breathed Scripture enters into the old creation, but it does so as a sign of the presence of the new creation. The renewal of language serves the gracious intention of God for humanity. Scripture has a servant form in its human aspects, but it is also redemptive; it indicates that God is Lord in salvation and in communicating with men.

In the faithful and true promises of Scripture the future is present before it actually happens. In the incarnation and resurrection of Christ the new humanity is already a new creation in the old (2 Cor. 5:17). Likewise, Scripture as divine revelation is tied to God's purpose in Christ, bringing the new from the old from the very start of redemptive history.

For this reason it is correct to speak of the 'oldness' of Scripture, but also of its 'newness' and its uniqueness. Its natural context and intention is the redemption of creation. Pagan 'of the earth', man is called to true humanity through the word of the Spirit in Scripture. Scripture reveals the grace of God because it is his redemptive word. Its humanity exists to restore men to true humanity.

Secondly, the humanity of Scripture is Christ-centred, not in terms of a Christological analogy, but because Christ is the conclusion of God's historical dealings with men. As the 'Alpha and Omega' he is the focus of God's works in the beginning, at the end, and in all that is in between; Scripture bears witness to this fact in its unfolding story of redemption in the following ways:

1. Christ is the creator (Col. 1:15–20, Heb. 1:1–2, John 1), the first and last who is promised by the prophets as the coming Messiah (Isa. 48:12–15) and the coming glorious Lord who will judge the earth and establish the new creation. (Rev. 1:1–8, 21:5–8, 22:12–15).
2. Scripture is God's Word tracing his history with humankind and providing, in the completed canon, the key to the unity of God's redemptive purposes in Christ.
3. Jesus Christ is the true image of God in the New Testament. Man, created in the image of God, is restored and adopted into the body of Christ. The progression of humanity towards this goal is described in the progressive historical revelation of Scripture, with its divine purpose: salvation of the people of God through transformation. This is the sphere of divine accommodation.

Finally, there is a link between the humanity of Scripture and new humanity formed by regeneration and new birth. The purpose of biblical revelation is to format the lives of people in whom the image of God is restored. God gave us not only his only Son but also the Holy Spirit to regenerate believers through the new birth, to write his law on their hearts and equip them for every good work.

God educates his children for freedom through the renewing teaching of Scripture that tells us about our regeneration, adoption, sanctification and glorification.

Conclusion

The renewal of human language in God's revelation and the impact it has in renewing our lives in the image of Christ is an exciting way of approaching the question of the humanity of Scripture. God is himself the source of language. He is the first communicator. He invests human words with a deep significance because he spoke to us personally in our humanity in Christ. His word nourishes true humanity in renewed personal relationships with God and man.

God renews human language in inspiration and the inscripturation of his word of revelation. He renews human beings through his life-giving Spirit. God's inspired word is the word of God and the Holy Spirit speaks through it here and now.

To grasp the true humanity of Scripture, we have to shake free from the shackles of negative attitudes and break out of the stockade that protects us from the battering of a politically correct culture. The scandals of the humanity of Scripture are never dissociated from the scandal of the gospel; God died and rose again in the human person of his Son.

Let God be true because every man *is* a liar.

11

Authority and Clarity

God has made himself known. His final act of special revelation was to inspire the written scriptures. The result is that Scripture as a whole is the word of God revealed and spoken to humanity. Because of its divine origin, it has a unique character as God's word in human words.

Four expressions are often used to describe this special claim about the nature of the Bible: authority, clarity, truth and unity. Each of them reflects an attribute of God himself and states something we believe about his revelation.

However it is not all plain sailing. Many questions are asked about the attributes of Scripture. How can we claim Scripture has authority when no one is listening, or maintain its clarity when many people have serious problems understanding it? Can Scripture be wholly true when it is accused of being flawed, both morally and factually? Or how is it possible to speak about its unity when it originated over such a long period of time and came from people in different cultures? These questions and many others show that we have to grapple to understand how these attributes work and what they mean.

In this chapter we will look at the authority and the clarity of Scripture because they go together. In the following one, we propose to examine the truth and the unity of Scripture.

Authority has to do with why we accept some things and not others. Clarity goes a long way to help us understand issues and take them on board. If we are not naïve, we do not simply accept things because we are told to do so; we need some pertinent reasons. On the other hand, being forced to accept something against our better judgment is a constraint nobody willingly accepts.

Authority and Scripture, a Definition

As a Christian I expect Scripture to have authority. I take it to be more important than what I think, than what others say and even than what churches teach. Even if I think Confessions of faith like the *Westminster Confession*, the *Chicago Declaration on Biblical Inerrancy* or the *Lausanne Declaration* are important and useful, I will always take the Bible over any or all of them, if there is an evident need to do so. This is the classic distinction between primary and secondary norms, and it is upheld by the Confessions themselves, as the following illustrates:

> The authority of the Holy Scripture, for which it ought to be believed, and obeyed, depends not upon the testimony of any man, or Church: but wholly upon God (who is truth itself) the author thereof: and therefore it is to be received because it is the Word of God[3].

For Christians, Scripture is the final authority in the following areas:

Knowledge: as far as truth is concerned, the Bible will always be taken to be true over against other sources and claims to truth, even when the odds seem stacked against it. For instance, I believe God to be the creator of all things not because of some notions about intelligent design or an absent watchmaker, but because I understand the Bible teaches it.

---

3 *Westminster Confession of Faith*, I. iv, cf. x.

Behaviour: in the realm of ethics, a Christian properly so called will seek to do what the Bible says, even if it hurts, telling the truth when a lie would be more comfortable, being honest when cheating would be more profitable, or simply not doing what everyone else around is doing.

Order: on the level of the nature of things (called ontology, their 'being'), the Bible is of a different order than human or relative things that are defined by reference to other realities in the visible world. The origin of the Bible as God's word that comes into the world makes it different from all else. This is the bottom line, and its special status determines the placing of the Bible above other considerations.

The Bible is a very diverse book. Something more different from a code with a series of instructions is difficult to imagine. Its variety comes from the long period of time over which it was written, but also from the numerous situations and the different people involved in its writing. All these things must be taken into account to define what the authority of the Bible means. But its authority is ultimately this: God speaks to us directly through his prophetic witnesses—Moses, Isaiah, John or Paul. What makes for the authority of the Bible is not the local colour, but that God gives principles for all time in various situations.

Before considering how we get these principles out of the Bible, we have to face some sticky issues that concern authority today.

Authority Complexes

Nowadays times are rough for any kind of authority and particularly for those who have to exercise it. Any parent or teacher will tell you that what was taken for granted a generation ago isn't any more.

People today seem to suffer from 'authority neuroses'. Their hackles go up to fend off what they consider to be infringements on their freedom or rights. We are all naturally, perhaps often sinfully, wary of authority and want to dodge it. That is why everyone drives well under the speed limit when there are police at the roadside, and accelerate as soon as the coast is clear. At least that's what happens where I live in the south of France.

Authority without clout is not much authority at all. Adding to the general social crisis of authority the fact that in the religious realm several conflicting authorities vie for attention means that an exclusive claim for any one of them is problematic. That is why the question of the authority of the Bible is so important.

Today's 'nowhere man' is a drifter. Often the line 'there are lots of gods, and I've never met one' is adopted to justify avoiding religious issues. People end up holding on to some minimal convictions that suit them—this is OK for me, I don't mind what you choose or do, whatever gets you through the night… This attitude often carries the fancy label of 'post-modernism'. In this context it seems hardly plausible to speak about any authority at all, much less the authority of an old book.

Authority in Three Points

What then does authority entail? Three basic ideas can be retained.

Firstly, authority contains the word 'author' and implies something that is 'authorised'. It's about where laws or ideas come from; their origin gives them clout and binding character. If you see a board saying 'Polite notice', you will not give it the same consideration as one saying 'Police notice'. Authority depends on who or what is behind things and gives them weight.

Secondly, authority implies establishing an order of importance between several available options. It is a hierarchical notion. Some people or ideas are accepted over others. If you are discussing a point of theology, all things being equal, you are more likely to take Donald Carson's word than your pastor's, your pastor's than that of another punter in your church, and the latter rather than a taxi driver. On things theological, Donald Carson is an authority. Ultimately, you will take the Bible over any of them, including Carson; their ideas will only be accepted if they line up with Scripture, at least on your understanding of what it says. We expect 'authorities' to be reliable because of their ranking and maybe because we have already checked them out. Then they can be accepted without more ado.

Finally, when we refer to the notion of authority we are in the realm of meaning, in a practical sense. The Highway Code is the recognised authority for driving rules. It says that you drive on the right in France but on the left in the UK. Road use is laid down in the code of each respective country. Anyone who flaunts the rules will soon suffer the consequences. Authority is important because it gives meaning to various areas and situations that crop up in our lives and keeps us in touch with reality.

So from a Christian viewpoint, the Bible has authority because it comes from God, because it has more clout than other opinions and because it gives us practical guidance how to live.

The authority of the Bible is the big issue for Christians because we believe that the message of the gospel has restored us to sanity in our relationship with God and that it impacts all of life. Straying from the meaning the Bible provides in various areas of our life—how we worship God, make decisions and act with respect to honesty, sexual ethics, or our role as citizens and more—leads to conflicts between what we believe and what we do.

The authority of the Bible tells us whether we are right with God and right in our other relationships. The question of authority is not a theoretical one; it involves what is pleasing to God and what is good for us.

On What Authority?

There are many answers to the question of what makes for authority. Outside the Christian church the options are legion, either in other religions and ideologies or in life-styles that range from consumerism to nihilism and much more.

Within Christianity so-called conflicting attitudes are also in evidence. Many people are content to follow the teaching of their church with its practices and traditions. Others follow an inner light, what they feel to be true, and still others just go with the flow without any thought about what is specifically Christian and what isn't. The problem is that these attitudes often have little to do with the Bible; what people think or feel about what is true and right can be totally off-centre. 'It doesn't matter if Christ rose from the dead,' a French protestant minister said to me, 'what's important is that I believe it.' This is not a Christian way of thinking, as it is not upheld by biblical authority. This is a serious issue. What the gentleman in question was doing was putting his own belief over Scripture. Similarly, one could also say: 'It doesn't matter if the moon is made of green cheese or not, what is important is that I believe it to be so.' That's not very satisfying is it?

Even when the Bible is taken to be our authority, there are several different ways of seeing exactly where authority lies in the Bible. For some it might be the Golden rule, for others it's the person of Jesus that stands out and yet again for others the community life of the early church with its gifts is to be our model today. All of these options might refer to the Bible, but they single out one aspect and use it as an authority against other teachings of the Bible. For instance, one might claim the authority of the Golden rule and reject the doctrine of divine judgment on that ground, or believe something about the person and teaching of Jesus but not in his resurrection from the dead, or one could believe that modern-day 'prophets' are superior to regular ministers in the church. All of these are in contradiction to the New Testament.

The problem of authority seems to have us coming and going! Where's the way out of the labyrinth?

What in The Bible, or Is It Who?

Perhaps it's stating the obvious, but the expression 'the authority of the Bible' is in itself rather strange. Recognising this might help.

It is evident that the Bible lying before me on my desk has no inherent authority over me. It cannot make me pick it up, read it or believe it. Mao Zedong said power comes from the barrel of a gun, and if a red guard was standing in front of me with a loaded Uzi he could make me pick up the little red book, read it and perhaps even believe it. But the Bible can do nothing of the sort. Its authority has nothing to do with a power to constrain. It must be of another kind.

The authority of the Bible is not primarily about a *what?* but about a *who?* The proper question is not *what* but *who* has authority. God reigns over all things because he is Lord of all. As the Lord,

God establishes the meaning of meaning before any other factors come into view and even before our thoughts and inclinations.

Authority is not impersonal, like power down a gun barrel. It is the personal rule of the living God over his creatures and over us, and his right to tell us what reality means. If the Bible is God's word, its authority must be presupposed, or taken as being real, simply because God is God. This means that we must listen to the message of Scripture expecting to find what God wants us to think and do.

What strikes us about the Bible is that whereas human claims to authority are invariably flawed and questionable, the witnesses who heard God's voice were inclined to accept it, even if they had to struggle to do so because what was asked of them was not easy. Think of Abraham who accepted God's call to leave Ur of the Chaldeans for foreign parts with little proof that it was a good thing, apart from that it was God doing the asking (Gen. 12:1). Or think about Job who accepted the wisdom of God even though he understood little about it, apart from accepting that God knows best (Job 1:21). Or think again of the disciples who left their jobs when Jesus called them, because *he* called them (John 1:47–51). Likewise, our capacity to accept the authority of the Bible depends on our capacity to hear God's word speaking to us in it. Apart from that, it just seems like another form of obscurantism to be laughed at.

Secondly, the Bible is also meaningful because of what it says. Its authority is expressed above all in what God intends to teach us through it. It is found in its teaching or its doctrine, the gospel, the good news of salvation. Bearing this in mind will keep us on track about the central issues and protect us from the wacky ideas some people seem to find in the Bible, like the earth being flat, that Jesus is coming back at a precise time next Saturday, or that Christians should wash each other's feet.

When we open the Bible, or when we hear it preached, we should come to it with great expectations and *want* God to teach us through it. If that is the case, we will be receptive even when the Bible's teaching runs contrary to political correctness or when it asks us to believe or do something that goes against the grain. If the gospel is a 'stumbling block to Jews and folly to Gentiles', no matter

—'the foolishness of God is wiser than men, and the weakness of God is stronger than men' (1 Cor. 1:23, 25).

The important thing from this perspective is that it is God who sets the agenda in the area of truth, not us. Too often we approach the Bible with the underlying attitude: What's in it for me? rather than expecting God to say something that we are called to trust and obey.

Finally, what God teaches in His word is useful. We accept the Bible as our authority for faith and life because it is 'profitable' in a great variety of ways, as Paul says in 2 Timothy 3:16. His list includes its teaching, persuasion about the truth, setting us straight on issues and training in what is right before God. When Christians are tuned in to its message they are kitted out for the game of life.

Hard and Soft

Sometimes a distinction is made between 'hard' and 'soft' authority. An authority is said to be 'hard' if we submit to it only because we have to. An example of this type of authority would be the police in a totalitarian state. This authority often exists in repression and tyranny and creates fear in those who have to knuckle under.

Time was when people accepted the Bible as a 'hard' authority, just because it was the Bible. It had a kind of untouchable status, and its sacred nature was beyond questioning. What is found there must be right, so no questions were asked, although a lot of doubts must have been ignored. Authority was the tissue of society, and the Bible fell in with that mentality. Few people today have this kind of attitude, mainly because all authority is questioned. As the old song goes, 'the things that you're liable to read in the Bible ain't necessarily so'.

'Soft' authority is what is accepted because something has been experienced to be useful and is valid for that reason. For instance, the use of medicine as prescribed is accepted because last time you took it you got better. So the Bible can be accepted in a 'soft' way, because it helped you last time around with a problem.

However, the distinction between hard and soft authority is not much use where the Bible is concerned. We cannot separate the origin and the content of the Bible. It is not accepted either because we take it for granted or because we have had a good experience with it. After all, there are many difficult things in the Bible, and it defies us to believe them. Because it is God's word it has intrinsic authority and that we find out full well when we understand and receive what it says. God's word will not fail or let us down. It is not a theoretical authority, but a living one.

The three aspects of authority we described above go together to make up the authority of the Bible as God's *saving* truth. Its authority lies in whom it comes from, in what it says and in its proven usefulness to get us out of the mess we have made with our lives. The apostle Paul speaks along these lines when he says that the gospel, the message of Scripture is 'the power of God for salvation to everyone who believes' (Rom. 1:16). He is not saying that the Scripture has no power for unbelievers; it certainly has the power to condemn unbelief. He means that the reality of God's power is demonstrated and certified when its message changes the lives of human beings. So we are encouraged to recognise and accept it.

Authority in the Works

All that has been said up till now may seem a little up in the air, but what does it mean in practice? How do we get to the authority of the Bible and how does it get to us to become meaningful in our lives?

Perhaps the following illustration will help you to see how authority works. Your boss has a certain authority over you and you relate to him or her on those terms. When she explains how some market trend affects your work you take the information on board; when she says next week you are on the road signing up clients, you accept the docket and make preparations; when you are chatting after work and she confides about some family problem, you sympathise. The first case is information, the second gives an order and the third is confidential. Each form of communication calls for a different and appropriate reaction. The way language is used and the particular situation together condition feedback, because different kinds of language have different functions and call for different reactions.

Authority comes via language and the way it works. We can recognise that the authority of Scripture is 'embedded' in two ways.

Firstly, authority is embedded in the words of Scripture. Its words are human and are part of the language stock people use to communicate; they function in the same way as other forms of speech. Many problems with understanding the Bible could be avoided if more attention were paid to the different kinds of language. In everyday speech we distinguish naturally between information, orders, exhortations, confidences, questions and exclamations. Also we distinguish between literary forms such as legal script, prose, poetry, proverbs, predictions, promises and threats. We know very well to take the facts in the newspaper or the TV news literally, but not the following from *The Idylls of the King*:

> Dry clashed his harness in the icy caves
> And barren chasms, and all to left and right
> The bare black cliff clanged round him…

The variety of biblical language impresses its authority on us in various ways, and so touches not only our intellect, but also our feelings and our will. Simple information would not necessarily be the dart to the heart that changes our attitudes, but the combination of commands, questions, affirmations, exhortations, promises and warnings we find in Scripture rouse us personally to faith and obedience. Through its variety, the words of the Bible touch us deeply.

Let's take a couple of examples to illustrate. Hebrews 6 raises lots of problems and some people, reading it, imagine that it is possible to lose their salvation. But observing the variety of language indicates what the intention of this passage is:

- Verse 1 begins with an *exhortation*,
- 1b and 2 give *information* about 'the foundation',
- 4–8 continue with *affirmations* in the form of *images* and give a *warning*,

- 9 is an *affirmation* and an *assurance* of 'things better',
- 10 presents a *general truth* about God who is 'not so unjust', and gives *commandments* formulated as *encouragements*.

Far from creating doubts about losing something, the whole literary structure aims at exhortation and encouragement. If it warns against the danger of apostasy, this exhortation follows close on a reference to the work of the Melchizedek who became the 'source of eternal salvation to all who obey him' (5:9).

Being sensitive to the language used helps us to see that the passage is not making a doctrinal statement (a proposition or an affirmation) about the possibility of losing salvation. It is warning against superficiality. Simply 'sharing' and 'tasting' the work of the Holy Spirit and the word of God, is like rain that falls on the ground and produces thorns and thistles, rather than the 'useful fruit' expected. Perhaps this is an indirect reference to Jesus' parable of the sower, and no one thinks that parable is about losing one's salvation. Hebrews 6, like the story of the sower speaks about two kinds of results stemming from the hearing of the word of God; the negative response produced by contempt (6:6) mirrors the attitude of those who crucified Christ. It is not about regenerate people losing something they had, but about people who turn away from something they might have had and people who have it and keep it. The passage is characterised by a tone of exhortation and warning.

Another example can be taken from a poetic context in Psalm 122.

Poetry

- Exclamations   v. 1, 2, 8, 9
- Affirmations   v. 3, 5, 9
- Exhortations   v. 6, 7
- Promises, warnings, commandments, questions—no uses

The exclamation found in the first verse sets the tone for the whole—the intense desire of the psalmist is to worship God in his temple. The text appeals to a feeling of gladness and longing to be in God's presence. The following verses reveal the reasons for this—God is present with his people and unites them as a God of justice. The 'I' of the first verse reappears again only at the end. Luther translated the final line of the psalm 'I will seek what is best for you' (v.9). The king (David) seeks justice and good for his people with an all-important motivation—'for the sake of the house of the Lord our God'. Love of neighbour, justice and peace all rest on the love of God and his presence. The exhortations in the middle verses to 'pray for peace' flow from an understanding that God is present in his 'house'. Unity, peace and justice are subjects of prayer for God's people as the consequence of worship in his presence.

This illustration can help us see how, in a strange way, biblical poetry can have an authority of its own, even if that notion is foreign to the post-romantic mentality that sees poets and musicians as not belonging to the same world as common mortals. Biblical poetry does not float in a mystical void, but deals with concrete issues. Psalm 122 shows how God unites his people by his presence so they may serve him, because he is their Saviour. God's people are a particular people formed for his praise. Poetry in the Bible is a celebration of the history of salvation and has an authority that is equal to that of prose in its attitude-forming functions.

Secondly, if authority is embedded in the words of Scripture, those words are part of a whole, and are to be understood as a part of the whole. Each particular text is embedded in the context of biblical revelation and its authority comes to light when the whole is considered. Francis Schaeffer used to say that we can think of what the whole of Scripture brings to each text and understand it in this perspective; the other way round we can think how the specifics of a text throw light on the whole.

This is not mental gymnastics. It is a consequence of thinking of things systematically, or in the context of a whole. For example, the engine of your car will not drive without a fan belt, but the belt will not run without the engine. It's part of a whole. So it is with individual passages of Scripture that have their own authority and meaning, but also contribute to the message of Scripture as a whole.

Let's return to our examples in Hebrews and the Psalms. In Hebrews, the writer is discouraging Jews from returning to Judaism. A major argument is that the new covenant is superior to the former one, because Christ is the 'Melchizedek' (chapters 5, 6 and

7:17) who is superior both to Abraham, the father of Israel, and to his descendants, the Levitical priests. Christ's priesthood is eternal and perfect and his sacrifice opens a new and final way into God's presence. Jesus is the 'guarantor of a better covenant' (7:22).

So the message of Hebrews 6 has its authority in the light of the contrast between the old and new covenants, the perfect salvation found in Christ and the final fulfilment of what went before. The fact that the promises of God are fulfilled in Christ is the best reason for not turning aside to the 'weakness and uselessness' of the law (7:18). The exhortation of chapter 6 comes with the weight of the history of redemption seen as a whole; it fits into this pattern because it is 'embedded' in the whole of revelation. Considered in this light, nothing could be further from the idea of the possibility of losing salvation, the exhortation being to hold onto Christ and the unshakeable salvation he has finalised. It is Christ-centred.

And Psalm 122? It's not, as I once heard preached, a eulogy about how nice it is to go to church (perish the thought!), or about the therapeutic value of songs of praise. Nor is it an exhortation to pray for Jerusalem and peace in Israel today. Both these ideas strip the Psalm of its biblical meaning and neutralise the authority of Scripture, replacing biblical ideas with ideas of our own, which is a real and present danger.

The amazing thing about the Psalm is that it was penned before the temple was built. In the Old Testament 'the house of the Lord' is used of the old tabernacle, the place of God's presence and worship in sacrifice. It also recalls 'Jacob's ladder' where the patriarch met God in his 'house' and received his promises (Gen. 28:17, 22). David's psalm is about the past and about the future to come. He received the promise that God would build a 'house' (2 Sam. 7:5–6, 11–13) for his family and establish his line forever. Psalm 122 concerns Sion, the city of God, and the promise that God will save his people through a Messiah.

So this Psalm speaks about Christ coming to purify the temple, the one who 'tabernacles' among God's people and who establishes peace and justice (John 1:14). Jesus cleansed the temple because zeal for God's house 'consumed him' (John 2:17, Ps. 69:9). Christ did 'what was best for us' by laying down his life for his people.

His resurrected body is the temple of his new people; in him unity, justice and peace are found.

Reading the psalm in this light, like David, we are thrown into the future, to the time when the new Jerusalem will descend from heaven, the 'dwelling place of God with men' (Rev. 21:2–3) and when Christ will establish his everlasting kingdom of joy and peace. So ultimately Psalm 122 is about the desire for the time when God will 'make all things new' (Rev. 21:5). In the context of the whole of Scripture, the authority of its message lies in turning our eyes away from the passing things of earth to the everlasting glory in the 'Father's house' where many 'rooms' are prepared by the Lord for his people (John 14:2). Ultimately it tells us that the 'house of God' is the place where God comes to save his people. In the New Testament that means the return of Jesus in glory. It is only when we get this straight that our lives on earth and service to God and others have any deep and lasting meaning.

To sum up: when the 'embedded' character of Scripture is seen in the two perspectives described, we can recognise how the authority of the Bible becomes tangible. Different texts become transparent to the message of salvation in Christ conveyed in all the Scripture. Biblical authority is real in the context of revelation. This saves us from the allegorisation that makes the story of Scripture into a moral or inspiring tale and also from the mistaken literalism that lifts the texts of the Bible right from the past into the present. Biblical authority becomes a reality for us when its teaching, precepts or principles are appropriated in mind and heart and arouse receptivity and obedience in our lives. Then the authority of Scripture becomes life-forming and directing, as we learn to obey God rather than human ideas.

The devil's best tactic, in preaching, in our reading of Scripture and in our living is always to get us to believe some human idea or practice instead of the authority of Scripture. Nothing is more successful in rendering the message of revelation null and void because the authority of *God's* word is lost. So we should be careful not to play games with Scripture.

The Best Authority

Perhaps you would like something even a little more concrete than this? The best I can do is to provide the following suggestion. In reading the Gospels, pay careful attention to how Jesus himself relates to the authority of Scripture throughout his life, both in word and deed.

If Jesus was the divine Son of God, he was also a human being who grew from infancy to adult maturity. Throughout his human development he had to learn that he was God's Son, the promised Messiah, from his knowledge of the Old Testament. As a human being, Jesus learnt the meaning of obedience to God and that his mission was to fulfil the Scriptures by fleshing out their authority in his life.

All the crucial moments of his life are placed in the light of the Scriptures—his baptism, the temptation, the first preaching at Nazareth, the Sermon on the Mount, his disputes with the Pharisees, the knowledge of his approaching death, the words on the cross and the resurrection. In all these things 'although he was a son, (Jesus) learned obedience through what he suffered' by his trust in Scripture (Heb. 5:8).

Crucial in this respect are the instances where Jesus shows himself to be consciously fulfilling the prophecies of the Old Testament. The following examples are a sample of the many instances where this is evidenced in his words:

- 'Today Scripture is fulfilled in your hearing' (Luke 4:21)
- 'Everything that is written of the Son of man by the prophets will be accomplished' (Luke 18:31–3)
- 'The Son of man goes as it is written of him' (Mark 9:12–13)
- 'These are days of vengeance to fulfil all that is written' (Luke 21:22)
- 'This Scripture must be fulfilled in me' (Luke 22:37)
- 'It is written, "I will strike the shepherd"...' (Matt. 26:31)
- 'All this has taken place, that the Scriptures of the prophets might be fulfilled' (Matt. 26:53–6)

- 'He interpreted to them in all the Scriptures the things concerning himself' (Luke 24:25–7)
- 'Thus it is written that the Christ should suffer...' (Luke 24:44–7)
- 'It is written in their law, they hated me without a cause'. (John 15:25)

These passages show that Jesus' recognition of the authority of the Scriptures was not only complete and articulate but it was also his road map for life.

Finally, if Jesus relied on the authority of the Old Testament his attitude toward it is underlined by the fact that all the Gospels, particularly Matthew, present Jesus as a new authority alongside the Old Testament. If Jesus fully accepted the authority of the law and the prophets and made himself subservient to them, he did so because his personal authority transcended them. It derived not only from his reliance on them, but also from his own unique person. He alone could say 'You know that it is written, but I say to you...' as he did repeatedly in the Sermon on the Mount. In this way Jesus validated the authority of the Old Testament. He was not tributary to it, but its Lord.

The Clarity of Scripture

While writing this book I have become more and more conscious of how little I know about Scripture. There is a depth we can't fathom. That does not mean that the Bible's message is not clear. The problem is our ignorance, an ignorance that is deep, and in some cases wilful. A complicated mathematical solution may be totally clear, logical and correct for the initiated, but to most of us it would be double–dutch because of our ineptitude.

The authority of Scripture, however, is recognisable because of its fundamental clarity, even if there are things that escape us. This is how the *Westminster Confession* puts it:

> All things in Scripture are not alike plain in themselves, not alike clear to all: yet those things which are necessary to be

> known, believed and observed for salvation, are so clearly propounded, and opened in some place of Scripture or other, that not only the learned, but the unlearned, in a due use of the ordinary means, may attain to a sufficient understanding of them. (I. vii)

There are difficult things taught in Scripture. When the apostle Peter talks of Paul's letters he was quite frank about it: 'there are some things in them that are hard to understand, which the ignorant and unstable twist to their own destruction, as they do the other Scriptures' (2 Pet. 3:17). So it is a fact that 'all things in Scripture are not alike plain' for everyone.

Peter attributes the problem of understanding to ignorance and instability. These characteristics imply a different type of person from those who are unlearned and who can still understand the main things taught by Scripture. One might be very learned and totally ignorant of Scripture, as in fact many intellectuals are. The Ethiopian eunuch was probably learned, and is an example of an ignorant person who needed someone to help him understand what he read in the scroll of Isaiah (Acts 8:26–35). Philip was sent to explain it to him. Instability on the other hand, could well refer to people who are influenced by all sorts of ideas because they have no real convictions themselves. However neither of these factors, nor people being 'unlearned', impugn the clarity of the biblical message.

Nor does the clarity of Scripture imply that I can understand or know everything about it. There are more than a few texts that the average Bible teacher or preacher would struggle to explain. Not even the most competent theologians are up to it in some instances. For example, I have never found a really a satisfying explanation of the meaning of the 'baptism for the dead' referred to by Paul in 1 Corinthians 15:29. No doubt the Corinthians knew, as the apostle had no need to explain it. Nor do I fully understand the *raison d'être* of the Song of Solomon. Some interpreters say it speaks of the beauty of human love as a gift of God; others spiritualise it and it becomes a parable about the love of Christ, the bridegroom, for the church, his bride. At present, I don't know one way or the other, although some people have set ideas on the subject. We should avoid adopting rigid positions out of a desire to minimise the difficulty.

However, these problems in no way militate against the clarity of Scripture as a whole. The story-line of the Bible as it develops is quite clear as to its central message. Even though there may be differences of opinion about some vexed questions and different interpretations of certain texts, so much is clear: in spite of these difficulties there is enough clarity in Scripture to allow the serious seeker to find the way of salvation. Once this central truth is in place, it enlightens the rest of the content of the Bible, even the dark corners and the mysteries of God (Rom. 16:25).

Finally, the clarity of Scripture itself does not make two further factors redundant. In fact, Scripture caters for both, although the first is more important than the second. Firstly, essential aid to reading Scripture aright is given by the Holy Spirit, the Spirit of truth and enlightenment. It is the Spirit that allows us to own its central message, that Jesus is Lord. Without the Spirit, none can make that confession (1 Cor. 12:3). Secondly, the New Testament allows for the office of teachers as aids to our understanding of the message of the Gospel. Throughout the history of the church teachers and preachers have been instruments of the Spirit to lead God's people into truth and true faith.

However, if this is so, teaching aids are only ever secondary. Every believer is called to be responsible before God for his conscience, which is to be informed by Scripture itself and not by a specialised class of super-clerics.

Between the believer and God there stands only one mediator, the one who is 'the way, the truth and the life' (John 14:6) and his word leads us from darkness to light. We should seek to know the 'whole counsel of God' (Acts 20:27) because that is the wisdom of Christ, and knowing it, to embrace it as the truth that impacts all our lives and makes us free.

Conclusion

To sum up: the authority of Scripture is a subject void of interest apart from the message of salvation that echoes through the Bible.

Our interest in its authority can never be simply a formal one, borne out of the desire to have an authority in our lives or the need to shore up our fragility. Our only reason for embracing this authority is because in Scripture God has given us a wonderful demonstration of his love for us in Christ. When we recognise this we are drawn out of ourselves to love him and serve him. If we keep the honour of Christ in the forefront then authority in the Christian life will not be the joyless and rigid straight jacket that seems to inhibit many Christians.

If we conclude, on the other hand, that Scripture does not or cannot bring us to salvation in Christ, it will have no effective authority and we may as well stop looking there. If we do not find healing and newness of life on the terms laid out in the Bible it's a tragedy, as we will not find them anywhere else either.

12

Truth and Unity

Truth is sacred because it ties us to reality and by tying us to reality it ties us to God who is behind it. The Bible is called the *holy* Bible or *sacred* Scriptures because through its truth God brings us back to our senses and so to reality.

'Thy word is truth' (John 17:17) states that God's word is totally trustworthy and by implication that the Bible is a book of unshakeable truth.

Sometimes the words *infallible* and *inerrant* are used to qualify the meaning of 'truth' although they seem like overkill to some people. These almost identical twins have generated as much debate in recent times as any other single topic related to the doctrine of Scripture. Wouldn't it be enough just to say that the Bible is true?

Rather than giving a drawn-out account of the ins and outs of the question, this chapter will consider why it's important. If the Bible is not entirely true, we can hardly speak about its unity. If it were a mixture of truth and error or of partial truths, it would be a hotchpotch of contradictions. Like a house divided against itself, its witness could not stand. The entire truth of Scripture is vital to its unity of intention and message. That's why the addition of the words inerrant or infallible to 'truth' is far from being redundant.

Difficulties

Some people run scared from the concepts of both infallibility and inerrancy, claiming these words aren't biblical whereas the word truth is and ought to be adequate for our needs. Truth is an attribute of God and using it with relation to the Scripture establishes an immediate link between God and his word. To this way of thinking, the legitimacy of going further than 'truth' is doubtful. Moreover, truth is a positive concept, whereas infallibility and inerrancy have a negative resonance. They give the impression that the truth Scripture is being holed-up in a defensive bunker. These reasons for reticence are understandable.

Other people prefer the word infallibility to inerrancy. Infallibility has a better theological pedigree, particularly in the European context. They marshal a good deal of historical evidence to prove that infallibility goes right back to the Church fathers and the Reformers. The *Westminster Confession of Faith* speaks about 'the infallible truth and divine authority' of Scripture (I,v). Support for it is drawn from the precedents of James Orr in Scotland or Herman Bavinck in Holland.

What those who choose infallibility over inerrancy don't appreciate is the context in which the word inerrancy became current. C. Hodge, A.A. Hodge and B.B. Warfield, Princeton theologians all, often come in for a bashing. The use of inerrancy, it is claimed, marks a rationalistic bent arising in the context of the nineteenth century struggle against scientific criticism of the Bible and evolutionism. In the twentieth century inerrancy became associated with dispensationalism and above all with fundamentalism. By adopting a position similar to that of the *Chicago Statement on Biblical Inerrancy*, one runs the risk of discrediting the truth of Scripture by claiming too much for it and defending extreme and unnecessarily rationalistic positions. Inerrancy is associated with redneck fundamentalism and bellicose attitudes displayed in books with titles like *The Battle for the Bible*.

Defenders of the infallibility of Scripture sometimes give the impression that infallibility provides more leeway in questions of detail and allows them to avoid haggling over minutiae while concentrating on the real issue of the theological infallibility of Scripture.

What's in a Word?

It is inexact to claim that infallibility is European shorthand for the complete truthfulness of Scripture, while inerrancy is the brainchild of transatlantic pragmatism. Apart from that, it is a tad condescending as well.

In fact, the word inerrancy has good pedigree on the European continent, in Roman Catholic scholarship in particular. A major Roman Catholic dictionary article on the subject in French bears the title 'Inspiration and inerrancy'. So it can hardly be claimed that inerrancy was the brain-child of encircled fundamentalists.

Also, from a Protestant perspective, infallibility is not without its own disadvantages. For a good while critics have taken the word infallibility as a pretext to conjure up a parallel between the authority of the pope and the Bible as 'paper pope.' In his notorious anti-Vatican polemic entitled *Infallible? An Enquiry*, the Roman catholic *bête noire* Hans Küng had a go at the pontiff and then extended his criticism to the infallibility of Scripture as well. Küng stated that infallibility should be jettisoned once and for all since the working of the Holy Spirit excludes neither defects nor errors. This is not edifying reading for the defenders of infallibility or inerrancy. For the likes of Küng, these notions are horses from the same stable and don't provide good mounts for open-minded jockeys.

So what's in a word? Is there any difference between infallibility and inerrancy? Is it just another theologians' debate, nothing really to write home about? The *Chicago Statement* in its section entitled 'Exposition' states: 'Holy Scripture, as the inspired Word of God witnessing authoritatively to Jesus Christ, may properly be called infallible and inerrant. These negative terms have a special value, for they explicitly safeguard crucial positive truths.'

Infallible signifies the quality of neither misleading nor being misled and so safeguards in categorical terms the truth that Holy Scripture is a sure, safe, and reliable rule and guide in all matters.

Similarly, inerrant signifies the quality of being free from all falsehood or mistake and so safeguards the truth that Holy Scripture is entirely true and trustworthy in all its assertions.

If this statement is taken at face value, there is little obvious reason why one should drive a wedge between the two terms. As it points out, they have a complementary function and the difference between the two seems wafer thin.

As I understand it, infallibility refers to Scripture as a 'rule' or 'guide'. It is more of a general principle. Infallibility indicates that we would not expect this rule of truth to lead us astray. It concerns our expectations about Scripture as the ultimate standard and how we can trust it.

Inerrancy has a different nuance. It indicates that the truth of Scripture extends to particular facts and details. All its statements are free from falsehood.

Infallibility then means the Bible is trustworthy and expected to be wholly true. Inerrancy claims that when Scripture states something, it is free from falsehood in fact and detail. If both expressions have their usefulness, inerrancy will involve us in defending the idea that the Bible got the age of Methuselah right when it says 969 years.

So why should we add infallible and inerrant to truth where Scripture is concerned? Truth is a slippery notion and we live in a world where skies are grey. Everyone thinks they know what truth is, but when pressed few can give an exact definition. 'Inerrant truth' and 'infallible truth' are like guarantees that back up the way we expect Scripture to work. Francis Schaeffer spoke of 'true truth' in a similar sense. The guarantee on my car doesn't make it run better, but it does enhance confidence in its roadworthiness because the maker stands by the viability of the product.

So to say Scripture is infallible or inerrant truth is a way of endorsing its trustworthiness. Because of its divine origin it is wholly true. Statements are not necessarily infallible or inerrant because they are true. On those grounds a textbook of mathematics or a telephone directory could be called inerrant. Even if human documents are true, they have not been through the divine quality control. Only divinely inspired Scripture can be called inerrant or infallible truth. It is the divine guarantee that makes it so.

The remainder of this chapter will firstly look at inerrancy as a form of biblical authority, an endorsement carried by the Scripture as part of the divine witness to its truth. We will use the term inerrancy rather than infallibility because we will be speaking about the factual nature of the truth of Scripture.

Secondly, since for many people inerrancy seems to be superfluous, we will seek to show that believing in an inerrant Scripture is quite consistent with the Christian faith as a whole.

Finally, something will be said about the unity of Scripture in the light of these ideas.

Inerrancy and Divine Authority

Many Christians claim to recognise *some* kind of biblical authority. However, only evangelical Christianity (as well as some traditional forms of Roman Catholicism) claims that this authority is expressed in terms of inerrancy and that Scripture itself witnesses to the fact. For this reason, inerrancy is important for evangelicals and it is also the object of criticism and misconceptions.

Inerrancy is a form of biblical authority expressed particularly in the informational or factual aspects of Scripture. The information in Scripture has its own authority because it is correct. Some salient points about inerrancy include the following considerations:

- Firstly, inerrancy is freedom from error arising from mistakes or deceit;
- Secondly, inerrancy is the result of the divine inspiration of the words of Scripture, which give a true record of God's revelation to his people, culminating in Jesus Christ;
- Thirdly, the authority of Scripture attached to inerrancy belongs ultimately to God. The idea of God's Word not being wholly true is in contradiction with the character of God himself;

- Finally, inerrancy is incompatible neither with the recognition that human nature is limited, weak and sinful, nor with human beings' proneness to error in other situations. It applies to the specific situation where divine inspiration is at work.

Inerrancy indicates two things about God's Word: God is its ultimate authority and Scripture carries marks of its nature and origin that encourage us to trust it.

Does Scripture Teach Its Own Inerrancy?

Most people today would either reply negatively to this question or deem it to be irrelevant, but a wealth of biblical evidence can be mustered in support of the idea that the Bible teaches its own inerrancy. Some considerations on the subject are as follows:

- In the Old Testament the people of God and the word of God come into existence at the same time. God speaks to his people (Deut. 27:9–11);
- The written word of the Law that God gives his people is surprisingly identified, as we saw in chapter 10, by the same attributes that belong to God alone (Ps. 119: 7, 9–11, 86, 129–30, 137, 142, Isa. 55:10ff);
- Jesus, as we have seen, attests the history of the Old Testament as being true, that it fulfils the Old Testament prophecies; he says that his people are identified by receiving his word as truth (John 17:6, 16–19); and he uses the Old Testament to interpret his resurrection (Luke 24:25, 44);
- The apostles attest the truth of their own teaching (Gal. 1:6–10, Eph. 3:2–5);
- No passage of the Bible ever infers that any other part of it is unreliable or wrong.

If Scripture nowhere affirms 'Scripture is inerrant', the attitude of Jesus and the writers of the Bible to the writings of others and to their own writing, is wholly consistent with this fact. It would also be inexplicable had they not thought Scripture to be inerrant.

What About Errors?

When inerrancy and infallibility are claimed for the Bible it is obviously difficult to avoid the question of alleged errors in Scripture. To err is to travel in the wrong direction, so what would constitute a 'wrong direction' in the Bible?

An error could be defined as being a fault of judgment coming between an observed fact and what is stated about it. To use the illustration about the car guarantee again, there is an error of manufacture if the car does not work in the way the maker claims.

In the case of Scripture, inerrancy implies that it is free from error *in general*, not only in matters of detail, but also in its broader affirmations. This includes freedom from internal contradictions, from misleading us about the nature of God, man and salvation, but also the absence of contradiction concerning facts known from sources other than the Bible. In practice, just as the car functions in the way the maker claims, Scripture upholds all its claims. For instance the Bible never infers that God is not a Trinity or that he is not the creator, that Jesus is not divine and human, that he told lies or that he will not return in glory, that this world is eternal or that there will not be a judgment day. Nor can any knowledge from outside the Bible ultimately put these teachings in doubt. The agreement in teaching is remarkable when one considers the length of time over which the Bible was written and how many authors participated in its writing.

A further definition regarding alleged error could be as follows: we cannot criticise the maker of a car if it does not run on diesel fuel, unless it is designed to. In the same way, Scripture does not err if it does not meet all our requirements of precision in every case. Error always depends on context and intentions. When going shopping, I might tell my wife I have 50 euros whereas I only have 47.50. This is not misleading, but it would be a serious error if I told that to a cashier at the bank when paying in. It's a question of context. In some cases too much precision hinders communication, while in others it is essential.

The Bible does not always claim absolute precision for its statements. It follows the conventions of its day in practices we have all observed: non-chronological narratives, imprecise quotations, historical telescoping, round figures, unpolished language or pre-scientific descriptions of the origin and workings of nature. The general purpose of Scripture is to motivate faith in God and Christ as John stated: 'these things are written so that you may believe that Jesus is the Christ, the Son of God, and in believing you may have life in his name' (John 20:31). John adds in the following chapter 'we know this testimony is true' (21:24). The language and presentation of the Bible is adapted to this fundamental aim. However it would be wrong to limit the purpose of the Bible in all cases to this alone, as if Scripture could never give information on history or the natural world. The contexts must determine how Scripture carries out its own purpose.

Big Issues and Details

The Bible cannot be accused of error if it doesn't answer all the questions we wish to ask. It cannot be taxed with insufficiency if it does not tell us how to drive a car or use a computer. Nor can our standards be imposed on it. It must be taken at its own face value. This issue can be approached on the following three levels:

AS TO DETAIL. We should seek to reconcile any apparent contradictions we find in the Bible, for example in the genealogies of Jesus, the different Gospel accounts of the cleansing of the temple, or the Old Testament chronologies. There are different ways of resolving these difficulties. For instance, we cannot rule out the fact that apparent discrepancies in parallel passages reflect the differing perspectives or purposes of their authors, that we do not always have all the details to explain everything, that often the solution is found in a more careful reading of the text, or even that a problem may be related to a sinful or wilful lack of understanding on our part. Sometimes we may have to wait years to find the solution to a particular difficulty. Perhaps, in some cases, we have to accept that no solution is forthcoming.

This was the case until recently with the chronologies of the post-resurrection appearances in the Synoptic gospels and in John.

Both Luther and Calvin were aware of the difficulties, but neither of them appeared willing to state that Scripture was in error on this point. Now we know different calendars were being used which can contribute to understanding the problem.

IN A BROAD SENSE. Inerrancy concerns the teachings of the Bible concerning the 'big issues'. Perhaps, as evangelicals, we have been too restrictive in limiting the debate about inerrancy to points of detail. The Bible says God is love, God created the world out of nothing, man fell into sin at a precise moment, the exodus happened, Jesus was the God-man, he worked miracles, rose from the dead, indwells believers by his Spirit and is alive for evermore. Are these things true? They are the essential questions and the real challenges to a way of thinking limited to what we observe now in the world around us.

If we believe these things, it is only because of our confidence in the witness of the Bible, for all of them are historically distant and none of them can be rationally demonstrated. They belong not to sight but to faith. However, they are neither irrational, mythical nor untrue. Within a Christian framework they are totally coherent and reasonable.

WORLD-VIEW. Inerrancy relates to the contrast between a Christian world-view and other perspectives. Ultimately, it refers not to isolated facts but to the harmony between different aspects of reality, because they are what they are in relation to God, their author. The inerrancy of Scripture expresses our relationship with God as human beings who need his truth. In the biblical revelation we see God as creator and Saviour in a way that corresponds to our deep longings. Inerrancy implies reliability and ultimate confidence. To take up the car illustration once again: we choose a make of car because it seems the best and the most road-worthy.

Spiritual Discernment

When we raise the question of the inerrancy of Scripture, we are not only asking about the Bible as a standard, or about its historical-cultural situation, but also about ourselves. Are we Bible-compatible?

To know how to use the Bible, we need spiritual wisdom. Our intelligence needs spiritual formatting for us to receive the truth of Scripture. Would this be why so many people cannot get past the first 'error' they supposedly find in Scripture? Could it be that God has given Scripture in its somewhat complicated, enigmatic form, precisely to remind us that the message of Scripture must be spiritually, not naturally, discerned?

Ephesians 4:17–24 presents a striking contrast between pagans whose thinking is futile and who are ignorant and hardened and those who, knowing Christ, have a new attitude of mind and a new nature created by God in righteousness and truth.

The goal of the inerrancy of Scripture is that the harmony found in the Bible be reproduced in our lives. By God's Spirit the truth of Scripture penetrates our lives and transforms us to the image of Christ, with his mind.

Inerrancy and Christian Truth

Recently, attacks have been levelled at the doctrine of inerrancy and this criticism makes people feel uneasy about this idea.

Inerrancy is often treated as rationalistic and accused of replacing a living experience of God with a dead letter, or of maintaining an anachronistic idea of a supernatural written revelation. Most of these criticisms focus on the idea that the inerrancy of Scripture replaces the authority of the living personal God with the authority of an abstract and impersonal code. The personal authority of God and the authority of a written revelation are taken to be mutually exclusive of each other.

However, the inerrant truth of Scripture is not a piece of antiquated rationalism; it goes hand in glove with the nature of the Christian faith itself. Moreover, faith is hard pushed to function properly without it. Five cases in point will serve to illustrate this.

INERRANCY DOES NOT CONTRADICT THE NATURE OF FAITH. It is often said that belief in inerrancy cannot stand up to the full range of facts presented by the Bible. If we consider *all* the evidence of Scripture some of the facts present us with problems. So, for some people, to claim the inerrancy of Scripture requires blind faith, the sort of faith that lacks adequate backing. Certain teachings of Scripture, they think, have to be assumed *a priori* as applying to all of Scripture. For this reason, from the time of Warfield to the present, some evangelicals have defended a theory of limited inerrancy, reserving the truth of Scripture to its central teaching.

What is the nature of faith and how does it work in a Christian setting? The criticism formulated above can be levelled against any Christian teaching. All Christian doctrine has some problems that remain apparently contradictory. All of it is in a certain sense paradoxical. Can we reconcile seemingly contradictory concepts like the divinity and humanity of Christ, divine predestination and human freedom, God's love and justice or faith as a gift of God and a human exercise?

Nor can we wait to have 'all the evidence' on any of these subjects before believing. We will never get it. What we believe about any major teaching of Scripture is founded on its most clear statements and then applied to the rest, the secondary factors.

The same is true for inerrancy. We believe it not because we have all the answers, but because some Scriptures clearly teach it and the problems are peripheral. In other words, we believe all Scripture was produced through the work of the Spirit, and is profitable and edifying, even if we do not find much that is *immediately* edifying in the chronological problems of Chronicles.

Moreover, Christian faith is about hearing God's voice and believing it, even though some of the facts may seem against it. The disasters of the last century *seem* to be against believing in God's control of history. Faith is trusting in God *in spite of* some evidence apparently to the contrary. Hebrews 11 is all about this.

The Christian approach is to hear what God says about something and then look at the other facts from this standpoint, not to look at the facts from our standpoint to find out whether what God says might be true. What God says is one of the facts of the situation and because of the divine witness it is the primary fact.

We accept inerrancy the same way as we accept other Christian doctrine. This leads us from thinking about faith to thinking about knowledge.

INERRANCY IS IMPLIED IN A CHRISTIAN WAY OF KNOWING. We have claimed that inerrancy is based on Scripture—*sola Scriptura*—and that it is implied in the nature of the divine witness. In other words, inerrancy is a consequence of other biblical teachings. Some critics accuse this approach of being *deductive* and claim that a correct method for approaching Scripture must be *inductive*, not starting with teachings, but looking at the range of facts to conclude whether or not there are errors in the Bible. A deductive argument runs like this:

- God cannot lie (Num. 23:1, Titus 1:2);
- God is not ignorant (Ps. 33:13ff, Heb. 4:13);
- Scripture is his Word (2 Tim. 3:16);
- Therefore Scripture is true.

What can we conclude from this argument about a Christian way of knowing?

First of all, our fundamental convictions affect our way of looking at things, even if we don't recognise it. Proper ways for understanding the Bible are provided by the Bible.

Secondly, the problem with an inductive approach that starts with the 'facts' is that it is not biblical facts that govern statements about Scripture, but *a human evaluation of some biblical facts*. The reader who says 'the biblical author made a mistake' replaces the self-witness of Scripture with a human idea. This is different from the witness of Scripture, which in the case of inerrancy is provided by Psalm 12 'the words of the Lord are pure words' or Jesus' statement 'Scripture cannot be broken'.

This question is vital for a Christian view of knowledge. We cannot start with an idea foreign to revelation and end up proving biblical truth. We cannot conjure up a doctrine of creation from the fact of the eternity of matter, human nature from an evolutionary process, the divinity of Christ from an idea about humanity, biblical conversion from a psychology of personality change or the return of

Christ from the predictions of the Davos forum. In every issue and with every question the witness of Scripture is the starting-point.

Inerrancy is an example of how Christian knowledge functions. Could there be Christian knowledge about anything other than from this perspective?

INERRANCY IS COMPATIBLE WITH THE CHARACTER OF GOD. It is often said that truth is a person, Jesus Christ, not a text. Faith refers to the living God, or to the living Christ and not to a dead letter. Sometimes we hear statements like 'there are no biblical norms to apply, only the living Christ to follow.'

However, biblical inerrancy is totally compatible with a personal God, for three reasons:

Firstly, Jesus himself never made any quality distinction between his own origin and the origin of Scripture. His attitude revealed that 'personal truth' and 'words' go together. Christ fulfilled Scripture, he declared his word to be the judge at the last day. He came from the Father, bringing the words of the Father. As he knows the Father, his word makes the Father known. In John 17 he says 'sanctify them through your word; your word is truth' and not 'sanctify them through me'.

Secondly, if Scripture were an imperfect and unreliable human witness to God's revelation, how could we know what Jesus came into the world to do? If there were no divine revelation, there would be no knowledge of divine salvation either. Any personal contact between God and man disappears altogether, if there is no way of having a personal knowledge of Christ through Scripture. If the witness to Christ were merely human, what could it truly tell us about the *divinity of Christ*?

Finally, for evangelicals, God is truly known, because his transcendence implies his immanence. God is infinite, the only living and true God, but he is also personal, self-revealing and communicating.

Once again, the inerrancy of Scripture is implied in our view of God and Christ and without it, we can have no real and true knowledge of God. If there is no Scripture, there is no Christ. This leads to the next point concerning the nature of salvation.

INERRANCY AND THE NATURE OF SALVATION. The Bible is not a book about a book, but a book about God and his salvation. Salvation therefore makes provision for God's words. The witness to this fact is as broad as the Bible itself. Salvation is deliverance from sin and from the bondage of unbelief, myths and untruth. A clear biblical example is in 2 Peter 1. There is nothing contradictory about God speaking on the mount of transfiguration and in his prophetic witness in Scripture. Both point to the divine revelation of salvation.

In addition, obedience to the spoken or written word is a necessary condition of discipleship. Jesus insists on this repeatedly.

Biblical salvation supposes true knowledge, substantial assurance, intelligent obedience and discipleship. For all of these the full truthfulness of Scripture is necessary. Where belief in inerrancy weakens, Christian salvation tends to be replaced by universalism, God's law by cultural relativism, the church militant by the church sociological and evangelism by good-works activism.

INERRANCY AND HUMANITY. It is often alleged that belief in inerrancy produces an impersonal Christianity as human freedom is replaced by a written code. To err is human and true humanity requires freedom. So humanity and the fragility of fallibility are closely linked.

How does the inerrancy of Scripture imply true humanity? Human beings were made by God to know the truth, to rejoice in God's plan for history and appreciate the diversity of cultural development. Sin is the root of error and produces a truncated view of humanity. God's renewal of humanity implies that man will be restored to the truth and will praise Christ as the head in whom the fullness of reality has its *raison d'être*.

The inerrancy of the prophetic words of Scripture points to a new hope for humanity. It is a specific case, related to God's giving his truth in revelation, which shows what God can and will do to transform human nature. It is an indication of the fact that in Christ the human race will be restored to truth. Our humanity will be a new humanity. As an aspect of the Holy Spirit's work in the inspiration of Scripture, inerrancy points in the present to a final state of truth and fellowship with God. Negatively, is it possible to imagine a new creation in which doctrinal error and untruth about God would be present?

Inerrancy is a sign and seal of what God's future work will be: it implies true humanity. How necessary it is for us to know that there will be true humanity in the future! What a stimulus for hope in Christ inerrancy is!

The humanity of Scripture in the fullest sense lies in the fact that by his Word God is making us truly human, because it reveals the new humanity, Jesus Christ.

The Unity of Scripture

The truth of Scripture is the framework for its unity. Its truth not only ensures that there are no real contradictions (other than apparent) in Scripture, but also that the biblical message is living and dynamic.

Unity is a complex idea and difficult to define in any case. What makes for the unity of the human body or of a person? Chemical composition, the nervous system or the intelligence? Is there something more to the unity of a motor engine than fine tuning?

Similarly, the unity of the Bible can be approached in several ways. It's not immediately evident how 66 books written by a diversity of people at different times can make up one book. Unity could be found in the non-contradictory nature of its teaching, in the development of its story-line or in the centrality of the person of Jesus as the one who holds it together. It could also be found in a less apparent factor such as human spirituality, or even in God willing it to be so. However, one thing is for sure, if we can't see the unity of Scripture in its truth, it will be a challenge to find it anywhere else.

Fundamentally it would be difficult to find the unity of Scripture in a human factor or in a historical process. If God is the ultimate author of Scripture, its unity must have its starting point in the divine person and in his willingness to communicate truth to his creatures. The instrument for doing this is the inspiration of the Scriptures that convey his truth to us. The unity of Scripture is its oneness in truth, which depends on inspiration, which depends in turn on God himself. To put it another way, there is a definite link between the oneness and unity of God and the unity of Scripture. Diversity in unity characterises both the person of God and his word, although on different levels.

This unity is of a spiritual nature. God is spirit, his word is spirit and truth and inspiration is the spiritual activity that unites his person to the given word. In its turn, this is the basis for another form of spiritual unity, the unity of his kingdom and his people, expressed visibly in the church. The New Testament expresses this in a triad—one Lord, one word (one truth) and one church. Three biblical illustrations can be given of this relationship.

In his discourse to his disciples in John 15 about the vineyard and the vines, Jesus says:

'I am the true vine and my Father is the vine dresser' (15:1).

'I am the vine; you are the branches' (5).

'If you abide in me, and my words abide in you, ask whatever you wish, and it will be done for you' (7).

In verse 7, Jesus is not inviting us to wish for a new BMW and promising that we will get one. The wish concerns bearing fruit (4) because the branches are in the vine. Jesus means the disciples *together* are to abide in him and bear fruit, as branches grafted into a vine. Note that when the disciples are one with Jesus, his words (7) are the expression of this unity. The unity flows from the Father to the Son, to the disciples who are one with him and through his words that make the unity a reality and bearing fruit a possibility. Obviously this does not prove the unity of Scripture, but it does illustrate the principle behind that unity. Oneness is a feature of God and it is expressed both in a spiritual relationship and in words. The same principle applies to the unity and truth of Scripture as a whole.

Jesus' high-priestly prayer in John 17 includes three subjects of intercession. Jesus prays for himself (17:1–5), he prays for his disciples (6–19) and he prays for those who will believe because of the witness the disciples will bear to him. In verses 20–26 Jesus prays that his work might be completed and carried forth into the world through the preaching of the good news by the apostles, as a manifestation of his unity with the Father. Jesus prays as one who has been given 'authority over all flesh to give eternal life' (2). How will this come about in practice? Jesus gives the key in his prayer:

'I have given them (the disciples) your (the Father's) word' (14).

'They are not of the world, just as I am not of the world. Sanctify them in the truth; your word is truth' (17).

'(I ask) for those (all believers, including us) who will believe in me through their word' (20).

'that they may all be one, just as you, Father, are in me, and I in you, that they also may be in us…' (22).

'that they may be perfectly one' (25).

This is *not* about any visible unity of churches in an ecumenical movement. It is about the unity of the Father and the Son, the unity of his disciples in them through the word from the Father that he has given them, and the perfect spiritual unity through the word. The unity of God, Father, Son and Spirit, is revealed in the word transmitted by the Son to his chosen ones and in the truth that sanctifies them and sets them apart. They are consecrated and made one by the truth through the word. The link between the unity of God, his word of truth and his people is unavoidable.

Finally, the well-known passage about the unity of the church as the body of Christ in Ephesians chapter 4 speaks about unity in God and unity in truth. The apostle Paul 'urges' his readers to 'maintain the unity of the Spirit' (4:3) as follows:

'there is one body and one Spirit'.

'one Lord, one faith, one baptism'.

'one God and Father of all, who is over all and through all and in all' (4–6).

Reading backwards we see that God is the source, Christ the Lord is the means and the Spirit is concretely the bond of the unity of the body of Christ.

Is the central expression 'one faith' in this instance subjective (the act of believing) or objective (the content of what is believed)? A good many people today would answer the first; unity is not found in doctrine or statements of faith or creeds, but in personal faith. I am inclined to think that it concerns the second, objective faith, because the faith in question refers to 'one Lord', as also in the case of baptism. Faith is defined by Christ the Lord, not Christ by our faith. In addition, the apostle goes on to indicate conditions for the well-being of the body (11–16). Teaching offices are given, under Christ's authority, apostles, prophets, evangelists, pastors and teachers, so that 'all attain to the unity of the faith and of the knowledge of the Son of God' and grow up 'speaking the truth in love'. Why would these special functions be given to the church unless the unity of the body depended in some way on the objective truth transmitted in the message of the gospel?

Once again we can see in this passage the links between the oneness of God, divine truth and the spiritual unity of the people of God in the 'faith'. Unity depends on oneness in truth and both depend on God who is one. The unity of Scripture depends on its truth content.

Conclusion

Speaking about inerrancy and objective truth at first sight may look unattractive. It seems to be negative and restrictive, but its pay-off is positive and constructive. It allows us to build up a biblical faith in all its dimensions in a spirit of confidence and trust that rests on God and his Word.

These considerations should be sufficient to show that biblical inerrancy is not genetically foreign to the nature of Christian faith, but of a piece with it. Truth so expressed is vital for an understanding of the unity of God's word.

Like faith itself, the truth of Scripture must touch all aspects of life, in order for God's grace to reach them all.

13

The Canon of Holy Scripture

The canon is the list of the books accepted as the authentic word of God and recognised as belonging to the body of Holy Scripture. It is not inclusion in the list that gives them authority. In other words, their authority does not come from the recognition implied in the act of canonisation.

The question of canon is fraught with historical problems and complexities; the sands of time have obscured lots of things about the process of canonisation. In addition, judgments about the canon are seldom made on purely historical grounds; theological presuppositions tend to interfere willy-nilly with historical judgments and it's best to be aware of that.

Someone who holds to a biblical view of inspiration and of the providence of God will have little difficulty accepting that if God chose to reveal himself through saving acts and inspired words that he should also have overseen the process by which they are made known. Our view of the canon will inevitably be conditioned by what we think about God. Although some questions may remain, we will accept that we know enough to satisfy our needs. In fact, rather than being perplexed, we will be impressed by the fact that these writings have been preserved through the meanders of time. God watched over his word from the autograph stage to the listing of canonical books and then down to us today in the translations we hold in our hands. Amidst so many uncertainties, it makes a rather surprising story, and one for which we can be thankful.

In this chapter, after a brief definition, we will look at how the canon of the Old and New Testaments came into existence and the problem of the apocryphal books (the non-canonical books not recognised by Protestants) before concluding with some theological considerations.

A Definition of Canon

Our word canon is derived from the Greek *kanon*. It originally referred to a measuring rod and later came to mean a rule or standard. It is used several times in this sense in the New Testament, for instance in Galatians 6:16: 'as for those who walk by this rule, peace and mercy be on them.' Clement of Rome, an early Church father, used it in the sense of a rule possessing authority. Later, in the third century, Origen used the word to denote the 'rule of faith', the standard by which truth is measured in the realm of religion. A century later Athanasius, the great defender of orthodox Christianity, spoke of the canon to refer to a list of writings that the Church accepts as the authoritative texts of divine revelation. So the word came to have a secondary meaning indicating the officially accepted list of books, the canon of Scripture and the books included in it.

The two meanings of canon are complementary. The Scriptures are recognised collectively as a rule of faith and the writings that possess the features associated with revelation and inspiration are included in the list of canonical books. For this reason the classical Confessions of faith, from the Reformation onwards, list the books deemed to be canonical in their statements about Scripture.

'Canon' has come to refer generally to this list of accepted books, although the idea that these books together provide the church with a 'rule of faith' is not excluded. Divine authority comes first and canonicity follows from authority and depends on it.

We can see this principle functioning already within the New Testament. The apostle Peter recognised Paul's writings to be on a par with the authority of the Old Testament. Paul he said, wrote about these things with the wisdom given him in all his letters that are misunderstood by the ignorant 'as they do the other Scriptures'. (2 Pet. 3:16) Paul himself claimed to write with the authority of the risen Lord; in 1 Corinthians 14:37 he affirmed, 'the things I write to you are a commandment of the Lord'. Consideration of these texts alone shows that the authority of these writings caused them to be recognised and included in the category of sacred writings.

To sum up: canonical texts were recognised because of their inherent qualities, among which can be numbered the following features:

- authority, because the Lord speaks in them;
- prophetic nature, as they bear the stamp of divine origin;
- authentic character, in contrast with spurious teachings;
- saving power, because of their divine wisdom.

Given the high conditions for acceptance, it is not surprising that some texts, such as the book of Esther, initially had difficulty meeting the required standards.

The Canon of the Old Testament

From the beginning of the Christian era the thirty-nine recognised books of the Old Testament were those that had been included in the Hebrew Bible. The reckoning was done slightly differently, because the Hebrew Bible was divided into three parts, the Law, the Prophets and the Writings. It included twenty-four books in all, the twelve Minor Prophets being counted as one book, as were the books of Samuel, Kings and Chronicles and also those of Ezra and Nehemiah.

About twenty years after the destruction of the Jerusalem temple in AD 70 and the dispersion of the Jews, an attempt was made to allay the catastrophe and preserve national identity. A new Sanhedrin or council of elders met at Jamnia near Jaffa.

They reviewed the fundamentals of Jewish religion and law and held lengthy discussions about the canon, and about which books should be admitted and which rejected. At the end of the day, their conclusions were quite conservative as they neither admitted any book that was not already recognised, nor did they exclude anything that had been formerly accepted. A good deal is sometimes made about this 'house of judgment' (*beth din*) as it is called in Jewish tradition. However the discussions at Jamnia seem to have been informal, no binding decisions were made and no formal pronouncement was made about the entire Old Testament.

Three other factors can be taken into account regarding the canon of the Old Testament: witnesses from extra-biblical sources, the words of Jesus and the evidence within the Old Testament.

EXTRA-BIBLICAL SOURCES. The oldest reference to the threefold division of the Old Testament is probably in the apocryphal book Ecclesiasticus (52:71, dated around 130 BC), which speaks about 'the Law and the prophets and the other books of the fathers'. Similarly, Josephus, the first century Jewish historian (in *Contra Apionem* 1.8), stated that since the time of Malachi, the last book of the Old Testament, many things have been written but none are worthy of what went before. Several references in the Talmud, the Jewish annotations of the Scriptures, are in the same vein, particularly the

The Hebrew Bible

The Law	the five books of Moses
The Prophets	the Former prophets, Joshua, Judges, Samuel and Kings, and the Latter prophets, Isaiah, Jeremiah, Ezekiel and the Minor Prophets
The Writings	the Psalms, Proverbs and Job; the 'five scrolls' made up of the Song of Solomon, Ruth, Lamentations, Ecclesiastes and Esther; finally Daniel, Ezra, Nehemiah and Chronicles

There is no apparent reason for this arrangement, as it follows neither chronological order nor subject matter. The order in the English Bible is based on the Septuagint, the Greek translation of the Hebrew Bible made in the second century BC.

tractate *Sanhedrin* (VII–VIII, 24) which comments 'after the latter prophets Haggai, Zachariah and Malachi, the Holy Spirit departed from Israel.'

In the Early Church the bishop Melito of Sardis drew up the oldest list of Old Testament books (around AD 170) and later Eusebius in his *Ecclesiastical History* (IV.26) commented on Melito's list, saying that he made it while travelling in Syria. This list includes all the books of the Old Testament, apart from Esther, which may not have been mentioned by those who provided this list for him.

JESUS AND THE CANON OF THE OLD TESTAMENT. When Jesus said, after the resurrection, 'that everything written about me in the Law of Moses and the Prophets and the Psalms must be fulfilled' (Luke 24:44), he was most probably referring to the Jewish canon as a whole. It can be added that on many occasions Jesus referred to the Old Testament as Scripture, but he never did do so with regard to any non-biblical writings, nor did any of his debates with the experts of his time have to do with questions of canonicity. Moreover, when he referred in Matthew 23:35 (Luke 11:51) to the 'blood of the innocent Abel to the blood of Zechariah son of Barachiah' he joined in his summary of former times an incident from Genesis 4:8 and one found in 2 Chronicles 24:21: 2 Chronicles is the final book of the Hebrew canon. So Jesus was in fact saying 'from Genesis to 2 Chronicles', including all the Old Testament in his statement.

THE OLD TESTAMENT ITSELF. It is widely supposed, although there is no direct evidence for the fact, that the threefold division of the Old Testament represents the stages in which the canon received recognition. Whether this is so or not, the triple division does indicate the basic shape of the Old Testament. Classifying the first five books together indicates that they are foundational, Moses being the pre-eminent figure as the servant of the Lord (Num. 12:1–7). As the one who received the Law, Moses occupied a position comparable to that of Christ, the founder of the New Testament economy (Heb. 3:2, 5).

When God gave the Law to his people it came with the instruction to place it beside the ark of the covenant, which represented the presence of God (Deut. 31:24–6). The priests were to read it to the people, notably on feast days or when the covenant was renewed (31:11). The king himself was to have a copy as it also included specific instructions for his rule (17:18–19).

The function of the Old Testament prophets was to apply the Law of Moses by recalling it to the people. They also warned them about the judgment that would follow disobedience. The prophets used the Law of Moses as evidence against the people and their words often took the form of a lawsuit in which they acted like prosecutors. The function of the wisdom books of the Old Testament (the writings) was to elaborate the practical benefits of following the ways indicated by the Lord.

The process of the reception of the canonical books may seem lax to modern western mentalities, with our criteria of authorship and copyright. It is true that there were no councils that registered approved writings and declared them to be individually or collectively authoritative. However, it was hardly necessary; the writings were recognised as God's revelation on reception and were accepted by his people. Ultimately, canonicity depended on the divine act of revelation, inspired writings belonging to the canon from the moment of composition. A human decision to make a text part of the canon is not what makes it canonical.

There are certain vital moments that stand out in the history of the reception of the books of the Old Testament. At the end of Moses' life the corpus of the Pentateuch was complete apart from some minor additions (called the 'post-mosaica'), which gave details about the end of Moses' life. Joshua, his successor, received the following mandate from the Lord himself: 'the Book of the Law shall not depart from your mouth, but you shall meditate on it day and night, so that you may be careful to do according to all that is written in it' (Josh. 1:8). Throughout the history of Israel the Law remained the yardstick of progress or regress for those who exercised office and for the people themselves.

Just as decisive as the giving of the Law is the way the prophets received divine revelation. The expressions used are telling. The word of the Lord 'comes' to them, they 'hear' it as God's word and they preface their statements with 'thus says the Lord'. They uniformly claim themselves to be vehicles for the communication of the final, absolute word of God (see for instance, Isa. 8:5, Jer. 3:6, Ezek. 21:1, Amos 3:1). Amos, who only prophesied for a few weeks, is a case in point. When challenged with treason about his message he countered: 'I was no prophet, nor a prophet's son, but I was a herdsman... but the Lord took me from following the flock, and the Lord said to me, "Go prophesy to the people of Israel." Now hear the word of the Lord...' (7:14–15) The striking thing about the work of many of the prophets is that in spite of the fact that they were censored because their message was unpalatable to those in authority, this message survived as God's witness and that at a time when making copies was a painstaking business.

What about 'the other books', the writings, referred to by Ecclesiasticus? There are no direct indications in Scripture as to how and when these books were collected or collectively recognised. They are certainly less uniform than the Law or the prophets; the name 'writings' was doubtless used to group them together a long time after their appearance.

At the time of Ezra, in the fifth century BC, after a remnant of deportees had returned to Israel, the Pentateuch was read out loud to the assembly (Neh. 8–10, Ezra 7). For the listeners, the writings of the major prophets had received historical confirmation by the predicted exile and return. The rebuilding of the temple may well have initiated a movement of renewed interest in the sacred books and their compilation. The individual writings of the third division of the canon may well have benefited from this reforming zeal. Ezra himself is described as a scribe (7:6); his mission was to see that the Scriptures were respected. Corroborative evidence is found in the apocryphal book 2 Maccabees (2:13ff) where reference is made to the fact that Nehemiah founded a library and collected books 'concerning the kings and prophets and those of David'. Although this tradition is dated from much later (see below), at least it bears witness to the idea that the return from exile was a time when the value of the former writings was fully recognised and steps were taken to preserve them.

The Old Testament Apocrypha

The books of the Jewish Apocrypha are those not included in the list of Old Testament canonical books. Apocrypha, from the Greek, means 'hidden things' and there is no little discussion about the real meaning of the name. These texts were either written in Greek or translated into Greek. Jerome was perhaps the first to use the word 'apocrypha' in the fourth century AD.

These writings were never thought to be canonical by the leaders of official Judaism. First century Jewish scholars like Philo of Alexandria or Josephus accepted only the Hebrew canon of the Old Testament. Nor did Jesus or the apostles quote the apocryphal books as being part of Scripture, even though they quoted the Old Testament in abundance.

Later many of the Church fathers made a distinction between the Apocrypha and Scripture. Jerome, who translated the Bible into Latin, rejected the apocryphal books from the canon. However he did introduce a distinction between what he called 'canonical books' and 'church books', which served to give the apocryphal books a secondary status. The Council of Carthage in 397 AD decided that the Apocrypha should be permitted as suitable for reading in the Church. So in spite of his reservations about these books, Jerome's distinction undermined his own position. Probably he would have disapproved of their being translated and included in his Latin Vulgate Bible after his death. On the other hand, many fathers of the Latin churches made no distinction between the two categories of book either in theory or in practice. This prepared the way for the acceptance of their canonical status by the Council of Trent in the 1546 (I and II Esdras and the Prayer of Manasses excepted).

Within Protestantism, Lutherans and Anglicans permit the reading of these books, but not as part of the rule of faith. *The Articles of Religion of the Anglican Church* (39 articles, VI) state 'the other books (as Jerome says) the Church reads for example of life and instruction of manners; but does not apply them to establish any doctrine.' Reformed and evangelical churches, on the other hand, do not recognise the Apocrypha, and few evangelical Christians will have even looked at them. One reason for this refusal is opposition

The Jewish Apocrypha
(as listed in the 39 articles of the Church of England, VI)

I and II Esdras. The first dates from about 150 BC and recounts the return from the exile. The second dating from 100 AD contains seven visions and is said to have so frustrated Martin Luther that he threw it into the river Elbe.

Tobias. Second century BC, it is a short story with emphasis on ritual practices.

Judith. Mid second century BC, the heroine, a beautiful widow saves the people by putting herself in a compromising situation and decapitating the attacking Assyrian general.

Additions to Esther. About 100 BC, mainly prayers of Esther and Mordecai that compensate the absence of the name of God in the biblical book.

Wisdom (of Solomon). AD 50, as in Proverbs, wisdom is personified and gives many proverbs to encourage piety in the context of paganism.

Jesus the Son of Sirach. Or Ecclesiasticus, the wisdom of Sirach, dated from around 200 BC. Maxims of religious practice, rather like Proverbs in the Old Testament.

Baruch the Prophet. Purports to be written by Baruch, Jeremiah's scribe in 582 BC, but actually from around 100 AD. After the fall of Jerusalem in AD 70, it urges civil obedience.

The Song of the Three Children. Borrowing from Psalm 148, it is placed after Daniel 3:23 in the Septuagint Greek translation of the Old Testament and in the Latin Vulgate.

The Story of Susanna. A final chapter (13) for the biblical book of Daniel about the virtuous wife of a leading Jew in Babylon, wrongly accused of dalliance by false witness, but saved by Daniel; from around 100 BC.

Bel and the Dragon. A further chapter for Daniel (14) with two fictional stories showing the danger of idolatry.

The Prayer of Manasses. Composed in the second century BC, it purports to be the prayer of Manasseh, the wicked king of Judah. No doubt inspired by the reference in 2 Chronicles 33:19.

I and II Maccabees. Both from the 1st century BC, these books describe the acts of the three Maccabean brothers, the second book concentrating on the exploits of Judas Maccabæus. This provides a valuable background to New Testament times.

to the Roman Catholic position, but the main argument is that these writings were neither recognised by the Jewish church nor by Jesus. The Christian church received the canon as recognised by the Jews and particularly by Jesus himself. On this point as on others, the authority of Jesus is canonical.

Apart from this, many other reasons have been evoked for the exclusion of the Apocrypha from the canon: the numerous factual inaccuracies, literary artifice of a type out of keeping with inspiration, teachings or practices that are not in tune with the doctrine of Scripture on subjects such as good works and the condition of the soul after death. In all, these writings do not have 'the feel', the divine authority and power that characterise the inspired word.

Perhaps more pertinent than these reasons is the fact that the New Testament speaks of a time of waiting that preceded the coming of the Messiah. Between the final prophesies of Malachi and the coming of John the Baptist the hands of the clock of the history of salvation stopped. As the rabbis said, the work of the Holy Spirit was absent from Israel during that period. Movement begins again with the 'beginning of the gospel of Jesus Christ' (Mark 1:1) and new events of salvation: the visitation of Mary, the revelation to Joseph, Elisabeth and Zachariah, the prophecies of Anna and Simeon in the Temple and the baptism of Jesus by John.

The New Testament Canon

The canon of the New Testament is the collection of the 27 books from Matthew to Revelation. There are three important questions concerning these books:

- on what grounds were these writings accepted?
- how can these books be dated?
- how and when did this canon came into existence?

If the teaching of Jesus is fundamental to the acceptance of the Old Testament canon, it is no less so for the New, although the principle applies differently; Jesus obviously said nothing concerning it as a body of existing writings. The canonicity of the New Testament rests on the inspiration of the texts, considered to be prophetic Scripture like the Old Testament, but also in a special way on the authority of Jesus.

THE GROUNDS OF CANONICITY. The person of Jesus is the crowning self-revelation of God and he fulfils the divine promises for the salvation of his people. However, this great work of salvation is not limited to the actual words and deeds of Jesus. There would be something incomplete about the saving revelation, on which Christianity stands or falls, if it were not preserved in authentic documents endorsed by the authority of God himself.

The four gospels are the written form of apostolic witness to Christ, recorded with the help of the Holy Spirit, which was promised by Jesus himself. Luke underlines this at the start of the Acts of the Apostles:

> In the first book, O Theophilus, I have dealt with all that Jesus began to do and teach, until the day when he was taken up, after he had given commands through the Holy Spirit to the apostles whom he had chosen… (Jesus) said to them… 'You will receive power when the Holy Spirit has come upon you, and you will be my witnesses in Jerusalem and in all Judea and Samaria, and to the end of the earth' (1:1–2, 8).

The 'first book', addressed to Theophilus, was the gospel of Luke, which begins in parallel fashion:

> Inasmuch as many have undertaken to compile a narrative of the things that have been accomplished among us, just as those who from the beginning were eyewitnesses and ministers of the word have delivered them to us, it seemed good to me also, having followed all things closely for some time past, to write an orderly account for you, most excellent Theophilus, that you may have certainty concerning the things you have been taught. (Luke 1:1–4)

Luke presents his credentials in a way that is acceptable in the Græco-Roman world. The form is comparable to that used by historians of the time. Luke claims that others before him have told the story, a reference to Matthew's or Mark's Gospel, or perhaps parts of the gospel circulating on pieces of papyrus. He also infers that it can be verified in the same way that he has done.

Luke refers here to witness and apostolicity, two notions that are capital for the formation of the canon. Those who had been eye-witnesses were sent as oral witnesses via the spoken and later written word. These were the apostles Jesus had chosen and to whom he had promised the power of the Holy Spirit. The message of the gospel is set before the church and the world by the witnesses, who claimed that these things really happened. Jesus did not leave it to chance; the apostles were authorised custodians of his truth. Hebrews 2:1–4 gives the order of things: this revelation came first from the Lord, then by those who heard it and finally through confirmation by the Holy Spirit with 'signs and wonders'. Hebrews compares the apostles to the angels who were messengers of God's truth in giving the Old Testament Law. Thus the apostolic gospel becomes the foundation of the church (Matt. 16:18, Eph. 2:21, Rev. 21:14). The apostolic witness represents the constitution of the Christian church, its trust deed.

Another important New Testament notion contributing to canonicity is that of tradition, mentioned in the second text above by the word 'delivered'. Tradition is what has been handed down (*paradosis*) or delivered over to the church with apostolic authority. The holy faith is transmitted to the church by the apostles who are custodians of the truth; the church is called to preserve this message and hold fast to it. The idea of holding fast the truth is prominent in the Pastoral Epistles (1 Tim. 6:20, 2 Tim. 1:14, 2:2) but it is already present in 1 Corinthians, in its famous fifteenth chapter: 'I remind you brothers, of the gospel I preached to you, which you received, in which you stand... I delivered to you as of first importance that Christ died for our sins in accordance with the Scriptures...' (15:1–11. Cf. 11:23, 1 Thess. 2:13).

It should not be overlooked that in this passage the apostle Paul is repeating in written form the oral message that he had received and had previously preached to his hearers. By writing it down the apostle is establishing the content of the gospel not only for his readers at Corinth but also for the church as a whole. Two frontiers are in view here: firstly the line of demarcation between the oral tradition and fixed in written form; secondly the frontier between what is the received gospel and what is not. Both of these are contributing factors in the formation of the New Testament canon as Scripture alongside the Old Testament.

Witness, apostolic character and 'delivery' are the three determinative factors for the canonicity of the New Testament scriptures. Apostolic authority and approval together constitute the primary test. This authority, whether it be that of the apostles in person, or that of their protégés, such as Mark and Luke, is never detached from the person of Jesus, both in his ministry on earth and in his resurrected power. Jesus as Lord speaks with authority to his church through his words and deeds on earth and in heaven.

THE QUESTION OF DATING. For a good while a nefarious tendency existed among New Testament historians to date its writings rather late, at the end of the first century or the beginning of the second. This meant of course that the texts could not be apostolic and that they came into being a long time after the events recounted. Sources behind the gospels were invented, such as the infamous 'Q' source (Q = *quelle*, meaning source in German), no fragment of which has ever been found. The fact that it never existed has not deterred academics from writing about the theology of Q!

These conjectures about dating are belied by several considerations. Firstly, the apostles worked in a cosmopolitan culture where libraries, scrolls and fragments of papyrus played an important role in circulating ideas. There were an estimated 60,000 Jews living in Rome alone in the first century and it would have been in the interest of the growing church to go to press sooner rather than later. Jesus had, after all, given them a universal mission and they would have had no justification for keeping it to themselves and this would even have countermanded their mission. In the light of this, how could a late dating be accounted for?

Secondly, the major event for Jews during the first century was not the fall of Jerusalem but the destruction of the Temple in AD 70 and with it the whole sacrificial system existing since the time of Moses

1400 years before. Writing any text in a Jewish context after this catastrophe without mentioning it would be like writing a history of modern America without reference to 9/11 and the Twin towers. However, there is not the slightest hint of this in all the New Testament, a remarkable thing indeed, particularly because the cessation of sacrifices would have been a prime argument for the superiority of the gospel. For this reason, even the liberal Bishop of Woolwich, John A.T. Robinson, of *Honest to God* fame, dated the fourth gospel between 40 and 65 and the Revelation of John in 68.

Earlier dating implies that apostolic authorship or supervision is possible for all of the books of the New Testament. In fact there are no real reasons why the apostles should not have started recording their memories of Jesus immediately after his death. It has been suggested recently that Matthew's Gospel could have been written much earlier than AD 40.

After Jerusalem was destroyed, in the last decade of the first century, two collections of Christian writings were in circulation: the fourfold gospel and the other writings, mainly the epistles of Paul. This was the first step toward a canonical collection beyond the recognition of each individual book by those who received it.

However, canonisation was a long process. Other comparable Christian texts existed and why they were not recognised as canonical is a valid question. For instance, Clement of Rome (perhaps mentioned in Philippians 4:3) wrote a letter to the church at Corinth that some historians date as early as AD 69 and others before the end of the century. This letter was included with the New Testament writings in an important collection of texts, the Codex Alexandrinus in the fifth century. Two other ancient Christian texts, the *Shepherd of Hermas* written largely by one of the Apostolic fathers and the *Epistle of Barnabas* (probably not by

Suggested Datings of New Testament Books

Matthew, 40; Mark, 45; Galatians, 48; 1 Thessalonians, 50; Luke, 54; 1 and 2 Corinthians, 55–6; Romans, 57; Timothy and Titus, 57–61; Philemon, 58; Philippians, 60–61; Acts, 62. Following John Wenham, *Redating Matthew, Mark and Luke*, London, Hodder and Stoughton, 1991.

the Barnabas of Acts) were included in the *Codex Sinaiticus* in the third century. These writings date from after the biblical texts but they bear witness to the growing amount of Christian and heretical literature in the post-apostolic generation.

Distinguishing the authentic from the spurious was a long haul and it involved a fallible church in all kinds of ecclesiastical meanderings.

HOW AND WHEN THE CANON CAME INTO EXISTENCE. A middle course must be steered between two extremes. On the one hand, it is easy to forget the complexity of the historical situation and maintain that a consensus has always existed implicitly in the church on the subject of canon. If this is the case concerning some texts, the question of the peripheral ones remains, to say nothing of a multitude of others claiming authority, often by using the names of the original apostles or even Judas! On the other hand, it would be wrong to claim that all the texts had equally valid claims to being accepted in the canon, just because they existed and were ancient. As the New Testament scholar Herman Ridderbos once remarked, the history of the canon is the process of the growing consciousness of the church concerning its biblical foundation.

Three reasons in particular forced upon the church the need to determine the extent of the canon. Firstly, others were doing it, not least the heretic Marcion who established his own list and published it in Rome around AD 140. Marcion rejected the Old Testament and produced a list made up of Luke's gospel and ten of Paul's epistles, all edited to his liking. Secondly, in the Eastern churches some biblical texts such as Revelation or Hebrews were rejected, because heretics had latched onto them, whereas other spurious texts were being used in worship. Finally, in 303 the emperor Diocletian issued an edict ordering the destruction of the sacred Christian books, which demanded differentiation between the various texts.

Looking backwards from the present, the first church assembly to list the 27 books of the New Testament was the synod of Hippo in 393, confirmed by the synod of Carthage four years later. Prior to that, the first complete list of books resembling our New Testament is found in a letter to the churches written by Athanasias of Alexandria in AD 357. A little later Jerome and Augustin indicated that the canon is made up of 27 books. Much earlier, the writings of Irenaeus, who became Bishop of Lyons in 180, indicated the uniqueness of the apostolic tradition. Irenaeus named 20 of the 27 books and he denied that revelatory truth exists outside these writings. This is significant as Irenaeus was a disciple of Polycarp from Asia Minor who himself had been a disciple of John. Polycarp and Clement in their writings quoted the Old and New Testament books prefixing them with the phrase 'as it is said in the scriptures'. Justin Martyr (100–165) refers to the reading of the apostles and the writings of the prophets during Sunday services. Ignatius in one of his letters used the phrase 'I do not wish to command you as Peter and Paul did because they were apostles'.

Because of the difference in character between the apostolic scriptures and other writings, which was clear from the beginning, and because of the Marcion effect, the contents of the New Testament were generally recognised by the last quarter of the second century, even if there was some indecision about the smaller books of the New Testament. Since Carthage, the canon has not been seriously called into question in the Christian church, although Martin Luther's doubts about the book of James and the epistle of Hebrews are well known. On this question, he let his theological assumptions overrule his biblical discernment, and even these unfortunate ideas did not lead him to question the notion of canon.

Finally, if it is evident that the canon cannot be demonstrated by historical arguments or even by the direct affirmations of the

Some New Testament Apocrypha (Approximate Dates)

1. Orthodox Christian texts include: The Epistle of (pseudo) Barnabas (AD 69–100), The Gospel according to the Hebrews (60–100), Epistle to the Corinthians (96), Shepherd of Hermas (96–115), The Epistles of Ignatius (100), The Didiche, or the Teaching of the Twelve (100–120), Epistle of Polycarp to the Philippians (110).

2. Heretical or Gnostic texts include: The Apocryphon of John, The Gospel of Thomas, Sophia Jesu Christi, Gospel of Truth, Gospel of Philip, Gospel of Peter, Gospel of Judas and many more…

New Testament texts, the notion of canon is fully consistent with the biblical idea that Christ is the foundation of his church, that this foundation is laid by the apostolic witnesses and that the church rests on it as being divine revelation. The New Testament Scriptures are the result of Jesus' word to Peter: 'You are Peter and on this rock I will build my church' (Matt. 16:18).

Theology of the Canon

A theological understanding of the canon beyond a description of the process of canonisation seeks to establish an overview of the factors that contribute to the notion of canon. Three important elements can be indicated: the rule or kingdom of God established through God's saving acts, the covenant that organises the life of the covenant people in relation with God and the texts themselves that are expressions of the covenant.

Modern approaches to the question of canon concerning both Testaments have been plagued by the idea that the limitation of the canon was essentially a human act. After much conflict and hesitation, a hitherto open canon was closed by the situation of consensus that had developed. Progress to this culminating point is often reconstructed along the lines of an evolutionary view of historical development.

Another perspective altogether has been presented in this chapter. The formation of the canon was a divine act because the words of God were given in inscripturated texts. The canon was formed by the appearance of one document after another and each bore the stamp of divine authority.

But what is the reason for the existence of these texts? Scripture appears at climactic moments in the history of divine redemption: when God calls Abraham, at the Exodus, to warn of the exile judgment, to restore his people and to give messianic promises for the future. The covenant is renewed in its final form because salvation is complete in Christ. In other words, when God intervenes in history on behalf of his people, his acts are accompanied by divine words in covenantal texts.

The origin of the Old Testament canon is found historically when God's people come into existence. God made a treaty with them at Sinai, a covenant of a verbal nature found in Exodus and Deuteronomy. The continuing history of God's dealings with Israel is recounted in the canonical texts that lead up to the appearing of God's final salvation. With its accomplishment in Christ, revelation is once again sealed verbally by the canonical texts of the New Testament. God's kingdom and rule are administered by his covenant and his covenant is sealed by texts that bind God and his people to each other. The Bible *is* the old and new covenant between God and his people and it is their only rule.

Today the canon is closed because there are no new acts of God to be recorded. Since Pentecost there are no fresh divine acts of salvation in the world. The regular work of the Holy Spirit in regeneration and sanctification unites God's people with Jesus Christ, their Lord. The church manifests the presence of the kingdom through the preaching of the gospel and the practice of the two sacraments given by Jesus.

God acted once for all in Christ; nothing more can be added to this because salvation is complete. The only new page of the history of redemption that lies in the future is the coming of Christ in glory to fulfil the promise of the Scripture, a promise that will hold good to the end of the age.

14

Reading the Bible

The point of this chapter is not to discuss modern theories and methods of biblical interpretation or hermeneutics, but to give a few practical pointers about reading the Bible. We will begin with something basic before becoming more specific.

What Kind of Reader Are You?

There may well be 57 varieties of Bible readers because there seem to be as many interpretations as there are readers. Is there any way out of this labyrinth?

Despite this impression, there are four fundamental types of Bible readers, leaving aside those who are simply disinterested or dismissive of the Bible.

Reader A feels that it is all a bit beyond them. Like the Ethiopian eunuch in Acts (8:26–40) who asked Philip how he could understand Isaiah if no one explained it to him, Reader A needs a helping hand. Honesty is not a bad policy; recognising that we are all at sea will at least encourage us to hope for a lifeboat. Sometimes we need help, and we should seek it from people like Philip who can teach us.

Reader B, on the contrary, has got it all sorted and is convinced of being right on almost everything. B is unteachable, a self-satisfied know-it-all and rather intolerant of people who think differently. B invariably has hobbyhorses that are ridden hard—subjects like Israel, discerning the times, predestination, spiritual gifts, worship or what bread should be used in the Lord's supper. Dogmatism means B wins debates and loses audiences.

Reader C is like a labourer on a construction site. A foundation has been put down and progress has been made, but there is still a long way to go and things are only 'known in part' (1 Cor. 13:9). Reader C tends to be modest about his achievements, is open to learning and will adopt as a principle that if anyone imagines that they know, then they don't know as they should (1 Cor. 8:2).

Reader D is a different kettle of fish altogether, the exact opposite of Reader B. For D there are many ways of reading the Bible and they're all legit. What's important is to be sincere about it. The line taken will be the following: 'that's your way of reading the Bible, but it's not mine'. If you want to talk about what the Bible means, or about its truth, you should always add 'from my way of looking at it'. A text may be as plain as pikestaff but D, not content with what it clearly says, will always be able to find another meaning than the one that is perfectly obvious.

D has a totally different approach from the other three readers and will not accept that there is any ultimate truth in the Bible, since everything is relative. Truth is not really distinguishable from error and every view is in some sense valid. D will not recognise that truth has limits and that what is outside these limits is wrong, at least not in the realm of belief. Finally, the idea that there is no ultimate truth will itself become an ultimate truth, even above the Apostles Creed, which everyone understands in their own way.

These cases illustrate that reading the Bible involves prior personal attitudes that fashion our expectations and hopes.

Great Expectations?

What we basically believe about the Bible affects the way we read it. Do we have great expectations or not? There is an enormous difference of attitude between someone who believes that the Bible is purely human, as D no doubt does, and A, B and C who believe it to be the inspired word of God.

Reader D will not expect there to be much coherence in the Bible and will be sniffy about looking for any harmony in it. Its texts are thought to be coloured by a diversity of authors and the times when they were written. The Bible will probably be understood to be a venerable artefact from the past, without much to contribute in the present. The most one might hope for would be some pearls of wisdom gleaned from sages of old, but one would not necessarily expect to find any ultimate truth about God or anything bearing directly on the way we think and live today. Reader D's expectations are rather low, so the role the Bible has in her life is probably rather marginal, perhaps even mystical. Members of Alcoholics Anonymous will attach more practical value to their 'Big Book' than reader D does to the Bible.

Readers A, B and C, despite their different attitudes, will entertain high hopes when opening the Bible. If this is God's inspired word over and above the diversity of the human authors, they will expect to find a unity of development in its story line and also a consistency in its teaching, even though some high points stand out in the landscape. A, B and C will seek to find principles for life, they will have expectations about how this book fashions thinking and living. If our individual lives are stories lived in different times and places, with changing scenes of trouble or joy, the big picture of sin and salvation that the Bible paints will provide a key to how to live as a Christian.

A Question of Attitude

Even though expectations count for a lot, in and of themselves they do not provide the actual tools that allow us to assimilate the Bible's message or 'rightly handle the word of truth' as the expression goes (2 Tim. 2:15). Right belief about the status of the Bible does not ensure correct understanding of it and even less does it justify slovenly interpretation.

Many people who do believe the Bible to be God's word do not show the requisite common sense when they read it. In fact they do not always have a method when they read the Bible, so their understanding is a hit and miss affair. For instance, some people believe that the Jerusalem temple will be rebuilt but few, in my experience, ever ask why there's nothing about this in the New Testament. They simply take references in the Old Testament that concern the rebuilding of the second temple in the time of Ezra, Nehemiah, Haggai and Zachariah and jump into the future from our present standpoint. This shows they have not really reflected about the history of salvation as a whole and in fact it plays little part in the way they approach the Bible.

So great expectations do not lead automatically to great results. Once I stayed a few days with some kind people in North America who had a small plastic loaf in their kitchen with 366 flash cards bearing the legend 'Daily Bread'. Every day at breakfast a card with an inspiring verse was extracted from the loaf. Biblical insight was dispensed via random verses lifted out of context.

The Bible has many inspiring verses, but I could not help thinking that much the same effect could have been produced with words from the works of Confucius or perhaps the Buddhist Scriptures. Although these people derived comfort from this practice, was the Bible meant to be used in this way? After all, God did not have to give us a book; if he had so wished he could have sent us brief and stimulating flashes like Pascal's *Thoughts*. However, God did choose a collection of books to reveal himself and for that reason it is difficult to think that the form of the Bible is purely incidental. It must be respected for what it is and read in accordance.

One of the things that never ceases to astonish is the great number of Christians who seem clueless about this and twist and turn the words of Scripture with pirouettes worthy of the Bolshoi ballet. Some people seem to be past masters in getting the weirdest ideas out of Scripture, totally perverting its clear sense and real meaning. We take far too many liberties with Scripture. No-holds barred Bible-studies are sometimes forums for what John or Jane Doe think, rather than what Scripture says in and of itself.

The fact, however, that the Bible was inspired with this chosen form tells us something important about it. When we read it, whether on the printed page, the iPhone or the computer screen, these are words inspired in a context designed by God. We can make sense of them only in that context and not in any other way. They are inspired there and not anywhere else.

For instance, the phrase 'all things work together for good' taken out of context can be used totally illegitimately. Once a woman said those words to me from a hospital bed. She was, unbeknown to her, dying of cancer without any apparent hope of eternity. Taken out of the context of Romans 8:28 the words had a different spin altogether, because she was thinking about getting well again. The meaning of that biblical phrase is determined by its context in that particular verse, by its place in Romans 8, which speaks about the unshakeable reasons Christians have for assurance of salvation in Christ, and in the broader context of the gospel that is the theme of Romans. 'Good' in Romans 8:28 doesn't mean that everything in this life will always turn out as we hope.

These considerations lead us to think about three fundamental aspects about what we are doing when we read the Bible: the basic rules, the principles they imply and the actual practices that arise from them both.

Basic Rules

When reading the Bible there are three basic rules to observe and these can also apply to other books to a lesser extent. They can be called the natural, the original and the general senses of the text. The first takes the words before us in their natural meaning, the second concerns what the authors meant by them and the third concerns how one part of the Bible may throw light on other parts.

God speaks to us in human words and these three rules say something about his character. We would expect God to speak clearly and intelligibly, to speak first and foremost to his chosen audience and to do so without obscuring the issues. Let's look at these basic rules in more detail, before moving on to some more general principles and practices.

The Natural Meaning

Sometimes people take it for granted that the Bible is inherently contradictory and so complex that getting at its meaning is impossible for the average punter. Look at the differences over the questions of baptism, the Lord's supper, church government or even the theories about the atonement, they say, implying that the Bible as a whole must be equally obscure. No one will deny that there are important differences on those issues, but there is a world of difference between the complexity of theological interpretations and the simplicity of Scripture and the two should not be confused.

For instance, when Jesus said 'I and my Father are one' or when he instituted the Lord's supper by saying 'this is my body' the words themselves are of an extreme simplicity and clear as a mountain stream. What we make of them is something else. The fact that there are differences of theological opinion does not mean that Scripture itself is not amazingly simple in its words and combinations of words.

When God, in his revelation, spoke to men through human witnesses he adopted not the highly technical language of academia, but common or garden talk. Ordinary language with its accepted rules of grammar, syntax and vocabulary present little difficulty to the average reader. When God spoke through human persons he used everyday language to speak of the most elevated subjects.

This baffles some people, but it implies that fundamentally the same literary rules are used to understand the Bible as are used to understand other books. Reading the Bible requires respect for its literary form and in particular its Jewish, Middle-Eastern origin. Did Jesus ever mean his hearers to pull out their eyes, cut off their arms, or give away their coats to enter heaven? An uncle of mine, a hardened atheist, tried to convince me when I was young that it was impossible to be a Christian because you never see Christians giving their coats away. Beyond his spiritual hostility to the Bible, he had no idea that the oriental mentality tends to repetition and exaggeration and that Jesus, who was not speaking to modern Europeans, used hyperbole to impress spiritual truth on his hearers.

What is literal in the Bible is to be taken literally, what is figurative is to be taken figuratively, the historical historically, the symbolic symbolically, the allegorical allegorically and parables as parables. Maybe there would be fewer discussions about the meaning of the 1000-year millennium of Revelation if its highly symbolic literary context were respected. Apart from the fact that the 1000 years are in heaven and not on earth, do we really think that the devil is literally chained in a pit for that duration, or that Christ will return on a white horse with a sword coming from his mouth? These are a literary litmus paper for understanding what we see in Revelation 19–20.

The true meaning of Scripture is its natural and obvious meaning. When the question is asked—how do we know if something is to be taken literally or not?—the answer is, by taking it like it is naturally. The meaning is then perfectly clear to those who want to understand, apart from those people who have an axe to grind by forcing everything into a literal or an allegorical straightjacket.

The Original Meaning

Secondly, the Bible should be read in its original sense, with an eye to what the authors meant in their context. It means what it meant for the authors when it was penned. What they wanted to say should not be eclipsed by our response to what we read, that is, what we want it to mean or feel it can mean today. Ideally, there should be no contradiction between what it meant for them and what it means for us today, although the way we apply it might be different from what they envisaged.

For instance, 'you shall not kill' is a commandment that aims at preserving the sanctity of life. When it was given, or repeated in different biblical contexts, the writers were not thinking of abortion, euthanasia or even 'character assassination'. Nor were they thinking about war, although many people take it to mean that. They were articulating a principle that might have a different bearing in new situations. What is important is the principle involved that can be applied to another context. The danger is for us to use our cultural perspective as a filter that imposes the tyranny of the present on what the Bible says.

So the question of the original sense indicates the importance of what the authors meant in their time, geographical location and cultural environment. What did they want to say and what did it originally mean for the people who heard it? What was said then may or may not apply to us directly. For example, many Christians take Jesus' promise of the Holy Spirit's coming: 'he will guide you into all the truth' (John 16:13), to apply to all Christians including ourselves. And so people say God promises to lead *me* into all truth today, I think this or that is true and it must be the work of the Spirit in my life. However, this does not consider that Jesus said these words to the disciples alone, just as when he said they must not worry about what to say when they were hauled before tribunals. What Jesus promised is that through the disciples, soon to be apostles, the Holy Spirit would lead his people into the truth. Jesus in fact said that the church receives the truth from the apostolic witness and that this is the foundation of the Christian community.

The Meaning of the Whole

Finally, we must be sensitive to the general sense of the Bible as a whole. From a simply human perspective, the Bible may seem to be a pick and mix of different people speaking in different times and places. However, contrary to appearances, the divine inspiration of Scripture assures us that it springs from one divine mind. The general sense of Scripture gives one tune even if it is played by a variety of instruments. The principle of harmony underlies any sound approach to God's word. We can understand one text by means of another because they are fundamentally complementary.

When, in 1561, Mary Queen of Scots had a private audience with the Scots reformer John Knox she remarked that he said one thing but the cardinals and the pope said another. Who is to be believed? Here is a paraphrase of Knox's reply:

> Believe God who speaks plainly in his word: and further than the word teaches, don't believe anyone. The word of God is plain in itself; and if there appears to be any obscurity in one

place, the Holy Spirit, who never contradicts himself, will explain the thing more clearly in other places.

So a proper understanding of Scripture requires the intra-biblical context to be added to the linguistic and historical contexts. Reading Scripture by the light of Scripture provides a system of checks and balances that help avoid misunderstanding.

Knox said three things about how this works:

- the Bible makes itself clear on its own terms;
- because of the Spirit's witness, we can expect to find a harmony of meaning;
- what is less clear is explained in other texts that are clearer.

The principle that the part is to be understood by the whole and that in the global perspective what is most clear functions as a guide for what is obscure will not lead us up the garden path. It will encourage us to seek to iron out discrepancies rather than blowing up the first problem out of proportion and declaring, 'Look! A mistake in the Bible'.

It is no mystery that most of the errors or major heresies found in church history or in sectarian movements find their origin in neglect of the principle of the harmony of Scripture. They can be divided into three categories.

Firstly, there are errors that come from taking an obscure text and making it into a major doctrine. For instance, the baptism of the dead practiced by Mormons, the 144,000 true believers of the Jehovah's witnesses, or the bizarre practice of snake handling found in the southern United States.

Secondly, problems arise because the progression of the Old to the New Testament is incorrectly understood. Examples might be the continuation of worship on the Jewish Saturday rather than on the first day of the week or the practice of polygamy. If the structure of development in the history of salvation is correctly observed this will foster a balanced view of the relationship between the two testaments and how Christ represents an accomplishment of things hoped for. This will help us to see, for example, that when

Christ is said to be the 'end (*telos*) of the law' in Romans this does not mean that he abolished it and that God's law has no place in the Christian life, but that he fulfilled it as its true embodiment.

Finally, logical errors occur when one series of biblical texts is selected and taken as telling the whole story about an issue without considering complementary texts. People find it hard to reconcile divine sovereignty and human responsibility so they plump for one strain of texts and minimise the other. Or they cannot accept the idea of God becoming man in the incarnation and they take the texts concerning Christ's divinity to be mythical and retain those that speak of his humanity. The principle of harmony encourages us to affirm one and the other even if we are called to recognise that logically speaking the result is paradoxical. But if the paradox is biblical it must be respected. We are not to forget that what is a paradox for us stems from our limited intelligence and could be easily reconciled in an infinite intelligence. The Bible tells us God's intelligence is infinite and a divine mind could know of links whose existence we do not even suspect.

Developing Skills

The Bible is the word of God, divine revelation, and it is revelation in the form God gave it. To hear its message we must learn to listen by developing some basic skills.

If the Bible is like other books because it is written in human language, it is also God's word, and as such we expect it to be different from other books. God speaks in Scripture and it is His word. For this reason the following considerations are important to our understanding.

It is important to realise that when we open Scripture we are coming into God's presence and that we cannot understand it without his help. Practically this means that:

- we must remember that the text of the Bible and its meaning belong first of all to its divine author;

- God spoke directly to men in specific situations to reply to their needs;
- the Bible is to be read not as an intellectual exercise but so as to hear God's enduring message for us today.

The word of God is destined for his people. It exists for the specific purpose that they may find forgiveness and communion with him.

- reading the Bible properly means letting it explain itself on its own terms;
- it does not exist to satisfy our curiosity, but to reply to our spiritual needs;
- the Bible is given to God's people and its message is to be received with others in a spirit of mutual exhortation;
- our best reply to its message is when we apply it to our lives and pray to be able to live it out.

From Genesis to Revelation is a long haul, but the scenery is harmonious, and can be described by one dominant feature, that is, the promise 'I will be your God, you will be my people'.

When we read the Bible our understanding is helped:

- by looking for what is new in this particular text concerning the covenant between God and his people;
- seeing this point in the light of the centre, the person of Jesus himself;

Pointers

The Bible is a book in which a person speaks to us. God reveals himself.

It presents God's covenant with his people and tells how he promised salvation in Jesus Christ.

Its doctrines are embedded in historical events. God intervened to save his people; the Bible talks of our salvation too.

God speaks to us so that we can speak and act as believers.

- asking how a particular text looks forward to his coming or back to his earthly ministry in the light of his second coming;
- by reading the Old Testament in the light of the New Testament fulfilment.

Some Things to Look for

If God, as we have claimed, is the author of the inspired word, He is also its only faithful interpreter, the only one who has an understanding of the whole and who can guide us in our reading of Scripture. The meaning is ultimately his and we only understand it in a secondary sense. A right understanding is one that is in line with divine truth as revealed in the whole of Scripture. It is correct when it approximates to the divine mind and is appropriated on our human level. We recognise that our interpretations are never the whole story, but they can be legitimate and they can be checked by what Scripture says.

Pointer

The Christian faith makes a definite claim to authority and this refers primarily to the authority of God. God himself is the originator of Scripture and its ultimate author. Because of this, the Bible also indicates the conditions of its own interpretation.

The key to the meaning of Scripture is therefore in Scripture itself and when we pay attention to it, the meaning becomes increasingly apparent to us. The following provides five considerations that can be borne in mind as we read the Bible.

ALL THE BIBLE INTERPRETS THE BIBLE. Because Scripture is divinely inspired it constitutes a whole. As with a car engine, all its parts are designed to work together and each has its importance for the running of the whole. Similarly, the teachings of Scripture are designed to work together. For example Genesis 1:1 is best understood when John 1:1, 1 John 1:1 and other texts that speak about the creation, such as Hebrews 1:1–2, are read together. The Bible comments on its own meaning. For example, king David's unfaithfulness recounted in 1 Samuel 21 and 22 and its consequences are commented upon by David himself in Psalms 52, 54, 56, 57.

THE BIBLICAL AUTHORS WERE 'BIBLE' READERS TOO. None of the biblical writers wrote in a vacuum, nor did they write off the top of their heads. They refer to those who went before them. Even Jesus backed up his teaching with the Old Testament when he said that all the Scripture spoke of him. Like the apostle Paul, Jesus had a profound understanding of Scripture and it nourished his human development (Luke 2:42). Reading Isaiah 1 or Jeremiah 2 illustrates how the writers related to existing texts. Both of these prophets apply the words God gave in the books of Moses to speak about Israel. Isaiah even calls Israel 'Sodom'. Or in the New Testament, the book of James makes constant reference to the sayings of Jesus and in particular the Sermon on the Mount. The book of Hebrews can hardly be understood without knowing about Melchizedek who as a type of Christ is superior to the Levitical priests.

PROMISE AND FULFILMENT. The basic structure of the Bible, as one would expect with an ongoing story, is one of progression. It is God's promises that create the dynamic of the story as they are fulfilled in stages. We find this in the bigger features, such as the Old Testament having its fulfilment in the New, but also in smaller stages. The exodus from Egypt fulfills the promise to Abraham, the covenant with David fulfills the promises given to Moses and the whole is fulfilled in Christ, as Hebrews 1:1ff. clearly states. The ultimate fulfilment is found in the work of Christ on the cross. When he said 'it is finished (or accomplished)', Jesus meant that not only his earthly work was at an end, but also that the Old Testament and its repeated promise of salvation is fulfilled in his person. He has done all that was required by God for salvation (see Heb. 9:15–28). Because salvation is complete in Christ, then in him also the promises God gave for his people to Abraham are also fulfilled, as Peter said in his speech on the day of Pentecost (Acts 2). If the New Testament fulfils the Old, then when we read the Old Testament we will look for how it is taken up in the New. A useful chapter to study on this theme is 1 Corinthians 10.

JESUS AT THE CENTRE. In all its parts the Bible speaks of Jesus, his person and work of salvation and we should look for him everywhere in the things that lead up to him and from him. To do this we consider the things in the life of Israel that prefigure him, but are never in themselves complete. We see how the prophets, priests and kings pointed to him, as he is the one who represents those things par excellence (see Matt. 12—he is more kingly than Solomon, more prophetic than Jonah and greater than the temple). Even if it is not always evident that Christ is found everywhere in Scripture, we can understand that he is the principal actor in the history of salvation and he is the one who is prefigured throughout it all. In the New Testament it is he who speaks to his people via the apostles as they bear witness to him (cf. Luke 24:13–48).

THE BIBLE ALONE. Scripture alone is the divine standard for faith and life and as such it is a closed norm. Nothing more can be added to it, neither apocryphal books nor church traditions. Any outside information or methods of reading the Bible are at best only aids. Nor can external information or new approaches to questions of interpretation ever make the Bible say the opposite of what was intended by the original authors. Three useful questions can be asked in this perspective:

- If this text were not in the Bible, how would it change my understanding of what I should believe?
- What does this text contribute concretely to what I believe?
- How is this biblical text important for me?

Pointers

'For whatever was written in the former days, was written for our instruction, that through endurance and through the encouragement of the Scriptures we might have hope' (Rom. 15:4).

'Concerning this salvation, the prophets who prophesied about the grace that was to be yours searched and enquired carefully, enquiring what person or time the Spirit of Christ in them was indicating when he predicted the sufferings of Christ and the subsequent glories. It was revealed to them that they were serving not themselves but you, in the things that have now been announced to you through those who preached the good news to you by the Holy Spirit sent from heaven, things into which angels long to look' (1 Pet. 1:10–12).

What to Do?

The fundamental fact about reading the Bible is that it provides its own key to unlock its meaning and the Holy Spirit applies its truths to our hearts. Our receptivity to the truth of the word therefore matters more than a simply intellectual understanding of what it says, but we can ask questions to help us get to its truth.

ABOUT THE TEXT ITSELF...

- What kind of text is it— is it poetry, history, wisdom, prophecy or a didactic passage?
- Where did it come from (time, place, author), what does it refer to in the past and point to in the future?
- How does it speak about Jesus and God's salvation?

REGARDING OURSELVES...

- What should I think and believe about God and Jesus Christ?
- What is my own situation and standing before God?
- What are my needs, insufficiencies, doubts, fears or sins?

FINDING REASONS FOR PRAYER AND PRAISE...

- What should I pray for after reading this text?
- What can I share from it with those closest to me?

CONFESSING THE AUTHORITY OF SCRIPTURE...

- What ought I to do in trust and obedience?
- What needs to change in my life because of this?
- What 'cross' am I called to bear today and what should I do?
- The key : 'If you love me keep my commandments...'

RECOGNISING THE TRUTH OF SCRIPTURE...

- How can I honour God in my thoughts?
- Am I conformed to the world's way of thinking?
- What needs to change?

WALKING THE WALK...

- Seek not only the Spirit's guidance but also desire that the word of God might be ever more present in shaping your life.
- Make it your aim that your life itself, in all its aspects, become like a prayer of thankfulness offered to God and that the Scripture might provide the foundation for this.
- Remember that God is the God of encouragement and hope and he gave the Scriptures so that we could put them to use. He is the God of life and his intention is that we live by them.

The Real Problem

Finally, when people refer to the fact that there are a great many interpretations of the Bible, some of which make opposite claims about its meaning, they often do so in a 'divide and rule' spirit. Their claim arises from self-interest and conveniently forgets two basic things.

Firstly, problems with the meaning of Scripture often come not from the text itself but from the meanings brought to Scripture and imposed upon it. We invariably have difficulties climbing down from the pedestal of arguments we have defended or views we have espoused and this prevents us from being open-minded about what the Bible teaches. We don't *want* it to accept something other than what we are comfortable with.

Secondly, we too often succumb to the current wisdom of the day without realising it. We accept the ideas around us rather uncritically. One of the most prevalent pieces of conventional wisdom is that human beings are inherently good and that we are doing the best we can. The latest is the best, something better lies ahead and people in the past, including the writers of the Bible, were rather unenlightened. Whether it concerns the way we live or the theories we adopt because they are accepted in our schools or work, we hold present knowledge in high esteem. To confess the truth of Scripture unabashedly is costly, un-politically correct and involves a loss of kudos. Christians are often tempted to live in two worlds, the biblical one with its norms and the modern one with its 'self-evident truths'. We negotiate endless compromises between the two worlds. This leads us to look for the most plausible solution to what the Bible means in terms of current humanistic values. When we do so, we wander unconsciously away from the truth.

These two factors highlight the fact that the problem is not with Scripture at all, but with us and our susceptibility to peer pressure. The product is a form of religion that may have the name 'christian', but is not the full packet of crisps. Our western world is awash with a churchianity that has little to do with Christianity or Scripture, but which makes people feel comfortable because it never challenges a thing they think. When this is the case, what is missing from the picture amounts to far more than what one might have. Who wants instant coffee when you can get an espresso?

There is nothing more exhilarating than opening Scripture and having *God's truth* jump right at you off the page. Who can know how much we would progress in the knowledge and the love of God if instead of putting up the barricades we were unreservedly open and applied it consistently in our daily lives?

15

Sola Scriptura, the Bible Alone

The Latin expression *sola Scriptura* is used to indicate that the Bible *alone* is an authority over all others for the faith and life of Christians and the church. Sometimes this is called 'the Scripture principle'.

The sixteenth century Reformation restored the principle of *sola Scriptura* which was operative in the church at the beginning. The apostles completed their divinely given task of witnessing to Christ by leaving written Scriptures which together with the Old Testament make up one united revelation from God.

The idea of *sola Scriptura* comes from the Scriptures themselves. Being inspired by God, the Scriptures are sufficient for knowing God, for salvation and for Christian living. They alone are the ultimate authority for the church and for Christians. No independent oral or written tradition can be added to them, either the teachings or the spiritual practices of the church or the so-called 'lost words' of Jesus found in apocryphal gospels. The Scriptures are in a class of their own.

Five 'Alones'

At the time of the Reformation the good news of salvation was summarised by using five 'sola' expressions. Taken together these give a résumé of the essence of Christian faith.

Salvation in all its aspects is attributed to the glory of God alone. It is experienced by faith alone, it is the fruit of grace alone, because of Christ alone and it is known by Scripture alone. We can represent this in a pentagon, with salvation in the centre.

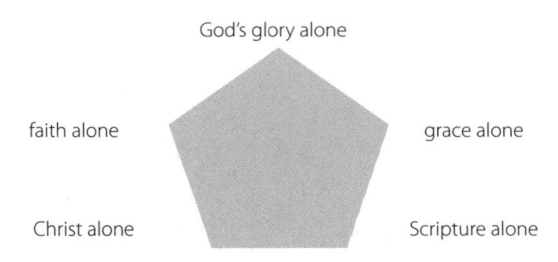

God's glory alone

faith alone

grace alone

Christ alone

Scripture alone

The word 'alone' added to these five factors of salvation points to the primacy of God and the helplessness of human beings to save themselves. God must do it because they can't.

The five factors qualified by the word 'alone' are complementary: if you remove one of them from the equation, the meaning of the others changes. For instance, if you say salvation is not by faith alone but by faith and good works the function of the other four is modified. If faith is not alone then neither can grace, the work of Christ on the cross or Scripture as God's revelation be alone. Man is God's co-worker and is called on everywhere to complete what God initiates. This is sometimes called synergism, that is the 'working together' of two complementary factors. It undermines the *soli deo gloria* that the Reformers fought for.

Today anything claiming to be unique, 'the only one' has difficulty standing up to the onslaught of relativism and may even appear to be dangerous. The five *solas* coined by the Reformation are attacked from all sides.

However, the fundamentals of the Christian faith must stand

against other options. There is only one salvation, as there is one God, one Christ, one grace given and one faith to believe. Scripture is our only way of knowing about any of these unique realities. No one can get to them by natural means from another holy book, through another mediator, or by the offices of a church. There is only one true faith, even if there are many beliefs and false faiths. The Christian message is not a both/and that leaves an open choice. It is unique and stands on its own because its claims rule out alternatives. If we lose this we lose everything. Presenting a broader way is foreign to the Bible approach: and therefore to Christianity. The apostle Paul had no complexes when he rejected the other gospel competing against 'the one we preached to you' (Gal. 1:7, 10).

People today don't like that attitude much and some think it encourages fundamentalistic attitudes and an intolerance of others that wants to set the world right. On the contrary: the 'alones' belong to God and cannot be implemented by any other means. They teach us to trust in God and to be critical of the usefulness of any human works and actions, even ours. The best argument ever against intolerance is that we can't do anything to change others, only God can. That is why Christ said, 'my kingdom is not of the world' and that those that take the sword will perish by it (John 18:36, Matt. 26:52).

Sola Scriptura in History

Roman catholic theologian Yves Congar has stated that since the Council of Trent in the sixteenth century the Roman Catholic Church has taught the insufficiency of Scripture. Revelation is contained partly in Scripture and partly in tradition. The second Vatican council in its *Constitution on Divine Revelation* went as far as to use the expression 'holy tradition' (11, 8).

The Reformers' quarrel was not with the early church, although they recognised its insufficiencies, but primarily with medieval theology. The early Church Fathers held to the principle of *sola Scriptura*, defending the faith against heresies without appeal to tradition. When, in the second century, Irenaeus and Tertullian used the notion of apostolic tradition to refer to the teaching handed down in the church in oral form, they understood it as being secondary to Scripture and acceptable only because it was found in Scripture. To back up their teaching they appealed to Scripture. Irenaeus of Lyon in his work *Against Heresies* stated:

> We have learned the plan of our salvation from none other than those through whom the gospel has come down to us. At one time they proclaimed it in public and at a later moment, by the will of God, they handed it down to us in the Scriptures, to be the ground and pillar of our faith.

Tradition was not considered as something that supplemented Scripture, but as something that coincided with it in the faithful teaching of the church. Appeals were not made to traditions independently of Scripture.

Later, in the fourth century, Gregory of Nyssa was representative of current opinion and practice when he stated: 'We make the Holy Scriptures the rule and the measure of every tenet; we necessarily fix our eyes upon that, and approve that alone which may be made to harmonise with the intention of those writings.'

This is the fundamental principle the Reformers sought to restore over against the corruption that non-biblical traditions had introduced into the church over the years.

In his famous defence against Eck at the diet of Worms (1521), Martin Luther set the 'infallible word of God' over against tradition:

> Unless I am convinced by the testimonies of Scripture or evident reason—for I believe neither the pope nor councils alone, since it is established that they have often erred and contradicted themselves—I am the prisoner of the Scriptures cited by me, and my conscience has been taken captive by the word of God; I neither can nor will recant anything, since it is neither safe nor right to act against the conscience. God help me. Amen.

The policy of the Reformers concerning Scripture was not one of discovery but one of recovery, in the context of proclaiming a full-orbed biblical gospel.

Scripture Alone and Tradition

Deprived of the *sola*, the status of Scripture inevitably slips from the pedestal on which the Reformers placed it on and junkets with other instances of authority. Authority, as we have seen in chapter 12, is a relational and a hierarchical concept. In the case of Scripture, when the 'alone' is minimised, other factors will be placed on a par with biblical revelation. The gospel will effectively be modified.

This scenario is unhappily current in what passes for Christianity today. The authority of Scripture is severely limited by what is acceptable now and what is done today. Few theologians hesitate to pay formal lip-service to the authority of the Bible, but how many have the audacity to affirm *sola Scriptura* in the classical sense? The way the Bible is used shows that there is a general shift from a 'hard' to a 'soft' form of authority and that the authority attributed to Scripture is of variable nature.

The evangelical view of Scripture stands in isolation from other views in so far as its doctrine of the authority of Scripture implies a vibrant 'Scripture alone'. Unfortunately evangelicals do not always live up to their standards and are as susceptible as other people to the tyranny of political correctness.

Historically, the question of tradition has been a bone of contention between Roman Catholicism and the protestant churches. The difference between the two does not lie in the choice between whether one has traditions or not, which is a common misunderstanding. Everyone has some traditions, and the Reformers were quick to recognise that 'good' practices, ones that have a biblical justification, are to be received and appreciated. The difference is rather as to how tradition functions.

Roman Catholicism's view of tradition is complex. It is far from just being a few teachings or ceremonies that are recognised and authorised by the church and are tacked on to Scripture. Tradition with a capital T can be summed up as being the dynamic truth of God's revelation in Jesus Christ, experienced in the whole life of the church. Tradition concerns the transmission of divine truth by the work of the Holy Spirit in the living body of the church. The definition given in the *Catechism of the Catholic Church*

(1992, Article 2) states that tradition, as distinct from the Scripture itself, is the process by which all that the church represents, and all that she believes in her doctrine, life and worship, is perpetuated in each generation. So what Catholicism is talking about is three things not two: Tradition, Scripture and traditions.

Tradition expresses the fact that God remains ever present and active in the church through the Word and the Holy Spirit. Three stages are recognised. Firstly Christ, the Word, announced the truth of God's revelation by his living presence. The apostles transmitted this truth in their oral proclamation and then later in written form in the inspired Scripture. Finally, the apostolic tradition was relayed through the successors of the apostles, who received their charge from them in order to keep the living truth intact in the church. This final aspect of tradition is distinct from written Scripture but linked to it as the instance through which the truth of Scripture is interpreted and enlarged upon. The fuller sense of the Scripture comes to light in the teaching office of the church and includes teachings and practices that are not found in Scripture but come down through the church as unwritten apostolic traditions.

The force of the Roman position comes from the fact that it claims that tradition in the unwritten sense existed before Scripture and gave birth to the written word. The Bible does not primarily generate traditions nor does it legitimize or discredit them. In a more fundamental way oral tradition gives birth to Scripture and for this reason has priority over it, both in a temporal and logical sense, and this oral tradition continues unbroken in the life of the church. This position is not unattractive to some biblical scholars who spend a good deal of time and energy trying to reconstruct the oral sources behind the New Testament.

The Biblical Meaning of Tradition

It hardly need saying that from a Catholic perspective the protestant *sola Scriptura* is not only invalid but also historically untenable. What then can be made of this seemingly impressive argument?

Firstly, there is a specific biblical reason for not accepting this point of view. In Matthew 28:20 Jesus' mandate to the apostles was to teach all nations 'to observe all that I have commanded you.' In the teaching of those selfsame apostles, historically attested in Scripture and in extra-biblical sources of the time, there is no mention of the things that the Roman catholic church has come to teach over the centuries in her 'constitutive traditions' about the mass, papal infallibility, Mariology, purgatory, etc. These traditions strike us as being light years away from what is contained in Scripture. More seriously, to bind people's consciences with teachings other than those found in Scripture is to go beyond what Jesus himself authorised when he said 'all that I have commanded you'. He did not authorise these teachings and practices.

Secondly, the Catholic notion of tradition does not correspond with the meaning of tradition in the New Testament. For the Church Fathers, tradition (Greek, *paradosis*) meant the revelation made by God through the prophets and apostles. It is not 'handed down' but 'handed over' or 'delivered'. It implies two things—that there is a 'deposit' that is handed over and that there are 'depositaries', those who are in possession of the deposit and who preserve and transmit it. This is the meaning we find in the New Testament itself:

> Maintain the traditions even as I delivered them to you (1 Cor. 11:2);

> Stand firm and hold to the traditions that were taught by us, either by our spoken word or by our letter (2 Thess. 2:15);

> Keep away from any brother who is walking in idleness and not in accord with the tradition that you received from us' (3:6).

The second of these passages shows there was an oral tradition embodied in the apostolic preaching that existed before it was written down. The apostles' preaching preceded the giving of Scripture, which was founded on it. But when the written attestation of revelation came, Scripture itself became the tradition to be handed over. From that point, all tradition outside Scripture, even if it was factually correct, bows to the authority of Scripture and is interpreted by it. The New Testament writings therefore constitute a tradition carefully fixed through inspiration and handed over to the church in order to be its supreme authority. This is a totally different meaning from the Roman one, in which tradition interprets and clarifies Scripture.

Finally, concerning the nature of human traditions. Recognised traditions are always corrupted by the passage of time and things once thought to be essential are rejected or replaced. If God saw fit to inspire Scripture to communicate his truth, no reason can be given as to why God would decide to give one part of his truth by written witness and the rest by a non-written form of tradition. This leads to the question of who decides that some traditions are authoritative and not others. The Roman church attributes this function to the teaching office. However, neither Old or New Testament church leaders were anything other than fallible and often sinful human beings. Inspiration accomplished something that the course of history cannot—it meant that human fallibility and sinfulness were overcome in the giving of the divine word.

The Roman catholic view of tradition gives the church a position and authority that has no biblical warrant.

The Self-Witness of Scripture

Sola scriptura implies that nothing outside of Scripture, neither the church, nor tradition, nor human reason, is required to bear witness to its authenticity. The Scripture bears witness to itself. It is self-authenticating.

The expression 'self-witness of Scripture' is part of the legal tender used to describe two things: what the Bible claims for itself and how this works out in practice in the way we interpret Scripture. It is, however, not immediately obvious what 'self-witness' means or how it contributes to our understanding.

In a sense, all acts of literary or cultural creation are self-witnessing in that they bespeak their character. The cover of some novels would not incite us to bother opening them. A telephone directory is obviously a list of names and is used only to find someone's number. One glance shows it's different from a hymnbook. So what is different about the Bible's self-witness and why is it important?

Historically, 'self-witness', like the *sola Scriptura*, was part of the Protestant polemic armoury used against Roman Catholicism. The Reformers believed you didn't need the church to know the meaning of the Bible or to do the believing for you. However, the idea of the self-witness of Scripture has more to it than that because it is of the essence of Christian faith.

God Is Self-Witnessing

God exists in and of himself. He alone can speak about and for himself; anything we know about God must come from him. This is true only of God. For human beings, if knowledge of who and what we are depends in some way on the extent to which we communicate our thoughts and feelings, that is not all that there is to be said. Our doctor may understand our pain better than we do or a psychiatrist may have more insight into a patient's condition than the person themself.

God, however, is self-evidencing by nature. Our thoughts are not on God's level. 'Proofs' about his existence will not add up to much, because they remain human ideas. Paul summed it up: 'who knows a person's thoughts except the spirit of that person which is in him? So also no one comprehends the thoughts of God except the Spirit of God' (1 Cor. 2:11). God alone can tell us meaningfully about God.

Consequently, as the word of God, the authority of the Bible is self-evidencing or self-authenticating. It impresses itself upon us naturally and we don't need to scrape the barrel of human reasons for arguments in its favour. Paul took the same line as above when he wrote: 'we have received not the spirit of the world, but the Spirit who is from God, that we might understand the things freely given us by God and we impart this in words not taught by human wisdom but taught by the Spirit' (12–13). Things given by God are imparted in words that are convincing because they bear the stamp of the God's Holy Spirit.

The Work of the Word

The self-witness of the word of God is illustrated in Jesus' encounter with the Samaritans recounted in John 4. After his conversation with the Samaritan woman Jesus stayed on with them for two more days. We read: 'And many more believed because of his word. They said to the woman "It is no longer because of what you said that we believe, for we have heard for ourselves and we know that this is indeed the Saviour of the world"' (John 4:41–2).

This striking account of the belief of the Samaritans shows the character of the word of salvation that comes with the gospel. Those who believed did not do so because of some convincing exterior proof coming from the Samaritan woman, from some other authority or from any in-depth theological research they might have done. They had 'heard for themselves' and responded. It was because of the word of Jesus itself that they believed. Its credibility and truth was self-authenticating. Many 'believed because of his word.' What this means is that the witness of Jesus was of such a character that it demanded immediate belief, whoever the hearers were, intellectuals, peasants, rich or poor, ignorant or learned. Christ's word itself called for trust and adequately demonstrated that he was speaking with divine sanction: 'I who speak am the Messiah' (4:26).

The faith that Christ's word called for was an informed belief, not blind faith, a leap in the dark or even an assent to something not fully understood. The word of Christ, like the word of Scripture as a whole, contains its own self-evidencing light. The Samaritans had come to know that Jesus was 'the saviour of the world'. They had exercised what Protestantism later called the 'right of private judgment' on the issue. Understanding Christ's claims they had been moved to faith in him through his word. They heard it for themselves, formed their opinion, and believed. No training in formal logic was required, as the words were clear enough for them. But belief cannot be without the content of the word any more than sight can be without light.

The conclusion that can be drawn from this is that the content of Christ's words demonstrated their own authenticity. The Samaritans needed neither a commentary on the text, the leisure to do some research into the question, nor qualified theologians to believe, because Jesus had made the supreme subject of salvation clear to them. His words were clothed with divine sanction; when the Samaritans honestly pondered them, they understood the demand of faith that was being made of them and believed in Christ. This was not a decision taken lightly; rather the substance of Christ's word produced the desired effects in them. What can be said about Christ's words is no less true of God's inspired witness to himself in revelation.

A final comment can be made, by way of contrast. The word of God is self-witnessing because it is situation-appropriate. The Samaritans understood it applied to them and to their expectations. It fitted them down to the ground. The question might however be raised, in comparison, as to the plight of the Ethiopian returning home from Jerusalem with a precious scroll of Isaiah (Acts 8:26–40). Here was someone who needed help to understand Scripture because he was totally in the dark and couldn't understand what he read. How then can we say that Scripture is self-witnessing in his case?

In a sense, the Ethiopian reading Isaiah in his chariot was in the same position as the Samaritans before they listened to Jesus. When Philip came along 'beginning with this Scripture he told him the good news about Jesus' (35), which is the same good news that Jesus announced to the Samaritans about his being the saviour of the world.

In so far as the Ethiopian is concerned, the Scripture he was reading was self-witnessing to the fact that it was incomplete. He knew something was missing in his understanding and so he was kept in the dark. When the missing pieces were added to the puzzle he understood it straight off, and wanted to be baptised on the spot.

This accounts for another important fact. The self-witness of Scripture is the witness to the whole of Scripture as the word of God. It implies a completed revelation to be a complete witness. Before the coming of Christ the witness of God to himself was not complete; the word of God that had been received, although totally reliable in itself, called for faith in the fulfilment of the promise it contained. Consequently, the self-witness of Scripture exists in harmony with two other aspects of understanding Scripture that the Protestant reformation brought to light, the analogy of Scripture and the idea of *tota Scriptura*—'the Scripture as a whole', to be understood as the word of God in its entirety. The completed canon of Scripture is essential to the notion of self-witness.

The Analogy of Scripture

It's impossible to speak about the self witness of Scripture without speaking about its infallible truth. If Scripture were self-contradictory it could not be a coherent witness about anything. This self-witness implies the notion of the analogy of Scripture.

The analogy of Scripture means that Scripture is understood by comparison with itself, one passage being understood in the light of what is found elsewhere. The self-witness of Scripture implies that to get the whole picture Scripture is compared with Scripture and clarity results from this broader vision. Sometimes this is also called 'the analogy of faith'. Belief in something that arises from one text of Scripture is completed by what is found elsewhere and so the river of faith runs deeper as many more sources flow into it.

For instance, almost everyone knows John 3:16, 'for God so loved the world'. Replete though this text may be, it does not tell us what 'the world' means. We get that from looking at the meaning of this word in a wide variety of contexts. It is a lost, fallen and dark world. It is the sinners who are in this lost situation who are objects of divine love before they even had any knowledge of it. But 'world' is also the created cosmos, God's own universe that he loves and will not abandon to sin. Through God's love in Christ what is lost to God is restored and, as in Romans 8:18–21, the salvation of God's children and the liberation of his creation go together, as both result from the work of Christ. So through the analogy of faith, wide vistas are opened up to enrich our understanding of the greatness of divine love.

Sola Scriptura implies that what is contained in Scripture is related to everything else because of the unity of the word. The biblical landscape contains no erratics. In Scripture there is also a fundamental coherence in the central themes. The analogy of faith is the fundamental perspective derived from *sola Scriptura* that contributes to reading Scripture at all levels, from the simple daily devotion to complex exegesis. When we read any biblical passage we necessarily have some notions, even vague ones, about the meaning of the text. We check, correct and deepen them as we study the word. The analogy of Scripture constitutes an 'outer limit', a final consideration about the well-foundedness of the meaning believed to be found in the text. It is because of the analogy of Scripture that we ultimately reject some interpretations that initially seem possible and attractive.

Both the self-witness and the analogy of faith rest on the ground of the coherence and trustworthiness of Scripture as God's inspired word. All its statements and facts are consistent with each other in their original meaning, if we have interpreted it aright. If this were not so, Scripture would neither be coherent nor trustworthy and there would be incompatible theologies in the New Testament, all claiming to be 'Christian'. However, coherence is valued in Scripture, as can be seen from the confidence of Jesus and his apostles in the unity of the Old Testament message.

There is something captivating about the permanence of God's truth, especially in an age like ours in which doubt and uncertainty have the upper hand.

Progressive Revelation

In practice, what Scripture clearly teaches will be used as a check when we run into more difficult issues as we read the Bible. What is crystal clear serves to illuminate what is more opaque.

The analogy of Scripture is not a static principle, because biblical revelation progressively unfolds divine truth. To be valid, the analogy of faith requires canonical enclosure, the constitution of the well-defined corpus we have described in the preceding chapter, which sets the word of God apart from other writings.

Concretely speaking, a given biblical text can be seen as having several perspectives which create a balance between its own contribution (the writer, the place and the moment) and the rest of the corpus of Scripture. When we read any biblical text we can understand it by moving from the particular to the more general. This can be understood in three stages:

1. the immediate context of the text, the author, the chapter and the book;
2. the interpretation based on the analogy of *antecedent* Scripture and how the author builds on previous revelation;
3. the analogy of *subsequent* revelation, which will bring out deeper meanings, perhaps unimagined by the original author.

This third level may seem artificial in the light of what the original author understood when he wrote the prophetic word. However, subsequent history always throws light on earlier history. Who knew, in 1926, how Hitler would turn out? The perspective of 1945 sheds new light on 1926. Likewise we understand much more about the virgin birth than Isaiah did when he wrote the words of chapter 9 verse 5. If we use the principle of the analogy of Scripture, it will lead us to translate the Hebrew word found there by 'virgin' and not 'young girl'.

Because revelation is progressive, the Old Testament cannot be understood in its full sense if the New Testament interpretations and fulfilments are not considered with it. Our understanding would remain at a 'Jewish' level.

Practically speaking, the analogy of Scripture, in the light of *sola Scriptura*, is a valuable way of reaching a proper understanding of the truth of Scripture in four ways:

- It will eliminate the subjective hunches and flights of fancy that inevitably take over when one text is isolated from the whole of Scripture;
- It will allow for checking and correcting the ideas (our presuppositions) that we bring to Scripture.
- It will shape our expectations, stimulate biblical imagination and allow horizons to be balanced. There is always something new to discover in Scripture, however deep we dig!
- It will encourage patience in looking for the solutions to complex problems rather than facile recourse to ideas such as contradiction and error to explain difficulties.

Finally, the most valuable contribution of the analogy of Scripture is that it is formulated in the context of *faith*. It encourages us to confess the perfect consistency of the revealed word. It enhances Christian discipleship because the Christian walks by faith and not by sight.

Tota Scriptura, the Whole Word

The analogy of Scripture is incomplete if we do not consider the Bible as a whole, *tota Scriptura*. All that is in Scripture contributes to the whole and the whole helps us to understand each part and to appropriate its meaning for ourselves.

The idea of 'all the Scripture' is vital if we are to have a correct view of the 'true truth' of the revealed word. This issue is important today in the light of the upsurge of 'reader-response' approaches to Scripture. These fix a great gulf between the message *of* the text and what is triggered because of how we feel about it. There may be many different reactions to any given text all of which are subjective and arbitrary. Each may claim to have a splinter of truth, but they may be miles away from what the text actually says. So people react in this way: 'I don't like a God who...', 'the apostle Paul was a tyrant', etc.

To most of us, objectivity seems a desirable commodity. However, because of presuppositions, facts are not the same for everyone. They are 'theory-laden' and made to fit in with what makes people 'tick'. How can any objectivity be attained? This is where the notion of 'all the Scripture' comes in.

Two poles can be considered in the light of this question. *Sola Scriptura* implies that no part of Scripture can be ignored. Objectivity is a goal aimed for in the context of *the whole*. All the Scripture is the data base under consideration. Objectivity, getting to the 'real meaning' of Scripture can be best served when interpretation is considered in three stages.

Firstly, the ideas we bring to the text are not infallibly *sufficient* and must be checked against the witness of the whole of Scripture. Sometimes our preconceived notions will be confirmed, sometimes they will have to be modified by allowing Scripture to speak for itself. Any doctrine Scripture is thought to teach is be open to testing, correcting and deepening. We 'travel the feedback circuit' to confirm what Scripture says from the 'whole counsel of God'.

Secondly, our ideas about what the Bible teaches must be tested by comparison with those of others, present and past. The latest ideas are not always the best. What others understood as they wrestled with Scripture in other times is a living witness, not just the stuff of libraries and museums.

Thirdly, we read the whole Scripture today with our questions in mind. We are called to appropriate the meaning of the text in such a way that it acquires an acute significance for our situation, without saying something entirely new and different. *Tota Scriptura* allows the changeless truths of Scripture to be appropriated without turning them on their heads. They are presented in a fresh way, without losing authoritative content. Their absolute nature is reaffirmed.

The Dual Witness of the Spirit

Sola Scriptura finds its necessary expression in the notions of the self-witness, the analogy of Scripture and the importance of considering the context of all the Scripture when we read it.

Taken together these factors make the idea of self-witness quite clear. When we receive and believe the Scripture we do so because it is *God's word*, and not for any other reasons, yet this is not all there is to it. If the Scripture is inherently clear in its self-witness, its truth is received in a saving way by the work of the Holy Spirit. The word itself and the Spirit are two complementary witnesses each of which has its own vital and specific function.

In and of itself, because of its self-witness, Scripture can be seen to be wholly true. But only the Holy Spirit impresses this truth on our hearts in such a way that it fulfils its purpose in bringing us to commitment to its truth and trust in its teaching. Because of the Holy Spirit, the truth is applied to us in a life-changing way, as it is impressed on our hearts and takes root in us.

Another way of putting this would be to say that the central message of Scripture is Jesus Christ and the salvation he accomplished. Because of the work of the Spirit, once this message is applied to us it unites us to Christ and we become spiritually one with him.

Sadly, it is possible to recognise that Scripture is the truth and even that it is God's word and yet remain foreign to it. One can know it and still not understand it. This is why the Westminster Confession of Faith states (I, vi):

> The whole counsel of God concerning all things necessary for His own glory, man's salvation, faith and life, is either expressly set down in Scripture, or by good and necessary consequence may be deduced from Scripture: unto which nothing at any time is to be added, whether by new revelations of the Spirit or traditions of men. Nevertheless, we acknowledge the inward illumination of the Spirit of God to be necessary for the saving understanding of such things as are revealed in the Word...

How can this be illustrated? Perhaps the best case of someone accepting the witness of Scripture but lacking the illumination of the Spirit is Agrippa in his reaction to the apostle Paul's teaching at Caesarea, as recounted in Acts 26:12–32. Brought before the proconsul Festus, King Herod Agrippa and Bernice, Paul recounted at length his conversion from Judaism when he had met Jesus on the Damascus road, the Jesus who had suffered the many things foretold and had been raised from the dead to be the light of the world. That was too much for Festus who shouted 'Paul, you're out of your mind, much learning has driven you mad'. The truth of the gospel often appears madness to those who can't see it. Paul replied, 'the king knows all about it' and appealed to him directly: 'King Agrippa, do you believe the prophets? I know that you believe' And Agrippa replied 'Almost you are persuading me to become a Christian' (27–9).

In this dispute, which has legal overtones, the apostle is defending the principle point of faith, the resurrection from the dead. Agrippa knows and believes the prophets of the Old Testament but his knowledge of this truth is worthless unless he looks to Christ, the giver of life foretold by the prophets. Festus' reaction shows blatantly how the truth is unprofitable without faith but the situation of Agrippa is more complex. He knows that the Scripture confirms Paul's teaching as being beyond all doubt. He believes it but doesn't have any real faith because he does not trust what it promises in the deepest sense. He believes the Scripture but without believing in terms of committing to its truth. So he is the 'almost Christian', the fence-sitter who recognises truth without having any real faith. Ultimately he is not persuaded. He will not answer Yes to the 'Bourne identity' question: 'will you commit to this programme?'

This tragic case underlines the predicament of knowing something and yet not putting one's personal trust in it. In fact, this is the last bastion of unbelief, to know something and not to believe it, because of the obstinacy of a heart that has not been brought to obedience by the work of the Holy Spirit. An unbeliever can recognise the self-witness of Scripture to its truth and not be changed by it. What Agrippa lacks is the internal witness of the Holy Spirit.

The Internal Witness

So the *sola Scriptura* without the internal witness of the Spirit is like a motor engine without oil. Everything is right as to design, but it will not run. Adolf von Harnack, a liberal theologian who had a bit of nous, at least on this subject, said that in Protestantism the internal witness occupies the position that tradition does in Roman Catholicism.

The classic formulation concerning the internal witness of the Spirit was penned by John Calvin in his *Institutes of the Christian Religion*. It is worth quoting:

> It is perfectly clear that only those who are inwardly taught by the Holy Spirit firmly embrace Scripture. Although Scripture provides a sure witness to its own truth and can be received without being subjected to proofs and arguments, we recognise its unshakeable truth by the testimony of the Spirit. Its intrinsic dignity justifies the respect we have for it; nevertheless, it begins to impress us when the Holy Spirit seals it in our hearts. When we are enlightened by the power of the Spirit, we no longer believe by our own judgment or by that of others that the

Scriptures are from God. In a way that surpasses any human judgment we confess without the slightest doubt that Scripture was given by the instrumentality of men from the very mouth of God, as if we beheld the nature of God himself in it.

We do not ask for proofs or legitimate evidences on which to rest our case, but we subject our judgment and our intelligence to it as a reality that is way beyond our human capacity.

(1, vii, 5, my translation)

Calvin makes four claims in this passage:

1. God is the author of the Scripture, which is self-authenticating. The evidence that Scripture is the word of God comes from God speaking in his word. Scripture is the word of God and the means of God's making himself known to us. Revelation brings with it its own 'external' witness to the truth.
2. Human reason with its arguments and proofs is not much use in so far as Scripture is concerned; faith in Scripture as God's word cannot be established by human logic.
3. The Holy Spirit and the 'internal' witness, sealing the truth in our hearts, alone bring the certainty of faith. Scripture is in and of itself true, as if God himself spoke to us, but without the witness of the Spirit the word does not produce faith in the hearts of sinners.
4. Scripture has a dual character, being divine and human. It comes via the ministry of men, but as if it were from the mouth of God himself. For this reason we see the very nature of God in it. This is one of the rare passages where Calvin speaks about the 'essence' of God, a term he usually avoids.

The complementary nature of the 'external' and 'internal' witnesses is the foundation of the notion of *sola Scriptura* and the self-witness of the Scripture as the word of God. Three comments can be made about it. Firstly, Scripture alone can be validated by the internal witness of the Spirit, because only God's truth can receive such an attestation. No other text or tradition is adequate to receive such a witness from the Spirit because it is not God's truth. Secondly, Scripture receives this complementary witness because of its nature, it is God's word given to us. Finally, if Scripture is beyond human judgment and cannot be proved by human reason, our rational capacities as human beings find their true function in the context and within the limits of faith in God.

Where exactly is this truth taught in Scripture? Right there in 2 Timothy 3:16—the holy Scriptures are *able* to make *wise to salvation*...and *profitable* for instruction in *righteousness*. The Holy Spirit alone is the instrument of God's saving power and progressive sanctification. We could add John 6:45, Galatians 1:8–9, and 1 Corinthians 2:9–12, but beyond this, experience teaches us that nobody is brought to saving faith in Christ by a message that is other than biblical or by a power other than that of the Spirit. This all born-again Christians know.

Conclusion

Word and Spirit go together both in the origin of Scripture as God's word given to us, in the life and ministry of Jesus, and in the renewed life that God gives to his children. The word is never without the Spirit and the Spirit is never without the word. They should never be played off one against the other, because their witness is always one and harmonious.

It follows that the best way for Christians to know the witness of the Spirit and his illumination is to search the Scripture that bears its own witness as the authentic and true word of God. Both word and Spirit point to Jesus Christ in whom we find salvation and who is the reason for their joint witness to his truth.

16

Conclusion

To round off, we will sum up what we have said eight practical propositions, each of which presents a major theme of Scripture. These features characterise its self-witness in its individual texts and as a whole.

Revelation

Because God acted to reveal himself we know him as our creator and saviour. We know truly what he has done in creation, throughout history, and how history will end. God reveals himself in all these aspects of the Bible's story. This encourages us to wait for what's coming next: the revelation of Christ in glory at the end of time, marking the beginning of a new creation. Revelation tells us *what* God has done and is doing in our world, *that* he did it, but never *how* or *why* he does it in the way he choses. Those two things belong to God alone, and are beyond our understanding.

The Word Of God

God has spoken. His word is true and personal. Knowing God's word is vital as it puts us in touch with reality. It helps us to see ourselves and other things as God sees them. Without God's word, we are lost in a morass of uncertainties and we will never be able to know God or even to pray meaningfully. His word is law and gospel. God gave his law in creation and in revealed words. 'Love the Lord with all your heart and love your neighbour as yourself'. The gospel teaches us what God's love means and how we are saved by grace.

Inspiration

It's wonderful that God's Spirit has been active in so many places, ways and times to communicate his truth to human beings. God expressed his truth through inspired witnesses. Each time he did so their human words were the result of the special action of the Holy Spirit. So human words are, in this case and in this case alone, God's own word. God accommodated himself to speak our language. The Spirit attests that the biblical word is God's revealed truth. We can have complete confidence that his word will not let us down because it is true; God does not make promises he can't keep.

Authority

'If you love me, keep my commandments', said Jesus (John 14:15). Loving God and obeying his word are one and the same thing. When we do God's will, it is for our good as well. Submitting to God is ultimate freedom, because when we give our life to him we get it back recycled. Belonging to God we are the freest of people and slaves to nobody or nothing. This is pleasing to God and liberating for us. It comes down to the smallest details of daily existence. In the words of the apostle Paul, 'Present your bodies as a living sacrifice, holy and acceptable to God, which is your spiritual worship' (Rom. 12:1).

Truth

Paul goes on: 'Do not be conformed to the world, but be transformed by the renewal of your mind, that by testing you may discern what is the will of God, what is good and acceptable and perfect' (Rom. 12:2). Knowledge of the truth works on the mind. It is objective 'true truth'. It puts us back in control of our lives and allows us to act for the good. The Christian develops a view of the world and of life in which God and his truth are the motivating factors. Truth makes us critical of the follies and obsessions of the world, but without bitterness or intolerance. Because God has delivered us from them, we can only have sympathy for those who are still caught in their web.

Christ-Centredness

Jesus Christ, the Son of God incarnate, is the Word made flesh. Holy Scripture is the word of God inscripturated. The incarnate Word is primary and the inspired word is secondary. Both are divine and human in their own particular way, Christ personally and Scripture verbally. Both have a role of mediation. Jesus Christ is the one bridge between God and his creation and the only way to God. Scripture bears witness to him and is the only way of knowing God. It mediates the truth of God. It is without error, just as Jesus was without sin. It is in our language, just as Jesus was in our flesh. Jesus Christ is the reason Scripture exists and he is its substance. He is the content of Scripture in the promise of the Old Testament and in its fulfilment in the New. His second coming is the one predicted act of revelation that remains for the future.

The Internal Witness of the Spirit

The Holy Spirit has a double function. The Spirit of inspiration is the Spirit of illumination. The Spirit works in giving the truth *for* us in Scripture and *to* us by writing it on our hearts. No saving truth exists outside Scripture that is not in Scripture. Nor does the Holy Spirit ever self-contradict. The truth is outside us before being in our hearts by the internal witness of the Spirit. What we feel can only be true if it harmonises with the objective truth of Scripture. Moreover, the Spirit seals the truth in our hearts and gives us assurance that we are children of God the Father. The Christian who knows the internal witness rests on Scripture and experiences the following three privileges: that of having God as Father; that of being certain prayer is heard and answered; and that of knowing that nothing can separate from the love of God in Christ (Rom. 8:15–17, 31–9).

Word and Spirit

God is Spirit and works in creation through the Holy Spirit, the third person of the Trinity. In the creation the Spirit comes before the word. But when God speaks to us in revelation, his word precedes the work of the Spirit. As we hear the word, the Spirit works and impresses the truth of the word on our hearts. Word and Spirit to together. When Jesus promises to send the disciples his Spirit, the 'other comforter' (John 14:16), he says 'I will not leave you as orphans; I will come to you.' To know the work of the Spirit is to know Christ, the word, and to know Christ is to know the work of the Spirit. The Spirit does not speak of himself, but points us to Christ. The Spirit never gives us something more than the word, but helps us to receive what is in the word. The function of the Spirit is to lead to Christ; the Spirit is given by Christ to achieve this specific purpose.

Through the inspired word of God we come into the light as the Spirit bears witness in us. We benefit from the truth God revealed through his prophetic servants:

> What no eye has seen, nor ear has heard, nor the heart of man imagined, what God has prepared for those who love him –
> these things God has revealed to us through the Spirit.
>
> (1 Cor. 2:9)

Appendix

Historical Criticism and After

> *'They claim to see fern seed and can't see an
> elephant ten yards away in broad daylight.'*
>
> C.S. Lewis

The subject of historical criticism is not of interest to everyone, nor is it particularly useful, but it is difficult to avoid it altogether. This appendix is a substitute for a whole chapter. The subject has interested me since I presented a doctoral thesis on the biblical scholar James Barr in the 1970's at the Vrije Universiteit in Amsterdam. The following gives just a sketchy outline on the subject.

The Protestant Reformers were fully aware of the historical character of the Bible and practiced a literary and historical approach to the text. Their fundamental principle was: 'Do not carry a meaning into Scripture but draw the meaning out of it'. The method of the analogy of Scripture, or of faith, presupposed the fundamental historical character of the text. With the linguistic tools made available by the Renaissance they took their distance from the allegorical hermeneutic increasingly practiced during the Middle Ages (called the 'four ways'), which became quasi-normative in Roman Catholic exegesis after its adoption by Thomas Aquinas.

The Reformers' approach was historical but it was not critical in the modern sense. The critical approach to history only began to emerge at the time of the Enlightenment as a result of the combination of the man-centred humanism of the Renaissance and the idea of autonomy related to a vision of the universe as a closed system. The rupture between religion and culture widened throughout the nineteenth century, not only between theology and the natural sciences but also the humanities, including historiography.

Early critical documentary analysis of the Old Testament was initiated by Spinoza, Eichhorn, Astruc, Graf and their ilk. Later, Baur and the Tübingen school applied criticism to the New Testament. Although they were a tributary of Cartesian rationalism and Kantian or Hegelian idealism, they lacked the formal structuring that came in later critical methodology. The groundwork of modern historiography was laid by Dilthey and, above all, by Troeltsch (1865–1923), called by his admirers the finest historian of religion since Hegel.

Troeltsch affirmed that any science worthy of the name, including theology, is obliged to work within the parameters of historical consciousness. No special pleading can be entertained either for dogmas or for events considered to have revelatory significance. Appeal to a special history of salvation is excluded as unscientific. The method advocated by Troeltsch was characterised by the principles of autonomy and naturalism: all facts, including the historian's own understanding, are to be interpreted in the light of natural explanations and thoroughgoing relativism.

In his famous essay 'Historical and Dogmatic Method in Theology' (1900/1913) Troeltsch outlined the three axiomatic methods of the historical approach: criticism, analogy and correlation.

Criticism, guided by freedom of examination and the contingency of all historical events, establishes plausibility in interpretation: an explanation may be possible or probable but never certain.

Analogy is the 'all powerful' means by which criticism is possible: it supposes that all historical events are homogenous and must take place in a similar way to events happening before our eyes.

Correlation is the analysis of the forces that drive history: each event has an antecedent cause and a subsequent result that must be explained rationally.

These three axioms, taken individually and collectively, mean that if history is totally haphazard or contingent, its meaning is rationally determined in a context of inflexible naturalism.

Troeltsch's description of the historical critical method was widely accepted as the starting point for historical examination in biblical studies and became the criterion of 'critical orthodoxy' and academic credibility in the last century. Where the reconstruction of biblical history or literary methods of interpretation were concerned, its influence was widespread. Its premises laid the foundations for Bultmann's demythologisation project and the methods practiced in the analysis of the formation of the synoptic gospels, called form and redaction criticism. Even conservatives who attempted to limit the historical method to prolegomena, such as Cullmann, and the neo-orthodox theologians of the Biblical Theology Movement (1930–70), who distinguished between 'history' and 'story', were obliged to do lip-service to it.

Evangelicals, particularly in the Anglo-Saxon world, were generally hostile to the critical method and drew support for their position not only from their view of revelation and inspiration, but also from archaeological studies and literary criticism. The temptation, however, was always present to adopt a critical methodology and moderate it by selecting the most conservative conclusions possible, a procedure scorned by Barr in his essay *Fundamentalism* (1977).

Criticisms of the method became more widespread across the theological spectrum during the last two decades of the twentieth century. As a method critical of theological special pleading, it seemed to be blind to its own intellectual dogmatism. Popper and others exposed the dangers of historicism. For all his talk of contingency, Troeltsch's method seemed to be a form of positivism that restricted the very openness it appealed to. Pannenberg and others criticised the notion of analogy used unilaterally by appealing to present knowledge. Barr, himself no enemy of critical methods, relativised the historical approach to the Bible by indicating the importance of the literary architecture of the text and semantics and opened the door to the growth of rhetorical criticism.

At present, the historical critical method as a scientific approach to the study of biblical history seems to be dying an agonising death. However, as with the evolutionary hypothesis in the realm of the natural sciences, no over-arching theory has arisen to replace it. Biblical scholars often seem to operate certain theoretical selections in their historical approach to the text, without having a formal method or a particularly coherent view of the presuppositions or the methodological coherence of historical theory.

In the light of this, it is perhaps more fitting than ever to note that 'the historical method' is a misnomer. It is not a unified method at all, all the more so in the context of post-modernity, but an assembly of methods, not always used in a coherent way. Often its results are speculative and far from being 'the assured results of scientific criticism' so impressive to the popular mind.

For the evangelical critic of historical criticism, this approach to Scripture will always seem to be pretentiously lacking in the humility that is appropriate with respect to divine revelation. It ignores the extent to which sin affects fallen humanity, including the lofty intellect.

Finally, the results of the historical critical method are scant. It has contributed little to a deeper understanding of the riches of Scripture, has never convinced anyone of its truth, nor can it be preached.